Notes from the Metalevel

STUDIES ON NEW MUSIC RESEARCH

Series Editor:
Marc Leman, Institute for Psychoacoustic and Electronic Music,
University of Ghent, Belgium

Notes from the Metalevel

Introduction to Algorithmic Music Composition

by
Heinrich K. Taube

Associate Professor Composition/Theory
School of Music,
University of Illinois at Urbana-Champaign, IL, USA

Taylor & Francis
Taylor & Francis Group

LONDON AND NEW YORK

Library of Congress Cataloging-in-Publication Data

A Catalogue record for the book is available from the Library of Congress

Cover image designed by Tobias Kunze Briseño

www.tandf.co.uk

ISBN 90 265 1957 5 (HB)
ISBN 90 265 1975 3 (PB)
ISBN 90 265 1958 3 (CD-Rom)

To my children
Konrad Gabriel, Maralena Valentin, and Florian Alexander Taube

There be none of beauty's daughters
With a magic like thee;
And like music on the waters
Is thy sweet voice to me

Contents

Preface

Notes From the Metalevel is a practical introduction to computer composition. It is primarily intended for student composers interested in learning how *computation* can provide them with a new paradigm for musical composition. Notes from the Metalevel explains through a practical, example-based approach the essential concepts and techniques of computer-based composition and demonstrates how these techniques can be integrated into the composer's own creative work. One of most exciting aspects of computer-based composition is that it is an essentially *empirical* activity that does not require years of formal music theory training to understand. For this reason, Notes from the Metalevel will be of interest to any reader with a high-school mathematics background interested in experimenting with music composition using MIDI and audio synthesis programs. The book will also be of use to computer science and engineering students who are interested in artistic applications of object-oriented programming techniques and music software design.

Every composer knows that learning how to write music takes an enormous amount of practice. It is only through practice that new techniques can become integrated into the composer's own approach to the craft. That is why this book takes a "hands on" approach to its subject matter, by combining a general theoretical discussion with real software examples. Notes from the Metalevel is filled with examples and exercises for the student to perform, study, modify and adapt to their own musical purposes. All of the examples as well as the software to work with them are available on the CD that accompanies the book. The reader is strongly encouraged to experiment with the chapter examples interactively, in parallel with reading the text. The vast majority of these examples are short, simple, and demonstrate only one or two points at a time so that the composer can begin to experiment with example code immediately after reading the explanatory text. In addition to the many chapter examples, Notes from the Metalevel contains a number of *Etudes* chapters that appear at regular intervals throughout the book. The Etudes are large structured projects that explore some particular technique or topic in greater detail.

Plan of the Book

Notes From the Metalevel is divided into two parts. The first nine chapters present an introduction to music programming in Lisp. Chapter 1 gives a brief history of Lisp and explains why the language is a particularly good choice for supporting the exploratory process of music composition. Chapters 2-9 give a *selective* introduction to computer programming techniques in Lisp. The term selective means that the material in these chapters has been selected specifically for its relevance to the material presented in the second part of the book and to musical programming in general.

The second half of the book (chapters 10-24) provides an introduction to the essential concepts and techniques of computer composition. The first few chapters discuss the representation of sound, musical structure, algorithms and processes. The material in the remaining chapters can be broadly grouped into four areas of discussion: algorithmic design, mapping and transformations, aleatoric composition and pattern based composition.

One of the really wonderful benefits of working in Lisp is that a composer does not have to become a Lisp expert in order to do meaningful and important work using the language. But some composers want to develop programming expertise in parallel with their artistic pursuits. An appendix to the book contains pointers to Lisp documentation that is freely available on the Internet. This material includes several famous Lisp text books, the Lisp and Scheme language specifications, and on-line Lisp tutorials. Some of this material is also provided on the accompanying CD. Readers who want to learn more about Lisp are strongly encouraged to take the additional time necessary to read and study this reference material in detail.

Programming Code and Lisp Interactions

Notes from the Metalevel contains two types of examples: programming code and Lisp interactions. Program code are Lisp expressions that define units of computation, for example, Lisp procedures or musical algorithms. Program code is usually saved in text files and then loaded or evaluated in Lisp. Lisp interactions are commands that the composer will input inside the Lisp application to produce some result, for example, to generate a musical score saved as a MIDI file.

All of the programming examples and Lisp interactions for each chapter can be found on the accompanying CD. The CD provides these examples in two different formats: HTML files and lisp source code files. The HTML files display the examples as they are shown in the book together with interactive links to the MIDI and audio files that each example generates. In the hard-copy book these audio links are printed with the file name and directory of the example on the CD so that the sound can be easily located.

The Lisp examples source code files contain the examples formatted as plain text. The source code files are suitable for editing in a programming editor such as XEmacs, or loaded and evaluated inside the Lisp application.

Programming example format

Programming examples are printed between dashed upper and lower borders to indicate that the example should be understood to be part of a larger source code file. Programming code is displayed using *syntax highlighting* to highlight important syntactic units. The hard-copy book and the HTML examples files differ in how this highlighting is depicted. The book displays important syntactic units such as definitions, *special forms* (forms like define and if) and keywords in bold face and lisp comments in italic face (Example 1).

Example 1. Example program code with syntax highlighting.

```
(define (fibonacci nth)
   ;; return the nth fibonacci number
   (if (<= 0 nth 1)
     1
     (+ (fibonacci (- nth 1))
        (fibonacci (- nth 2)))))
```

The HTML examples files on the CD use text colors for syntax highlighting. Normal code appears in black face, definitions and special forms appear dark red, user comments are blue, text strings are green and keyword symbols (symbols starting with a colon) are red.

Lisp interactions

Lisp interactions are commands that the user will type inside the *Lisp Listener*, a window that runs an interactive Lisp command shell. Lisp interactions are depicted inside a solid box with a light gray. A single interaction consists of the Lisp input prompt:

cm>

followed by the user's command expression shown in bold face on the same line. Results from the command (if any) appears in regular face on the next line. If no output is produced then the next line is left blank. More than one command may appear within a single interaction example, in which case the more recent commands appear toward the bottom of the example. The last line in an interaction example usually shows the prompt without an input command to indicate that the Lisp Listener is waiting for the user to type the next command expression (Interaction 1).

Interaction 1. Example interactions in the Lisp Listener.

```
cm> (list 1 2 3)
(1 2 3)
cm> (define 2pi (* 2 pi))

cm> 2pi
6.283185307179586
cm>
```

Chapter source text
The best way to read Notes from the Metalevel is to run the Common Music application in parallel as you study each chapter. This will allow you to test out each interaction and experiment with the programming examples as you encounter them in the book. The source code for all of the program examples and interactions in each chapter can be found in a ".cm" file (Common Music source file) located in the same directory as the HTML example file for the chapter. Etudes, op. 1 describes two different ways to work with example material. The best way is to edit source examples in a text editor that allows Lisp expressions to be remotely evaluated inside the Common Music application. See Chapter 4 for more information about this topic.

Sound examples
Every musical score example in the book has one or more sound files associated with it that contain the musical output generated by the example. Audio files are stored in stereo MP3 format and MIDI files are stored in Level 0 (single track) MIDI format. Except for a few noted cases example MIDI files do not contain program changes so that the reader can experiment with different instrumentation when playing back the examples. If no instrumentation is suggested in an example then a Grand Piano sound may be assumed.

Each sound example is marked by an arrow. Examples in the book also contain the location of the sound file on the CD. Sound examples in the HTML example files are actual links that play the example. A short description of a a sound example may appear after its listing:

→ nm/00/snd/sines.mid Two midi "sine waves" at slightly different rates.
→ nm/00/snd/thunder.mp3 Tuned thunder clap from Aeolian Harp.

Special notes
Special notes highlight points of difference between Lisp implementations or operating systems that affect how examples appear or execute on the various different systems. A special note consists of a styled label and an explanatory text:

CLTL Note:
 Common Lisp defines `nil` to mean both boolean false and the empty set.

Definitions

Functions and variables defined by Common Music are only briefly explained in the main chapter text. The full explanation for these entries can be found in the on-line Common Music Dictionary (http://commonmusic.sf.net/doc/index.html) and also located on the CD in the file "doc/dict/index.html" under the Common Music source directory.

Definitions are printed in a special typographic format. Definition terms, literals (code that you type) and program code are printed in fixed width font. Variables and metavariables (names that stand for pieces of code) are printed in italic face. Terms separated by | are exclusive choices. Braces {} and brackets [] are used to associate or group the enclosed terms in a syntax declaration and are never actually written in code. Brackets [] mean that the enclosed terms are optional. An optional term may appear at most one time. Braces {} simply group the enclosed terms. A star * appearing after a bracket means that the enclosed terms may be specified zero or more times. A plus + after braces means that the terms may be specified one or more times. A sample syntax definition:

`(hertz `*x*` [:in `*scale*`])`   [Function]

In the sample above `hertz` is the name of the function, *x* is a required argument and *scale* is an optional keyword argument. Italicized variables in a definition may have descriptive names or may consist of a single letter such as *x*. Single letter names generally provide an indication as to the type of data the user is expected to specify. The meaning of the letter variables are shown in Table 1.

Table 1. Single letter variable names.

Letter	Description	Letter	Description
x	any value	*b*	boolean
n	number	*s*	symbol or keyword
f	float	*l*	list
i	integer	*g*	string

Acknowledgments

I would like to thank the Research Board at the University of Illinois for its grant toward the completion of this manuscript. The author is indebted to the Center for Computer Research and Acoustics (CCRMA) at Stanford University and to the Zentrum für Kunst und Medientechnologie (ZKM, http://www.zkm.de) in Karlsruhe, Germany for their contributions to the Common Music software project on which this book is based. I would like to thank Johannes Goebel, director of the Audio group while I was working at ZKM, for his commitment to the Common Music project while I was employed at the center. The author would like to acknowledge

William Schottstaedt at CCRMA for his contributions to computer music programming in general and for his Common Lisp Music (CLM) synthesis language which the author used to produce the Aeolian Harp examples included on the CD. The author is greatly indebted to Tobias Kunze for his many contributions to Common Music and for his help in the preparation of this document. Tobias implemented many of the MIDI features in Common Music, wrote several examples on which Etudes chapters in this book are based, designed Common Music's glowing lambda logo and developed the CSS style for the HTML version of the book. I am also indebted to Michael Klingbeil for writing several programming examples in the book, for allowing me to use exerpts from his composition *1706°F* and also for producing the EPS illustrations that appear in the hardcopy version of the book. I would also like to express my thanks to Richard Karpen and the Center for Advanced Research Technology in the Arts and Humanities (CARTAH) at the University of Washington for their friendly encouragement and for the many good improvements and suggestions that they have made over the years. And finally, I would like to thank Carl Edwards and David Phillips for their careful reading of this manuscript and for their sound editorial advice.

Colophon

This book was written in the XEmacs text editor using the ispell spelling program and a lisp-based mark-up language developed by the author. This mark-up language generated the HTML for the book's publication as well as all the chapter example files. HTML output was then imported into Microsoft Word to produce the camera-ready manuscript. All of the graphic plots that appear in the book were created in Plotter, a plotting tool included in the Macintosh/OS 9.2 version of Common Music.

1

Introduction

The one crowded space in Father Perry's house was his bookshelves. I gradually came to understand that the marks on the pages were trapped words. Anyone could learn to decipher the symbols and turn the trapped words loose again into speech. The ink of the print trapped the thoughts; they could no more get away than a doomboo could get out of a pit. When the full realization of what this meant flooded over me, I experienced the same thrill and amazement as when I had my first glimpse of the bright lights of Konakry. I shivered with the intensity of my desire to learn to do this wondrous thing myself.

spoken by Prince Modupe, a west African prince who learned to read as an adult.

— Leonard Schlain *The Alphabet Versus the Goddess*

It is impossible to know exactly how Prince Modupe felt when he discovered a process by which his very thoughts could be trapped and released at will again into speech. But I think his epiphany must be close to what I experienced when, as a young composer, I was first shown how I could use a computer to represent my musical ideas and then "release them" at will into musical compositions. At that time I was a masters student in composition at Stanford University. My teachers

John Chowning and Leland Smith had just demonstrated to our introductory computer music class how a music language called SCORE (Smith) could capture musical ideas and, at the push of a button, trigger an almost magical process in which fantastically complex scores were computed and then realized by instruments unimpeded by the laws of physics. At that instant it became clear to me that there was an entire level of notation above the scores that I had been writing in my regular composition classes, a level I knew nothing about! But I could see that in this level it was possible to notate my compositional ideas in a precise manner and work with them in an almost physical way, as "trapped words" that could be unleashed into musical sound at the push of a button. Equally important was the realization that this new (to me) level was essentially devoid of any preconceived notions of "musical correctness" and so offered me an attractive alternative to the symbols and glyphs of Common Practice music, which I increasing felt were too tied to historical tradition. I too, "shivered with a desire to do this wondrous thing myself" and, as I look back on it now more than twenty years later, I realize that this moment was one in which my life's path was irrevocably altered.

The first several years that I was associated with the Center for Computer Research in Music and Acoustics (CCRMA, http://www-ccrma.stanford.edu) were among the most intellectually stimulating experiences I have ever had. Our computer music classes were located in the D. C. Power Laboratory (named for a person, not a current), an off-campus facility that was devoted primarily to research in Artificial Intelligence. The Lab housed a PDP-10 mainframe computer that students in the computer music group were allowed to use during the night from 2-7am. As I learned more about music languages during my studies I also took time to learn about the software languages that AI researchers were using at the Lab. I cannot say with certainty why I did this since I had never taken a class in computer science and was not particularly good at mathematics! There were two primary languages in use: SAIL (Stanford Artificial Intelligence Language) and LISP, a language developed by John McCarthy at Stanford. I was immediately attracted to the power and beauty of the Lisp language for many of the reasons that are discussed in the next chapter of this book and I began to use it in my musical life.

All things change, particularly in the digital world, and one day the SAMBOX digital synthesizer that was at the center of my artistic life was retired without any immediate replacement. My software world — which was hopelessly tied to the retired hardware — vanished at the speed of an electron, and all of the programs and libraries I had used for years were suddenly useless. I decided at that point that I would develop a generalized and portable replacement to that world, one that would run on any machine, and could be customized and redefined even to the core of the language. The result was the Common Music software system, written in Lisp, that continues to evolve today. Though born of necessity, Common Music developed in response to the explosive growth of new hardware and music systems that resulted from the introduction of the personal computer in the 1980's. As the number of computers, operating systems, sound synthesis languages and music applications increased, the need for a portable composition language that could function with all of these systems became obvious. The Common Music software project started in 1989 when I was a Rockefeller Fellow at CCRMA. Much of the system as it exists today was implemented at the Institut für Musik und Akustik at the Zentrum für Kunst und Medientechnologie in Karlsruhe, Germany, where I worked for the first half of the 1990's. In 1996 Common Music received First Prize in the computer-assisted composition category at the 1er Concours International de Logiciels Musicaux in Bourges, France. Common Music continues to evolve today at the University of Illinois at Urbana-Champaign, where the author is now an associate professor of music composition.

Notes from the Metalevel

Every musician is familiar with performing music from a score. The score is not the same thing as the music, it is a *representation* of music — a notation designed to capture information about creating sound with an instrument. But musical sound can be represented in a number of different ways and on a number of different levels. For example, a recording captures music at a very low level, by storing a representation of the music's acoustic waveform. Of course, the recording does not contain any performance information — musical notes and other kinds of performance instructions can be thought of as constituting a *level of abstraction* above the sonic waveform.

If we compare the score of a composition with its recording there are several observations that can be made. First, the score is a much more condensed representation than the recording. By definition, the process of abstraction eliminates, or hides, a certain amount of detail that exists in the lower, unabstracted layer. In addition to hiding detail, an abstraction can also be a more *general* representation than the information in the unabstracted layer. Another way of saying this is that, while the abstraction is more concise it may also be less precise. Imprecision does not mean that something is wrong with the abstraction, just that there is not an exact correspondence between it and the lower level. For example, given a musical score a performer can create different versions at the acoustic level simply by performing the score a number of times. In fact, it is the imprecision of traditional scores that allows for musical interpretation and makes performance art interesting.

A score such as the one Bach is holding in Figure 1 is notated in a language that allows a composer to convey information to a performer. This language provides a set of *symbols* — the musical marks that appear on the page — and a *syntax*, or grammar, for stringing the symbols together to form meaningful statements. Given the existence of the score representation one might ask if there is yet another representation that constitutes a level of abstraction above the performance information? The answer, of course, is yes; it is what this book terms the *metalevel*. If the score represents the composition then the metalevel represents the *composition of the composition*. A metalevel representation of music is concerned with representing the activity, or *process*, of musical composition as opposed to its artifact, the score. If the metalevel seems more ephemeral than the performance level it may be due to the fact that it is more closely related to the mysterious cognitive processes that occur within the composer. In addition, there is no common physical artifact, such as a score or a CD, to represent the metalevel. This book is about using the computer to *instantiate* the metalevel: to define, model and represent the compositional processes, formalism and structures that are articulated in a musical score and acoustic performance but are not literally represented there. By using a computer the composer works with an explicit metalevel notation, or language, that makes the metalevel as tangible as the performance and acoustic levels. But unlike the bits on a CD or the notes on a score, statements in the metalevel representation are active representations of the processes, methods, algorithms and techniques that a composer develops to craft the sounds in his or her compositions.

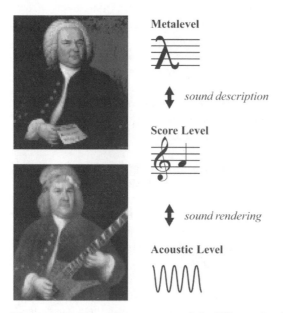

Figure 1. Music can be represented on different levels of abstraction, acoustic, performance and metalevel. (The metalevel is depicted using the Greek lambda superimposed on a music staff.

Computer Composition

Over the course of the last few decades the computer has played an ever increasing role in the professional lives of composers. Computers are now involved in all phases of a composer's work, from pre-composition exploration to sound generation, score notation and CD recording (Figure 2). Composers have been using the computer as a compositional tool for almost as long as the modern computer has been in existence. Lejaren Hiller and Leonard Isaacson are generally regarded to be the first "computer composers" and their *Illiac Suite* for string quartet was premiered August 9, 1956 at the University of Illinois at Urbana-Champaign, where the author is on the composition faculty. As computer hardware and software has improved the computer has come to take on an increasing role in music composition. It is now useful to distinguish between several different ways that computers can be applied to music composition. In *computer assisted composition* the computer facilitates compositional tasks such as computing pre-compositional data, event editing, performing playback and so on. In some sense the computer is applied before or after the composer has a compositional idea rather than as a representation of compositional formalisms.The term *automatic composition* can be applied to computer systems that are designed to compose music "independently". Software such as David Cope's Experiments in Musical Intelligence (Cope) and some types of sound installations are examples of this kind of system. *Computer-based composition* means to use the computer to explicitly represent compositional ideas at a level higher than the performance score. An explicit metalevel representation means that the relationships and processes that constitute a composition (the composition of the composition) are represented inside the machine apart from the composer thinking about them.

Why would a composer be interested in computer composition? I think the main reason is to think about music and to write music differently than one would without using a computer. Thus, computer based composition affects the compositional process as well as the composition in a number of different ways:

- Computer-based composition becomes an essentially *empirical* activity, one in which the composer experiments with ideas and rapidly tests them out as they develop from an initial curiosity into their final compositional form. Regardless of whether or not a composer writes "experimental music", computer-based composition practically insures that the composer writes "experimenting music".
- An explicit metalevel representation allows compositional ideas to be represented as reusable building blocks that may be used in a variety of musical contexts and in different musical pieces.
- Compositional tasks can be solved by applying generic algorithms to solve specific problems or tasks. These algorithms can be organized into "toolboxes" that provide services over and over again.
- Just as it is possible to generate different acoustic representations from a single score, so it is possible to generate different versions of a score from the same metalevel representation.
- Complex probability and chance procedures can be incorporated into the compositional process very easily.
- Very small changes at the metalevel can have a profound impact on the score level representation.
- Relationships that are simple to express in the metalevel can generate extremely complex performance scores.
- Changes in the metalevel can lead to unintended or unanticipated consequences that trigger new compositional ideas or take the compositional process in a totally new direction. Any composer who has integrated computers their compositional process in an experimental way can cite examples of this phenomena in their own music.
- An explicit metalevel representation means that compositional ideas can be manipulated and processed by machines. If the composer can construct a

metalevel representation, then so can a program. This means the metalevel (the composition of the composition) could be an artifact of other, higher order abstractions in the machine.

- Metalevel compositions can explore domains too complex or too large to imagine doing without a computer. Of course, since a computer is deterministic then strictly speaking there is no calculation that can be accomplished with a computer that cannot also be accomplished with pen and paper. But the quantitative difference in speed and processing power between computer-based and pen-and-paper-based computation is of such a magnitude that for all intents and purposes it is a qualitative difference for the metalevel composer.

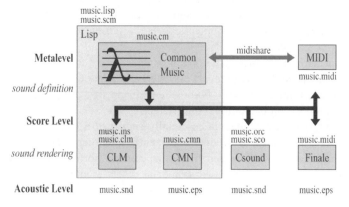

Figure 2. The composition abstraction levels represented in a computer and their relation to the software systems described in this book.

References

Smith, L. (1972). Score: A Musician's Approach to Computer Music.. *Journal of the Audio Engineering Society, 20,* 7-14.
Cope, D. (1996). *Experiments in Musical Intelligence.* Madison: A-R Editions.

2

The Language of Lisp

Just as its hard to describe what makes a piece of music or a painting aesthetically pleasing, it's equally difficult to describe what makes a mathematical theorem or a physical theory beautiful. A beautiful theory will be simple, compact, and spare; it will give a sense of completeness and often an eerie sense of symmetry.

— Charles Seife, *Zero, The Biography of a Dangerous Idea*

What is Lisp?

Lisp is a computer programming language written in Lisp. Behind this tautology lies one of the most unique and interesting facts about the language, namely, that Lisp does not make a distinction between data, the grist of computation, and programs, the software agents that act on data. A Lisp program *is* Lisp data. This symmetry between programs and data reflects a very different "world view" than computer languages like C or Fortran. What are some of the consequences of Lisp's unique approach to language design that are relevant to the activity of music composition?

Lisp is easy to learn

Lisp's syntax is simple, compact and spare. Only a handful of "rules" are needed. This is why Lisp is sometimes taught as the first programming language in university-level computer science courses. For the composer it means that useful work can begin almost immediately, before the composer understands much about the underlying mechanics of Lisp or the art of programming in general. In Lisp one learns by doing and experimenting, just as in music composition.

Lisp is beautiful

It might seem odd to call a programming language beautiful but many people who use Lisp are attracted to it as much by its elegance as by its efficacy. Like the M. C. Escher hand that draws itself, the recursive, self-similar nature of Lisp can be inspiring. The symmetry between data and programs gives the whole language a sense of circularity and completeness that makes working in Lisp, for many people, as much an aesthetic experience as it is a practical one. This is, I think, an important quality for the novice Lisp composer to be aware of and one that composers are particularly well suited to appreciate. Aesthetics can play an important role at the compositional metalevel just as it does in the performance level.

Lisp is interactive and dynamic

By its very nature Lisp supports the exploratory and incremental process of music composition. When a Lisp application runs, a window called the Listener is available for the composer to interact with the Lisp environment. This interaction allows the composer to rapidly develop new ideas and test them out "on the fly". Lisp's interactive nature also encourages the composer to start developing a musical program even before fully understanding how it will work or what its final outcome will be. This style of programming is called prototyping . In prototyping, an application is developed incrementally, through a process of experimentation and change.

Lisp is a programmable language

The fact that Lisp is written in Lisp means that the language itself can be programmed and extended. Lisp's programmable nature makes it an ideal metalanguage in which to implement other languages and large software systems. The abstraction levels in computer music — composition, synthesis and sound production — can be easily represented by different Lisp software "layers" all of which work together to further a common goal.

Lisp makes symbolic computation possible

Lisp makes it very easy to represent and manipulate compositional structure. All programming languages calculate with numbers but Lisp is designed from the bottom up to also support symbolic expressions . A symbolic expression is an expression that consists of words and groups of words. Lisp programs can manipulate symbolic expressions for language processing. Music is a symbolic language and the ability to group symbols is fundamental to music composition. The ability to work with symbols and groups of symbols in Lisp means that it easy for the composer to create and manipulate musical expressions.

Lisp conforms to a language standard

Lisp's language standard insures that all Lisp implementations operate in the same way manner across all the different computers and operating systems currently available. A number of these implementations are free and can be downloaded from the internet. This means the Lisp composer can work on practically every computer available today and at no software expense.

The History of Lisp

Lisp is one of the oldest computer programming languages. It was invented by John McCarthy in the 1950's to support research into symbolic computation and artificial intelligence (AI). As a simple demonstration of what symbolic expressions are and what a Lisp AI program might do with them, consider the following two expressions:

1. Bach is a composer
2. All composers are mortal

A program that implements pattern matching and logical inference can conclude a new fact, namely:

3. Bach is a mortal

This is interesting, in part, because if you read the first two sentences (or listen to Bach's music!) you wouldn't necessarily conclude that Bach is a mortal. But by applying generic inference rules to a database of expressions the program can add new expressions to its knowledge base. In some sense, then, such a program has "learned" since the "knowledge" at its disposal has measurably increased.

Although research in Artificial Intelligence was one of the initial reasons for developing Lisp, AI has long since ceased to be the central focus of the language. Over the last few decades Lisp has evolved into a general purpose programming language that is used for many different types of applications: CAD systems, notation programs, text editors, HTML servers, window managers, even airline reservation systems. But at its core, Lisp remains a language that is particularly well suited to research and, by extension, to creative domains with a strong exploratory nature, like music composition.

Dialects and Implementations

Adialect is a version of a language. As research into symbolic computing progressed in the 1960s and 1970s a number of different Lisp dialects emerged. Scheme and Common Lisp (CL) are the two most important Lisp dialects in existence today. Each dialect has its own particular strengths: Scheme is a small, elegant, consistent and "pure" version of Lisp; Common Lisp is a much larger, faster and a more "industrial strength" version of Lisp.

Within a single Lisp dialect there are likely to be a number of different language *implementations*. An implementation is the computer software that makes a specific instance of a language specification. Some Lisp implementations are free, others are products sold by companies. In general, all implementations of a given dialect agree on a common set of features as defined in its *language specification*. A language specification is a document that defines the exact syntax and semantics of the language. The specification for Common Lisp is Common Lisp: the Language (2nd Edition), by Guy Steele (http://www-2.cs.cmu.edu/Groups/AI/html/cltl/cltl2.html). The language specification for Scheme is The Revised (5) Report on the Algorithmic Language Scheme (http://www.swiss.ai.mit.edu/~jaffer/r5rs_toc.html).

Lisp implementations are allowed add extensions and extra features to the core language as defined in the language specification, which means that features not explicitly covered in the specification tend to vary widely from implementation to implementation. Common extensions include "developer tools" such as compilers, graphic libraries, foreign language interfaces, program code analyzers, optimizers, debuggers and so on.

Common Music and Lisp

The music software system that accompanies this book is called Common Music (CM). Common Music produces sound by transforming a metalevel representation of music into a variety of different protocols for controlling sound production and display. The system was originally written in Common Lisp but now includes both Scheme and Common Lisp bindings (Table 1). Because Scheme is smaller and conceptually more consistent than Common Lisp it is the dialect that is used and documented in Notes from the Metalevel.

There are several things to keep in mind while working through the book. First, although the book adopts Scheme syntax for pedagogical reasons all of the examples and program code in Notes from the Metalevel will work with *any* implementation of Common Music that is listed in Table 1. Secondly, language extensions provided by the host Lisp implementation are available to the user when working with Common Music, but Common Music itself does not depend on them. And lastly, the vast majority of examples in the book do not depend on any operating system specific features. Where such differences do exist they are documented using one of the special notes discussed in the Preface.

Composers who would like to examine CM's program code to learn how a particular feature or function was implemented can access the source code on the accompanying CD. Common Music's Scheme sources have a .scm extensions and Common Lisp sources have a .lisp extension. The sources included on the CD are a "snapshot" of the software as it was at the time this book went to press. Common Music continues to evolve and the reader may wish at some point to install a newer version of the system than the one that was shipped on the book's CD. Source code to the most recent version of Common Music can always be downloaded via the Internet from the CM project home page.

Table 1. Lisp Implementations for Common Music

Implementation	Dialect	Linux	OSX	MacOS	Windows
ACL	CL	x		x	x
CLISP	CL	x		x	x
CMUCL	CL	x			
Guile	Scheme	x	x		x
MCL	CL		x	x	
OpenMCL	CL	x	x		

3

Functions and Data

Lisp is a *functional language*, which means that all actions are accomplished by functions acting on data. A Lisp function is a program, or procedure, that accomplishes a task. Most tasks require a function to manipulate some sort of data. The term *data* refers to the information that a function acts on, or processes. The idea of functions in Lisp comes from the Lambda Calculus, a branch of mathematical logic developed by Alonzo Church in the 1930s. The Lambda Calculus defines mathematical computation in terms of anonymous functions, called *lambda expressions*, that are applied to input values to produce output values. This basic computational model is adopted by Lisp but with two important additions. First, most Lisp functions are not "anonymous", they have names associated with them. A name makes it easy to refer to a function and also gives an indication of what purpose the function serves. Secondly, not all functions in Lisp return results. Most Lisp functions behave like lambda expressions — they calculate useful values. But some functions are used for the *effects* they produce rather than for a value they return. For example, the purpose of the Lisp function define is to add a new definition to the language rather than to compute a result. Interaction 1 shows the two uses of functions. In the first expression the function * is called to return the product of its inputs 2 and *pi*. In the next line the function define adds a new variable definition to Lisp and does not return a value.

Interaction 1. Examples of calling Lisp functions.

```
cm> (* 2 pi)
6.283185307179586
cm> (define 2pi (* 2 pi))

cm> (list 2pi 2pi)
(6.283185307179586  6.283185307179586)
cm>
```

The terms *function, lambda body, procedure, special function, macro,* and *closure* are used at various times in this book to refer to types of Lisp functions. Two of these terms deserve mention here because they will be used in the next several chapters of this book. A *special function* is a basic building block of the Lisp language. Special functions are "special" because they have their own unique syntax that provides some essential feature of the Lisp language. The define function is one such special function. A *macro* is a function that rewrites expressions. A macro takes an input expression exactly as the user typed it and then *transforms* it into a different expression which Lisp then executes. This is a subtle but important point because it means that the notation of the external expression may follow its own special rules of grammar. The loop and process macros appear in many of the music composition programs discussed in this book.

Data and Datatypes

The term *data* refers to the information that a function acts on, or processes. Most functions receive input data, perform a computation, and return an output value back to the caller. In some sense, then, a function can simply be thought of as an object that maps input values to output values (Table 1).

Table 1. Functions map inputs to outputs.

Inputs:	1 2	1 2 3	60
	\ /	\ | /	|
Function:	+	list	keynum->hertz
	|	|	|
Outputs:	3	(1 2 3)	261.625

Since we only interact with functions by passing inputs and receiving outputs we do not need to understand how they are implemented in order to use them. For the moment we will just treat them as "black boxes" that provide useful programming services.

One of the most important skills that the beginning music programmer can develop is an ability to understand what sorts of information will be needed for given musical project and how best to represent that information in the actual data that a Lisp program will process. The composition programs and algorithms that appear in this book process many different kinds of information, from simple numbers to complex and multifaceted objects in object-oriented programming. One of the basic features of the Lisp language is that all data are classified according to their *type*. Consider a program that converts a MIDI key number to a Hertz frequency value. If key number 60 (Middle C) is the input the program would output 261.625 Hertz. While both the input and output are numbers they are actually different *types* of numbers. The number 60 is an exact number called an integer. The value 261.625 is an inexact, or real number. The terms integer, real and number are examples of Lisp *datatypes* that classify the data that Lisp programs process. The novice Lisp composer must develop an ability to recognize the most common types of data used in Lisp programming, to understand how these datatypes can be used to represent musical information, and to be able to specify this data in proper Lisp notation. We will cover each of these points in the remaining sections of this chapter.

Symbolic Expressions

The Lisp language was invented, in part, to support *symbolic computation*, a type of programming in which tokens, called symbols, are processed along with quantitative information. A symbol can be thought of as a word. For example, the symbol debussy denotes a great French composer. In symbolic computation, symbols and groups of symbols are manipulated as if they were words and sentences. Of course the symbols and symbol groups do not have to reflect a natural language, they might reflect other languages as well, for example those of mathematics or music. For historical reasons, symbolic expressions came to be divided into two groups that reflect the basic distinction between words and groups of words. An *atom* is a basic, elementary thing like a symbol or a number. A *list* is group of things. A list can hold atoms and other lists. Lists are the central hallmark of the Lisp language. In fact, the name "Lisp" is an abbreviation for <u>Lis</u>t processing. The following graph depicts the most common types of symbolic expressions, or *s-expressions* that will be encountered in this book.

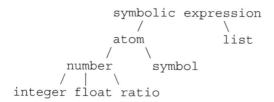

```
              symbolic expression
                 /           \
              atom           list
             /    \
        number     symbol
       / | \
integer float ratio
```

The symbolic expressions listed in the graph are actually just a tiny fraction of the total number of datatypes represented in Lisp. Lisp also provides the means to add user-defined datatypes to the language. But the graph contains the most basic and important types of data that the Lisp composer will work with on a daily basis. We will now examine each of these types in more detail.

Integers

An integer is an exact counting number like 1, 0 or -99. Digits can be optionally preceded by a + or - sign. For all practical purposes there is no limit on the size of an integer in Lisp. The special prefix #x allows an integer to be notated in base 16 (hexadecimal), #o is the prefix for octal notation and #b for binary.

Integers are a basic feature of almost all programming languages. In addition to their role in mathematical expressions, many programs use integers for counting the number of times some action is performed. In terms of purely musical information, integers are a natural choice to represent pitch classes and interval distances expressed as half steps. Integers are also ideal for representing MIDI information such as *key numbers*. A key number is an integer between 0 and 127 that represents the position of a key on a "virtual" MIDI keyboard. The first key on the keyboard is key number 0; Middle C on the keyboard is key number 60.

Example 1. Samples of integer notation.

```
- - - - - - - - - - - - - - - - - - - - - - - - - - - - - - - - - - - - - - - - - - - - - .
44100
-1
102003012303023024402323133329382381
60
#xFFFF
#b-11110000
- - - - - - - - - - - - - - - - - - - - - - - - - - - - - - - - - - - - - - - - - - - - - .
```

Real Numbers

A real, or floating point number, is a fractional number like 1.25 or -.45. Very large or small real values can be written using exponential notation. In exponential notation the real number is followed by a suffix e+n or e-n where n is the appropriate power of ten. For example the large real number 1230000000000.0 can be written more concisely as 1.23e+12 in exponential notation.

Real numbers, like integers, are ubiquitous in programming. But unlike integers, there are a few issues to keep in mind when using real numbers. First, a real value is an inexact representation of a quantity. For example, 0.333 is only an approximation of the quantity 1/3. The value 0.333333 is a closer approximation to 1/3 than 0.333 but it is still not exact. A real approximation can only go to a certain *precision* because there is a limit to the size of floating point numbers in a computer. The maximum precision and size of a real number depends on each Lisp implementation. Secondly, when an inexact number is used in a calculation a slight error is introduced into the result. If this result accumulates over many repetitions of a computation then what was originally an insignificant difference may compound itself into a serious error in the final result. And finally, mixed arithmetic — mathematical expressions that contain both real and rational numbers (integers and ratios) — will always produce a real result. Multiplying 10 by 1.0 produces 10.0 not 10. This conversion into the inexact representation happens automatically and so it may be the source of confusion for the novice programmer.

Despite these caveats real numbers are a very effective way to represent measurements, and many types of musical quantities that only need to be "good enough". These include such things as frequency in Hertz and time values in seconds. Values like Hertz and seconds only need to be good enough because humans can only discriminate their precision up to a certain point. Real numbers between 0.0 and 1.0 can also be used in composition to represent "normalized" values. A normalized value is like a percentage except that it may directly scale another quantity to produce the desired value.

Example 2. Samples of real number notation.

```
440.0
4.3E+2
-.25
33.33333333333333
6.5E-10
```

Ratios

A ratio is a fraction of two integers, for example 1/2 or -3/4. The numerator and denominator are separated by a / with no spaces. Lisp automatically reduces ratios to their simplest canonical form, for example 2/4 becomes 1/2 and 6/3 becomes 2.

Ratios are exact fractional quantities. They are useful in music for expressing exact proportions like those found in mensural notation, the harmonic series or even the Fibbonaci series. For example, if 1 represents a whole note then the ratio 2/3 is the proportion of 2 triplet half notes, 1/5 is 1 quintuplet quarter note, 7/8 is 7 eighth notes and so on. Ratios can be used to represent intervals in the harmonic series and to produce *justly tuned* values by scaling (multiplying) Hertz frequencies. For example, $3/2f$ is the frequency a just fifth up from f, $8/9f$ is a just major second down, and so on. Despite their obvious utility, one potential problem with ratios is that they can be difficult to interpret sometimes. For example, how much is $160929076/151896821f$?

Example 3. Samples of ratio notation.

```
13/21
5/3
-3/4
```

Symbols

A symbol is a sequence of alphanumeric characters, like music or 5th-symphony. Hyphenated symbols are very common in Lisp. Symbols can be thought of as words. Most combinations of letters, digits and hyphens can be included in a symbol's name. However, there are a few characters that have a special significance in Lisp notation and should not be used in symbol names. These characters are:

```
    `  #  (  )  \  :  ;  "  '  ,
```

Lisp can be either case sensitive or case insensitive. Case sensitive means that a lower case letter is not recognized to be the same as its upper case equivalent. In a case sensitive Lisp the three symbols machaut, Machaut and MACHAUT would all be different symbols. In a case insensitive Lisp the three notations would refer to the exact same symbol. For simplicity's sake, and because standard Lisp programming style uses lower case letters exclusively, this book assumes a case sensitive lisp and symbols are always notated in lower case letters.

Symbols appear everywhere in Lisp. In addition to their role as words and tokens they have a special significance as names for Lisp programs and variables. A *keyword* is a special type of symbol that starts with a colon, for example :retrograde. The colon is not actually part of the symbol's name, it is a special character that defines the symbol to be a keyword. Keywords have a special role in programming that will be discussed in the next few chapters. For now just remember that keywords can be used as tokens just like regular symbols can be used.

Example 4. Samples of symbol notation.

```
- - - - - - - - - - - - - - - - - - - - - - - - - - - - - - - - - - - - - - - - - -
c-sharp-minor
+
*tempo*
sfz
:sounds-good
- - - - - - - - - - - - - - - - - - - - - - - - - - - - - - - - - - - - - - - - - -
```

Lists

How data are organized is often just as important as what the data represents! The idea of grouping things together to form larger units of structure permeates the activity of music composition and it is also a fundamental property of Lisp data representation. All but the simplest programs in this book exhibit data grouping that forms higher level units of information out of constituent elements. For example, a twelve-tone composition project might use integers to represent the twelve pitch classes and then group pitch classes together to form "rows". The twelve-tone program would then operate on each row as a single unit of information. Note that a grouping like a twelve-tone row is homogeneous — all of its elements are of the same datatype and represent the same type of information. But this need not be the case — grouping can reflect an association between complex and heterogeneous information as well. For example, a project that involves Forte sets might represent each set as a group of three elements: the name of the set, the prime form of the set and the interval vector of the set. Each of these values means something quite different in the representation and would likely be implemented using different Lisp datatypes. To understand more about how data can be grouped into bundles to form "higher level" representations requires some knowledge about how Lisp itself represents and organizes data.

A *Lisp list* is a container. The contents of a list are called its elements. Any kind of data, including lists, can be placed inside of lists. The ability to organize different things inside of lists makes them an extremely versatile tool and their *recursive* nature means that there is practically no limit to the depth and complexity of information that they can represent. However, a few very simple formats for organizing list elements have proven to be especially effective for representing many different types of information. The most basic of these formats is called the *property list*. The property list format will be discussed in a later section of this chapter.

It is not possible to categorize all the ways in which lists can be used in music composition — sets, rows, notes, chords, measures, phrases, sections, movements, pieces, staves, sequences, matrices, envelopes — the list goes on and on. But before learning how musical information might be represented with lists we must first understand how lists are notated.

List notation

Lists are beautiful. They are simple, powerful, flexible and extremely easy to work with. There are only four very simple rules to proper list notation:

1. The starting and ending points of a list are marked by parentheses: (). The left, or open, parentheses (marks the start of a list and the right, or close, parenthesis) marks its end.
2. Every open parenthesis must be matched, or balanced, by exactly one close parenthesis.
3. A close parenthesis matches the nearest unmatched open parenthesis to its left.
4. Spaces, tabs or lines can separate elements in a list.

It is very important to realize that the ability to understand and implement Lisp music programs depends on the ability to read and write lists. So if you understand the preceding rules then you are ready to start programming!

Example 5. Samples of list notation.

```
-------------------------------------------------
()
(0  3  7  11  2  5  9  1  4  6  8  10)
(how many violists does it
     take to screw in a light bulb?)
(3-7 (0 2 5) (0 1 1 0 1 0))
(staff violin-1
        (clef treble)
        (signature c-minor)
        (meter 2 4)
        (measure (rest 8th)
                 (note g4 8th ff)
                 (note g4 8th)
                 (note g4 8th))
        (measure (note e4 half fermata)))
-------------------------------------------------
```

The first list in Example 5 has no elements. A list with no elements is called the empty list. In other words, the empty list is still a list — a list without elements is not the same as no list at all. The second list in the example has 12 elements, each element is an integer. This list is one possible way to represent the twelve tone row from Berg's Violin Concerto. The third list demonstrates how sentences can be represented by symbols grouped into lists. The fourth list demonstrates one possible representation of a Forte set. It includes the name, prime form and interval vector of [025]. The last list in the example shows one possible way to represent the opening violin part of a very famous symphony.

Property lists
Lists are collections that associate or group information together. Although lists can reflect a multitude of different organizations there are a few list formats that have proven to be very effective for representing different types of information. The most important of these list formats is called the *property list*. A property list is a list whose elements are interpreted pair wise. The first element of each pair is called the property and the second element is called the value. Since a pair consists of two elements a property list will always have an even number of elements. The entire list can be interpreted as the description of the properties, or attributes, of some entity. How might this be used to represent music? Consider a program that computes flute compositions. Each note for this composition might be defined to have the acoustic properties of duration, frequency, amplitude, and timbre. Given this set of properties, individual notes in a composition could be specified by computing the appropriate values for each property of each note. For example the program might start out the composition by computing the following note description:

Table 2. Property and value pairs.

Property	Value
duration	7/8
frequency	440
amplitude	ff
timbre	breathy

The information in this table is easily represented in the composition program as a property list (Example 6).

Example 6. Property list notation.

```
(duration 7/8 frequency 440
            amplitude ff timbre breathy)
```

It is quite common for keywords (symbols that start with ":") to be used as the property names in lists such as the one shown above. There are several reasons for this. First, using keyword names gives a visual cue as to what is serving as name and what is value in a property list (Example 7).

Example 7. Keyword names in property lists.

```
(:duration 7/8 :frequency 440
          :amplitude ff :timbre breathy)
```

Secondly, some functions we will encounter later in this book allow *keyword arguments* to be passed to the function. A keyword argument is an optional input value that is referred by its keyword name. The syntax for these arguments shares the same keyword and value pairing as seen in the list above.

Function call lists

Passing input values to a function and receiving its output value is referred to as *calling* a function, or *applying* a function to its arguments. *Arguments* are the data passed to the function as input. Function calls follow a very consistent format in Lisp: a function call is a list whose first element is the name of the function and the rest of the elements (if any) are arguments to the function.

This type of notation — in which the function always appears before the data passed to it — is called *prefix notation*. Prefix notation makes it easy to determine when symbols are used as functions and when they are not: for a symbol to act as a function it must always be in the first position of a list. In the third line of Example 8, the symbols * list and expt are functions because each is in the first position of a list. The symbol pi is not used as a function because it is the not the first element of a list.

Example 8. Function call notation.

```
(* 2 pi)
(list 2 pi)
(* 440 (expt 2 1/12))
```

Note that function calls may be *nested*. In the last line of Example 8 the second argument to the * function is itself a function call. Embedding function calls inside other function calls is very typical of Lisp programming style.

Other Common Datatypes

This chapter has introduced the basic building blocks of symbolic expressions — numbers, symbols and lists — that are used by the composition programs in this book. There are two other datatypes that historically were not considered to be symbolic expressions but nevertheless appear in many of the programming examples in this book.

Boolean

Both the integer and real datatypes represent an infinite number of values. The boolean datatype represents only two possible values: true and false. Computer programs use boolean values to express *conditional actions*, actions that are only performed if a certain test is either true or false. For example, a music composition program might start by first randomly generating interval sets until a set with a certain interval vector content has been generated. If that test is true then the program begins to compose using the set, otherwise (the test was false) the program keeps picking random interval sets until it finds one that it "likes". Logic tells us that if something is not false then it must be true. In other words, since false is false then truth is anything that is not explicitly false. So some computer programs in Lisp do not test for an explicit boolean true value, they simply check to see that values are not boolean false. This allows *predicate functions*, functions that test the truth or falsity of an input expression, to return useful "true" values other than explicit boolean true.

Example 9. Samples of boolean notation.

- ·
```
#f
#t
```
- ·

Lisp Note:

> Scheme defines `#t` as boolean true and `#f` as boolean false. Common Lisp defines the symbol `t` to mean true and the symbol `nil` to mean false. This book generally refers to these values as simply true or false.

Text Strings

A string is a sequence of text characters delimited by double quotes at the start and end of the string, for example `"Music"` or `"Das Lied von der Erde"`. Strings are simply blocks of text, they have no other significance to Lisp. The text within a string may contain any combination of characters, even the special characters listed in the section describing symbols. (To include the `"` character as part of the text it must be preceded by the special *escape character* \ which tells lisp that the quote following the escape character is not interpreted as the end of the string.)

Strings are used primarily for displaying messages or printing text to files. They are also frequently used to specify *pathnames*, the names of files and directories on the computer.

Do not confuse strings with symbols or lists. `"Music"` is word-like but the pair of double-quotes makes it a string not a symbol. `"Music is an art"` contains words separated by spaces but it is not a list. These differences can be seen in the following summary table:

Table 3. Strings, symbols and lists.

Type	Example
symbol:	`music`
text string:	`"music"`
list of symbols:	`(music is an art)`
text string:	`"music is an art"`
text string:	`"(music is an art)"`
list of strings:	`("music" "is" "an" "art")`

4

Etudes, Op. 1: The Lisp Listener

Etudes Op. 1 introduces the Common Music application and the Lisp Listener. This chapter assumes that you have copied the contents of the CD onto your computer's hard drive. The exercises discussed below represent a "bare bones" method for working with Lisp and Common Music. Once you have performed these Etudes you should download the latest version of Common Music from http://sourceforge.net/projects/commonmusic and learn how to work with Lisp and Common Music from inside the Emacs or XEmacs text editors. These editors "understand" Lisp syntax and will allow you to evaluate Lisp code interactively, as you edit and develop your programs. Please consult the last section in this chapter for more information on working with Emacs or XEmacs.

Op. 1, No. 1: Running the Common Music Application

To start the Common Music application first locate the directory that contains the contents copied from the CD. This directory will be referred to as the "NM project directory". Once this directory has been located the Common Music application can be started by performing one of the instructions listed below that matches your computer's operating system.

MacOS:

> Double-click the Common Music application icon located in the NM project directory.

OSX and Linux:

> Open a Terminal window and execute the "cm" script in the bin/ subdirectory of the NM project directory. This example assumes NM project directory was restored under the author's home directory:
>
> ```
> /User/hkt% ~/NM/bin/cm
> ```

Windows:

> Double-click the file "cm.bat" located in the NM bin project directory.

Op. 1, No. 2: The Lisp Interpreter

The Lisp Interpreter is a program that allows the composer to interact directly with Lisp inside a window called the Lisp Listener. The user interacts with Lisp by typing input expressions into the window and then observing what Lisp returns as an output value on the next line. You might think of the interpreter as a fancy calculator that determines the value of any Lisp expression you type to it. Whenever the interpreter is waiting for the user to enter an input expression it displays an *input prompt* and the cursor bar just after the prompt marks the *insertion point*, the position in the window where the next input expression should be typed. Since input prompts tend to vary with each Lisp implementation, this book always displays the input prompt as:

```
cm>
```

The letters are an abbreviation for the Common Music application that is running inside the Listener. The user's input expressions that follow the prompt are printed in bold face to distinguish them from the output values that Lisp prints back to the Listener window. An output value (if any) appears on the line directly beneath the input expression that produced it.

Click on the Listener window to make sure it is active and then type the following expression at the insertion point at the very end of the last prompt line in the window. Then press the Return key to enter the expression into Lisp. The Return key is not displayed in the examples, it is assumed that the user presses Return at the end of every input expression.

Interaction 1. Evaluating numbers.

```
cm> 440
440
cm> 44100.0
44100.0
cm>
```

As the user works inside the interpreter the entire interaction history is visible in the window but only the insertion point at the end of the last line is available for input. Try entering a few different types of numbers and symbols into the interpreter:

Interaction 2. Evaluating symbols.

```
cm> pi
3.141592653589793
cm> *scale*
#<tuning "standard-chromatic-scale">
cm> stravinsky
*** - EVAL: variable STRAVINISKY has no value
1. Break [4]> abort
cm>
```

Entering the first two symbols caused each variable's value to be printed (variables are discussed in the next chapter). Entering the third symbol stravinsky triggered a *Lisp error*.

Op. 1, No. 3: Lisp Errors

Whenever Lisp encounters a problem it prints an *error message* that helps the user identify and fix the problem. Each Lisp implementation has its own method for handling errors. Some versions of Lisp immediately return the user back to the Lisp prompt after the error message is printed. Other implementations may enter an *error break* that allows a programmer to "inspect" the Lisp environment in order to determine the exact cause of the error. Error breaks are usually indicated by the Lisp prompt changing to a special *break prompt* immediately after the error message has been printed. Break prompts look a bit different than the normal top-level Lisp prompt and often include a number that shows the current *error level* the user is working in. The error level indicates how many errors must be resolved before Lisp is back in its normal, "top-level" working environment.

Lisp errors should never cause the application to "crash" or the computer to freeze. An error is really just a kind of report that attempts to explain what was wrong with the expression that caused the error. Note that while Lisp may be able to determine exactly what went wrong with an expression it cannot determine why something went wrong. This is because Lisp cannot know all the conditions that led to the problem. For example, when an *unbound variable* occurs in the Listener it may be due to the user misspelling the name of an actual variable or it may be the correct name of a variable that the user forgot to define. Because Lisp cannot know the intentions of a user, error messages may seem cryptic at times, or may not give very helpful information for correcting the problem. The novice Lisp composer should prepare for this eventuality by developing a consistent strategy for resolving errors, and by always resolving each error immediately after it occurs. This is called *debugging* a problem. Here are a few simple strategies to follow:

- Read the error message carefully and completely.
- Attempt to determine exactly what symbols or expressions are involved in the error.
- Locate these expression in the code you were just using.
- Study the code and its surroundings to see if you can identify the problem.
- If you cannot locate the problem, reduce the expression to smaller pieces until you have isolated the exact source of the problem.

There is practically no limit to the type and number of errors a human can make! The good news is that most problems are easy to resolve because they are simple mistakes like mistyping a name. The novice Lisp composer should pay particular attention symbol spelling and proper list formatting. Here is a list of the most common errors that the beginning Lisp composer may make:

- Misspelled symbol
- Improperly formatted list
- Improper function call syntax
- Function call list whose first element is not a function
- Symbol or list not quoted

Once you have determined what the error is you should always *resolve* the error before continuing to input Lisp expressions into the Listener. The easiest way to resolve errors is to simply *abort* them. Aborting an error will stop the current program from executing any further and return the user back to the "top-level" input prompt in the Listener. Each implementation of Lisp has its own mechanism for aborting errors:

OSX, Linux and Windows:
> Type the symbol `abort` to the break prompt (Interaction 2).

MacOS:
> Press the Apple command key and type "." (Command-.) or select the Abort Error item in the Lisp menu.

Lisp evaluation and errors are discussed in more detail in Chapter 5.

Op. 1, No. 4: The Lisp Editor

A composer spends most of the time in Lisp developing music programs. This means that a large portion of your time will be devoted to writing and editing your *source code* in a text editor. Emacs (or XEmacs) is without a doubt the best editor to use when you work with Lisp code and Common Music. Both Emacs and XEmacs are mouse-and-menu graphical editors that "understand" Lisp syntax and can even run the Common Music application in a special window inside the editor. This tight integration between Emacs and the Common Music application will allow you to edit your Lisp source code and then *remotely evaluate* Lisp expressions from your edit window as you develop your program. For more information on installing and using Emacs or XEmacs with Common Music, please consult the Common Music document http://commonmusic.sf.net/doc/emacs.html.

Example 1 shows what a Lisp file looks like inside the Emacs editor. If you are looking at the HTML example page, notice that different parts of the code are colored according to what type of syntactic unit it is: comments (lines beginning with one or more semi-colon characters), definitions, special forms and keywords. Emacs calls this colorized display *syntax highlighting*. If you do not see different colors, select "Syntax Highlighting" from the Options menu to turn highlighting on. Note that in the book these syntax highlights will be displayed in black and white.

To edit the example file from inside Emacs, choose the "Open File" menu item from the File menu. When the dialog window pops up locate the file "opus-1.lisp" in the examples subdirectory of the NM project directory and select the file. You can navigate through the list of files in the Open File dialog using the Up and down arrows. Press the Return key to select a file or to enter a highlighted directory. Once you have selected the file it will be displayed in an editor window. If you have installed Emacs according to the Common Music documentation you can select the "Lisp Listener" item in the Lisp menu to start Common Music running in its own Emacs window. Then examine the file and perform the suggested actions. Here is the contents of the example file (Example 1). If you do not have Emacs installed, you can type each expression (skipping the comment lines beginning with semi-colons) directly to the Lisp interpreter.

Example 1. A Lisp file

```
- - - - - - - - - - - - - - - - - - - - - - - - - - - - - - - - - - - - - - - - -
;;; This is a sample lisp source file and you are
;;; reading a Lisp comment.  A comment begins with ;
;;; and continues to the end of the line. Lisp
;;; ignores comments when it process source code.
;;;
;;; To evaluate a lisp expression inside Emacs,
;;; first select the expression by double-clicking it
;;; and then use the Eval Expression command in the
;;; Lisp menu. Try evaluating the following expressions
;;; in the manner just described. The results from  each
;;; evaluation will appear in the Listener window.

2
pi
1/4


;;; To evaluate a list double-click one of the outer
;;; parentheses to select the whole expression. Then
;;; use Eval Selection to evaluate it.
;;; You can also evaluate expressions by placing the
;;; cursor on the start or just after the expression
;;; and then typing: C-x C-e (control-x control-e).

(* 2 pi )
(list 2 pi)
(sin (* 2 pi ))
(define albans-row '(0 3 7 11 2 5 9 1 4 6 8 10))
- - - - - - - - - - - - - - - - - - - - - - - - - - - - - - - - - - - - - - - - -
```

```
(define (row->matrix row)
   ;; this function is discussed in Chapter 8
   (loop for i in row
         collect
         (loop for j in row
               collect (mod (+ (- i) j) 12)))))
(pprint (row->matrix albans-row))
```

Op. 1, No. 5: Improvisation

Try typing a few expressions of your own inside the text editor's window and then evaluating them. Once you have finished experimenting with the sample code you can quit Common Music by selection "Quit" from the File menu in the Listener window.

Chapter Source Code

The source code to all of the examples and interactions in this chapter can be found in the file cmapp.cm located in the same directory as the HTML file for this chapter. The source file can be edited in a text editor or evaluated inside the Common Music application.

5

Lisp Evaluation

In this chapter we examine the process by which Lisp *evaluates*, or interprets, Lisp expressions in order to produce results. Since Lisp programs are built out of Lisp expressions, understanding this evaluation process is key to understanding Lisp notation and the behavior of the music programs we will develop over the course of this book. In a very real sense the process of evaluation defines how Lisp operates as a programming language.

The Interpreter

In Chapter 4 we learned how to interact with Lisp by typing input expressions into the Listener window and then observing the results that Lisp prints back to the window. The Listener window supports this interaction using a program called the *interpreter*, or *read-eval-print loop* (Figure 1). The terms *read*, *eval* and *print* define three different stages in the processing of Lisp input expressions. These stages are literally implemented by three separate Lisp functions called `read`, `eval` and `print`. At the beginning of each cycle through the loop the interpreter waits for the user to input an expression. Once a user enters some text — either by typing it and pressing the Return key or by remotely evaluating a block of text in an Emacs buffer — the interpreter processes the input by invoking the three steps of

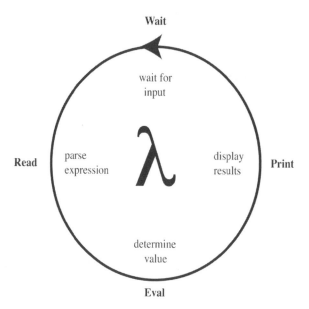

Figure 1. The Lisp interpreter continuously processes input in its read-eval-print loop.

the read-eval-print loop in successive order. We now examine each of these steps in more detail.

Read
In the read step the text string that the user inputs into the Listener window is first *parsed* from the window and then assembled into a true Lisp expression. If a valid Lisp expression results then the interpreter goes on to the next step (eval) in the process. If a Lisp object cannot be parsed from the input then the interpreter signals an error and waits for the user to correct the problem.

Eval
During the eval step the interpreter determines the *value*, or result, of an input Lisp expression. This evaluation process lies at the very heart of the language. Unfortunately, the evaluation process is not actually visible in the Listener window — it happens "behind the scenes", before any output is printed back for the user to see. This may make the effects of evaluation seem a bit mysterious to the novice Lisp composer. But the mechanism is simple to understand if the rules that govern its behavior are first understood. These evaluation rules are covered in the next few sections of this chapter.

Print
In the print step the interpreter displays the results of evaluation back to the Listener window. The print step is in some sense the "reverse" of the read step — the Lisp expression that results from the eval step is translated into a text string and then displayed on a new line in the window. Once this output has been printed the interpreter starts the read-eval-print loop all over again by displaying the input prompt and waiting for the user to enter the next command string.

Lisp Evaluation

The "goal" of Lisp is to determine the value of Lisp expressions. Evaluation is accomplished by applying a small number of "interpretation rules" to an input expression. The applicability of these rules is determined by the datatype of the input expression. This means that the easiest way to learn about the evaluation process is to observe its effects on the basic datatypes that were presented in Chapter 2.

The evaluation of numbers, booleans and strings
Numbers, booleans and strings are *self-evaluating* expressions. A self-evaluating expression means that the expression does not change as a result of evaluation. Common sense tells us that numbers and booleans must be self-evaluating because, if they were not, the laws of mathematics and logic would make no sense — zero, one, true and false must remain ever so! Strings are self-evaluating expressions because Lisp simply declares them to be so.

Note that — although self-evaluating expressions remain unchanged by the evaluation process — their "appearance" in the print step may be different than in the read step. This difference does not mean that the value has actually changed, but only that the print step has *notated* the value differently than how the user first entered it.

Interaction 1. Some self-evaluating expressions.

```
cm> 44100
44100
cm> #xFFFF
65535
cm> .500
0.5
cm> "Ondes Martenot"
"Ondes Martenot"
cm>
```

We can summarize our observations about self-evaluating expressions in a simple rule to remember:

Lisp Evaluation Rule 1:
   A number, boolean or string evaluates to itself.

Symbol Evaluation and Variables

In Chapter 2 we learned that symbols can be treated as words and grouped into lists
to form symbolic expressions. But here are two symbolic expressions that use the
symbol pi differently:
```
(pi is a greek letter)
(* 2 pi)
```
The first expression treats the symbol pi as the name of a Greek letter. But the
second expression appears to represent an *action*: "multiply 2 and pi together." In
this case the symbol pi would clearly be standing for a particular numerical value:
3.141592653589793.

   A symbol that stands for a value is called a *variable*. It is important to
understand that a symbol and a variable are not exactly the same thing. A symbol
names a variable. A symbol is created just by typing its name but a variable can only
be created by *defining* it using special mechanisms provided by Lisp. Although Lisp
symbols appear to be just words they are actually complex objects that possess a
number of different properties. One of the properties of a symbol is it's *print name*,
the text that you see printed on the screen. A symbol also has a *value cell* property.
This value cell allows a value (any Lisp expression) to be associated with the
symbol. This association is called a *variable binding*. It is only through the eval step
that symbols can be treated as variables. When the eval step encounters a bound
symbol its value is returned instead of the symbol. If the symbol is not bound before
it is evaluated then Lisp will signal an "unbound variable" error. One of the
interesting features of Lisp that distinguishes it from many other programming
languages is that a symbol's value cell can hold *any* Lisp value. Most programming
languages constrain variables to hold only one particular type of data. But in Lisp it
is the data itself that is typed, or classified, rather than the variable. This makes it
simple to work with variables in Lisp because the composer does not have to
"declare" a variable's type or insure that the variable is set to only one specific type
of data.

Interaction 2. Symbols are evaluated as variables.

```
cm> pi
3.141592653589793
cm> messiaen
> Error: Unbound variable: messiaen Aborted
cm>
```

In Interaction 2 the result of evaluating pi produced a value because the symbol pi
was defined to represent that value. The evaluation of the symbol messiaen
signaled an error because this symbol was not defined to have a value before it was
evaluated. We summarize symbols used as variables in a second rule of evaluation:

Lisp Evaluation Rule 2:
   A symbol evaluates to its variable value. Lisp signals an "unbound variable"
   error if the variable does not have a value.

Evaluation of Function Call Lists

A *function call* is the application of a Lisp program to input data. Function calls are
notated as lists: the first element of the list is the function and the rest of the
elements are called the *arguments* to the function. In the expression:
   (* 2 pi)
the symbol * is the function and 2 pi are its two arguments. The evaluation of a
function call requires that each argument to the function be evaluated before the
function is actually called. This process can be demonstrated using the example
above. Before the multiplication can occur the two arguments 2 and pi are first
evaluated in left to right order to produce the values that are to be multiplied. The
first argument 2 is a number and therefore evaluates according to our Rule 1 to
produce the value 2. The second argument pi is a symbol and so it is evaluated as a
variable, according to Rule 2. The application of the second rule results in the value
3.141592653589793. Since neither argument produced an error, their values are
passed to the function *, which multiplies them together and produces the result
6.283185307179586 that is is then returned as the *value* of the function call.

   Since each argument in a function call is evaluated before the function is called,
arguments may include variables and other function calls. It is very common to see
nested function calls in lisp programming. A nested function call is an argument to a
function that is itself a function call. In the last input expression in Interaction 3 the
function call (* 2 pi 1/4) is nested as the argument to the sin function.

Interaction 3. Function call notation.

```
cm> (* 2 pi)
6.283185307179586
cm> (list 2 pi)
(2 3.141592653589793)
cm> (sin (* 2 pi 1/4))
1.0
cm>
```

Each of the input lists in Interaction 3 are function calls. Recall that the first element
in a function call is a function and the rest of the elements are arguments to the
function. This means that in the expressions above the symbols *, list and sin
are treated as functions because they are symbols in the first position of a list. The
symbol pi is not a function because it is not the first element of a list. Arguments in
a function call are evaluated in left to right order to produce input values to the
function. The inputs are passed to the function and the result returned by the
function becomes the value of the function call expression. Lisp signals an error if

the first element is not a function or if any argument cannot be evaluated. We summarize function call lists in a third evaluation rule:

Lisp Evaluation Rule 3:
    A Lisp list is evaluated as a function call. Lisp signals an "undefined function" error if the first element is not a function.

Blocking Evaluation

The previous two sections have described how the eval step processes symbols and lists. This brings up the obvious question: how can symbols be tokens or lists be used as data if the evaluator always treats them as programming variables and function calls? For example, how can pi ever be used as a word rather than a value? The answer is that Lisp provides a simple mechanism that allows us to selectively "turn off" evaluation such that an input expression becomes data, with no special interpretation made by the eval step.

The lisp quote
The single quote character: ' is a very special prefix character that "defeats" evaluation, by forcing Lisp to accept the expression that appears just after the quote exactly as the user typed it. Another way of saying this is that the eval step evaluates a quoted expression by stripping off the quote and returning the (now unquoted) expression as the value. The quote character can be applied to any Lisp expression. In the case of numbers, booleans and strings the quote will have no effect since these are self-evaluating anyway (Interaction 4).

Interaction 4. The effect of quote on evaluated expressions.

```
cm> '44100
44100
cm> '"Ondes Martenot"
"Ondes Martenot"
cm> pi
3.141592653589793
cm> 'pi
pi
cm> ''pi
'pi
cm> '(0 2 5)
(0 2 5)
cm> (* 2 pi)
6.283185307179586
cm> '(* 2 pi)
(* 2 pi)
cm>
```

A quote in front of a symbol or list causes Lisp to "see" just the expression itself rather than its value. We summarize this behavior in a fourth evaluation rule:

Lisp Evaluation Rule 4:
A quoted expression evaluates to the expression without the quote.

To quote or not to quote...
It is easy for a novice Lisp composer to become confused about when and when not to use quote in the Lisp Listener. A few simple guidelines should help make this determination less confusing:
- Numbers, booleans and strings never need to be quoted..
- Symbols need to be quoted unless they have been defined as variables or they are *keywords* (symbols starting with the colon character)
- Lists need to be quoted unless they are function calls.

The lisp backquote
The Lisp *backquote* character: ` is related to the quote character. But rather than block evaluation altogether, the backquote performs *selective* evaluation. Backquote can be used to specify lists in which some elements are evaluated and others not. A backquoted list acts as a *template*: elements are constant unless preceded by a comma, in which case that element will be *replaced* by its evaluated value (Interaction 5).

Interaction 5. The effects of quote and backquote on lists.

```
cm> '(a b pi c)
(a b pi c)
cm> `(a b ,pi c)
(a b 3.141592653589793 c)
cm>
```

The first input expression in Interaction 5 is a quoted list and so Lisp returns the entire list exactly as it was typed as the evaluated result. The second input expression is a backquoted list that selectively evaluates the variable pi and replaces it with its evaluated result in the list. Since each unevaluated expression would otherwise have to be quoted in an evaluated list, the backquote can substantially reduce the size and complexity of a notated expression by eliminating the need for explicit quotes. The following two expressions are equivalent:

Interaction 6. Equivalent expressions using list and backquote

```
cm> (list 'a 'b pi 'c)
(a b 3.141592653589793 c)
cm> `(a b ,pi c)
(a b 3.141592653589793 c)
cm>
```

Chapter Source Code

The source code to all of the examples and interactions in this chapter can be found in the file eval.cm located in the same directory as the HTML file for this chapter. The source file can be edited in a text editor or evaluated inside the Common Music application.

6

The Art of Lisp Programming

> The process of preparing programs for a digital computer is especially attractive, not only because it can be economically and scientifically rewarding, but also because it can be an aesthetic experience much like composing poetry or music.
>
> — Donald E. Knuth

A program in Lisp is a sequence of Lisp expressions that — when evaluated — produce an intended result. Once a programming task is understood, implementing the code really consists of only three things:
1. defining variables that hold data
2. defining functions that operate on data
3. calling the functions to produce the results

The clear, consistent, and functional nature of Lisp makes this process easy to learn. The little music program shown in Example 1 should be readily understandable by the reader even before the specific content can be explained. (Looping is discussed in Chapter 7.) After studying the example, start the Common Music application and evaluate each expression in the Listener to see what the function `transpose-row` returns.

Example 1. A small Lisp program.

- -

```
(define middle-c 60)

(define albans-row '(0 3 7 11 2 5 9 1 4 6 8 10))

(define (transpose-row row offset)
  (loop for pc in row collect (+ pc offset)))
```

- -

Try calling the program several times, as demonstrated in Interaction 1.

Interaction 1. Using the program

```
cm> (transpose-row albans-row middle-c)
(60 63 67 71 62 65 69 61 64 66 68 70)
cm> (transpose-row '(0 2 5) 90)
(90 92 95)
cm> (transpose-row albans-row (random 80))
(17 20 24 28 19 22 26 18 21 23 25 27)
cm>
```

Programs are Functions

Because all actions in Lisp are accomplished by calling functions, learning how to write music in Lisp amounts to learning how to call functions and knowing which functions to call in a given situation. A large part of this learning process is simply becoming familiar with the most frequently used functions encountered in music programming. To "become familiar" with a function means to learn its name, to know what results it returns, and to remember the number and type of input values the function accepts in a function call. This chapter introduces a core set of Lisp functions that the composition programs presented in the rest of the book depend on. This core set includes the basic arithmetic and boolean operators, list accessors, and the special function define that adds new variables and functions to Lisp. The next chapter presents several small and simple music programs that use some of the functions defined in this chapter.

The core set of functions presented here are actually only a very small portion of the total number of functions available to the Lisp programmer. The reader is strongly encouraged to consult the language specifications for Scheme or Common Lisp to learn about the complete set of functions available for use. The language specifications for Scheme and Common Lisp are indispensable tools for beginning and advanced Lisp users. One way to quickly gain familiarity with Lisp is to examine all of the entries that are related to the function definition you look up in the specification.

Function names and function types

The name of a function will usually give a good indication of what its purpose is. For example, the function named + calculates the sum of its input values. Lisp programmers have developed an informal set of *naming conventions* that provide additional information about what role or purpose a function has. It will be helpful to keep some of these conventions in mind as new functions are introduced in the coming chapters. The naming conventions depend on the type of function involved:

- A *predicate* is a function that returns true or false based on a test that it applies to its input. Predicates can usually be identified by the suffix ? appended to their names. For example, the predicate list? returns true if its argument is a list otherwise it returns false. The function odd? is a numerical predicate that returns true if its input is an odd number.

- A *getter* is a function that returns a value from a Lisp object. For example, the getter first returns the first element in a list. Getters may have the suffix -ref appended to their names ("ref" is shorthand for "reference"). For example, the function list-ref returns an element from a specified location in a list.

- A *setter* is a function that sets a value in a Lisp object. For example, the setter list-set! puts a value at a specified location in a list. Setters almost always have the suffix ! appended to their name. The ! informs the user that the function literally alters the object that it sets.

- A *constructor* is a function that creates a Lisp object. For example, the constructor list creates a Lisp list out of the values specified to the function. Constructors sometimes have the prefix make- added to their name. For example, the constructor make-list creates a list of a specified length.

- A *converter* is a function that converts one type of Lisp object into another type. For example, the converter symbol->string returns a Lisp string containing the name of a specified symbol. Converter names usually contain the "arrow" -> between their input and output types.

Function call syntax

Every Lisp function has a particular convention for accepting input values. Most functions expect a fixed number of input values. Some functions support what are called *optional arguments* — arguments that may be specified or not in a function call. A few common functions like *, + and list allow any number of arguments to be specified in the function call, including none. The function call syntax for each function documented in this book is described using a special format. Arguments to the function are shown as italicized *meta-variables*, like *x*, that stand for an input value in the function call. The special meta-variable ... means that any number of additional input arguments may be specified from that point on in the function call. An input variable enclosed in square brackets, like [*x*], means that the enclosed argument is *optional*. An optional argument is an argument that can be specified or not in the function call. An optional argument always has a *default value* if the argument is not specified. Unless otherwise indicated, this default value is boolean false. Consult the section Definitions in the Preface for additional information about the format used to describe function call syntax in this book.

The Core Functions

The following sections in this chapter present an overview of the most basic functions encountered in the programs discussed in this book. This core set includes arithmetic operators, list functions and the special function define that adds variables and functions to the language. Documentation for each function entry includes the name of the function, its function call syntax, and a brief description of what the function does.

Numerical functions

Lisp provides many numerical functions, only the most common are listed here. Consult the Scheme or Common Lisp references for the complete listing.

Numerical predicates

(number? *x*)	[Function]
(even? *n*)	[Function]
(odd? *n*)	[Function]

The numerical predicates return boolean true or false based on a test of their arguments. number? returns true if *x* is a number, otherwise false. even? is true if *n* is an even number and odd? is true if *n* is odd.

Interaction 2. Examples of numerical predicates.

```
cm> (number? 1)
#t
cm> (number? '(1))
#f
cm> (even? 0)
#t
cm> (odd? -2)
#f
cm>
```

Arithmetic relations

(= *n* ...)	[Function]
(< *n* ...)	[Function]
(> *n* ...)	[Function]
(<= *n* ...)	[Function]
(>= *n* ...)	[Function]

The arithmetic relations return boolean true if the relation is true for all arguments, otherwise false. Inequalities of more than two arguments test the ordering of the input values.

Interaction 3. Examples of arithmetic relations.

```
cm> (= 1 1.0)
#t
cm> (< 1 1)
#f
cm> (> 3 2 1)
#t
cm> (>= -1 0 1 1 100)
#f
cm> (<= -1 0 1 1 100)
#t
cm>
```

Arithmetic operators

(+ ...)	[Function]
(* ...)	[Function]
(- n ...)	[Function]
(/ n ...)	[Function]

Return the sum, product, difference and quotient of their arguments, respectively. + and * return the operator identity (zero and one, respectively) if no arguments are specified. - returns the negative inverse of one argument or subtraction of two or more arguments. / returns the reciprocal of one argument or the quotient of two or more arguments.

Interaction 4. Example arithmetic operators.

```
cm> (+ 1 2 3 4)
10
cm> (* 10 10)
100
cm> (- 1)
-1
cm> (- 1 .5)
0.5
cm> (/ 1)
1
cm> (/ 1 .25)
4.0
cm> (/ 30 5 -2)
-3
cm> (+)
0
cm> (*)
1
```

```
cm>
```

Other numerical functions

(min *n1 n2* ...)	[Function]
(max *n1 n2* ...)	[Function]
(mod *n divisor*)	[Function]
(expt *n power*)	[Function]
(log *n*)	[Function]
(sin *n*)	[Function]
(cos *n*)	[Function]
(random *n*)	[Function]

The min and max functions return the smallest and largest of their arguments, respectively. mod returns *n* modulus the *divisor*. expt returns *n* raised to the exponent *power* and log returns the exponent of *n* base *e*. sin and cos are the trigonometric functions sine and cosine, respectively. Both sin and cos take a single argument *n* in radians. The random function returns a uniform random number between zero less than *n*. If *n* is an integer then random returns an integer, if *n* is a real then a real value is returned. This means the random function can generate values in both discrete and continuous distributions (see Chapter 18 for a discussion of random distributions.)

List functions
Lists are an essential feature of Lisp and are used everywhere in this book. The core arithmetic and list functions will form the foundation of your programming vocabulary. Take the time necessary to work with these functions in the interpreter until you are familiar with their behavior.

List predicates

(list? *x*)	[Function]
(null? *x*)	[Function]

The list? predicate returns true if *x* is a list and null? returns true if *x* is the empty list.

Interaction 5. The list predicates.

```
cm> (list? '())
#t
cm> (list? 1)
#f
cm> (list? '(1))
#t
cm> (null? '())
```

```
#+
cm> (null? '(1))
#f
cm>
```

List constructors

(list ...)	[Function]
(list* *x* *list*)	[Function]
(make-list *len*)	[Function]

list returns a list that contains the arguments as elements. list* returns a list with *x* added to the front of *list*. make-list creates a list of length *len* with list elements initialized to false.

Interaction 6. List constructors.

```
cm> (list)
()
cm> (list 1 2 3)
(1 2 3)
cm> (list* 1 '(2 3))
(1 2 3)
cm>
```

List getters

(first *list*)	[Function]
(second *list*)	[Function]
(third *list*)	[Function]
(fourth *list*)	[Function]
(rest *list*)	[Function]
(list-ref *list index*)	[Function]

The functions first through fourth return the first, second, third and fourth elements in a list. The function rest returns all but the first element in *list*. The function list-ref returns the element at the *index* position in *list*. The first element in a list is at index zero.

Interaction 7. List accessors.

```
cm> (define my-notes '(a b c d e))

cm> (first my-notes)
a
cm> (rest my-notes)
(b c d e)
cm> (list-ref my-notes 0)
a
cm> (list-ref my-notes (random 5))
d
cm>
```

List setters

(list-set! *list index x*)   [Function]

Sets the element at position *index* in *list* to *x*.

Interaction 8. List setting

```
cm> (list-set! my-notes 0 'f)

cm> my-notes
(f b c d e)
cm>
```

Take care using setters as they "destructively" modify, or alter, what they set. We will not have occasion to use setters very often in this book.

Other list functions

(length *list*)	[Function]
(reverse *list*)	[Function]
(append ...)	[Function]
(member *x* *list*)	[Function]
(position *x* *list*)	[Function]

length returns the number of elements in *list*. reverse returns a copy of *list* with its elements in reverse order. The append function concatenates all of its arguments into a single list. Each argument to the function must therefore be a list. member returns true if *x* is an element of *list*, otherwise false. position returns the position of *x* in *list* or false if *x* is not in the list.

Interaction 9. List setting

```
cm> (define my-notes '(a b c d e))

cm> (length my-notes)
5
cm> (reverse my-notes)
(e d c b a)
cm> (append my-notes (reverse my-notes) my-notes)
(a b c d e e d c b a a b c d e)
cm> (member 'g my-notes)
#f
cm> (member 'e my-notes)
#t
cm> (position 'b my-notes)
1
cm> (position 'g my-notes)
#f
cm>
```

Boolean operators

The boolean operators return either true or false based on a test applied to their arguments. Remember that Lisp considers any value to be true unless the value is strictly boolean false.

(and ...)	[Function]
(or ...)	[Function]
(not *b*)	[Function]
(if *test* *then* [*else*])	[Function]

The function and returns true if all of its arguments are true, and or returns true if any of its arguments are true. not returns the logical negation of *b*. The special function if first evaluates the *test* expression. If the expression is true then the *then* expression is evaluated, otherwise the optional *else* expression is evaluated.

Interaction 10. Example of boolean operators.

```
cm> (and #t #t #t)
#t
cm> (and #f #t)
#f
cm> (and (= 1 1) (< 10 11))
#t
cm> (or #f #f #t #f)
#t
cm> (or #f #f)
#f
cm> (not #f)
#t
cm> (not (not #f))
#f
cm> (if #t 1 2)
1
cm> (if #f 1 2)
2
cm> (if (> pi 4) 'yes)
#f
cm> (if (< 1 3) 'winner 'loser)
winner
cm>
```

Object functions

Lisp *objects* are a way to represent user defined data and are the foundation for representing musical structure in Common Music. Objects and the functions that operate on them are introduced in Chapter 11.

Input and output

```
(print x)                                                      [Function]
(pprint x)                                                     [Function]
(describe x)                                                   [Function]
(load file)                                                    [Function]
```

The print function prints *x* to the Lisp Listener window and returns *x* as its value while pprint "pretty prints" *x* by insuring that list structures are displayed with proper indenting so that they are more easily readable. The describe function prints information about *x*. The load function loads *file* into Lisp and evaluates all of the expressions contained in the file.

Sequencing

A number of special functions in Lisp *sequence* a series of expressions, which means that each expression is evaluated one after the other in left-to-right order. Several of these functions are discussed in this chapter, we introduce only the most basic sequencing operator here.

```
(begin ...)                                                    [Function]
```

begin evaluates every argument in sequential order and returns the value of the last expression. Use begin to form a single expression out of a series of expressions.

Interaction 11. Sequential evaluation.

```
cm>  (begin 1 2 3 'go)
go
cm>  (if (< (random 3) 2)
         (begin (print 'winner)
                'payday)
         (begin (print 'loser)
                'go-to-jail))
loser
go-to-jail
cm>
```

In Interaction 11 two begin expressions are used to define *then* and *else* clauses, each of which holds two sub-expressions. The first sub-expression in each clause is a print statement that displays either winner or loser to the window depending on which clause is triggered by the *test*.

The Special Function define

Define is a *special function* that defines either variables or functions in Lisp.

Defining variables

(define *symbol* *value*)   [Function]

Defines *symbol* as a variable bound to *value*.

Interaction 12. Defining variables.

```
cm> (define two-pi (* pi 2))

cm> two-pi
6.283185307179586
cm> (define lotsa-pi (* pi pi pi))

cm> lotsa-pi
31.006276680299816
cm> (define favorite-pie 'apple-crunch)

cm> favorite-pie
apple-crunch
cm>
```

If one studies these last interactions carefully it is possible to discover that define "breaks the rules" of Lisp evaluation. In the last chapter we learned that each argument in a function call is evaluated before the function is called. Indeed, the interactions above clearly show that the expressions (* 2 pi), (* pi pi pi) and 'apple-crunch were evaluated. But notice that the first arguments to define — the variable names — were *not* evaluated. If these symbols had been evaluated, all three expressions would have produced "unbound variable" errors according to Evaluation Rule 2. No error occurred because define is a special function that does not evaluate its first argument. Instead, the first argument simply *names* the variable or function being defined.

Variables can be defined for a number of different reasons. One reason is simply to give a name to a value. A name provides a level of abstraction up from the raw data and helps indicate something about the role that the data plays in the program. For example, the variable pi used in place of the value 3.141592653589793 gives a much better indication of what role that quantity serves in a program. Of course, Lisp does not actually care what name is chosen for a variable — pi could just as well be called pie or hamburger. But taking time to select appropriate names is an important programming task because it helps to make code "self-documenting" and more intelligible to the reader.

Variables are also useful for saving the results of a calculation so that the same value does have to be recalculated. While in principle there is nothing wrong with calculating the same value over and over again, it is important to understand that every instruction a computer executes takes some amount of time to perform and a program that calculates the same value more than once uses more time without any additional benefit. If the calculations are time intensive (or if the computer is slow) the time wasted recalculating values can become a significant issue for someone using the program.

Variables can also stand for quantities whose values change over time or usage. Consider a program that generates twelve-tone music. If the program defines a global variable to hold the twelve tone row then new pieces can be generated by the exact same program by simply *redefining* the variable to hold a new row form. The define function can be used to define new variables or to redefine an existing variable to hold a new value. When a variable is redefined its old value is simply "thrown away" and replaced by the new value.

Another way to specify a new value for an existing variable is to use the special *assignment* function set!:

(set! *symbol value*)   [Function]

The set! operator sets the variable named *symbol* to *value*. The difference between define and set! is that set! only assigns a variable a value, it does not actually declare the symbol to be a variable.

Interaction 13. Redefining and assigning variables.

```
cm> (define favorite-row '(0 7 8 3 4 11 10 5 6 1 2 9))

cm> favorite-row
(0 7 8 3 4 11 10 5 6 1 2 9)
cm> (define reverse-row (reverse favorite-row))

cm> reverse-row
(9 2 1 6 5 10 11 4 3 8 7 0)
cm> (set! favorite-row reverse-row)

cm> favorite-row
(9 2 1 6 5 10 11 4 3 8 7 0)
cm>
```

Defining functions

(define (*name* [*arg* ...]) *body* ...)   [Function]

The definition of a function involves the specification of three pieces of information:

1. The name of the function.
2. The *input parameters* to the function — the "windows" through which the function receives input arguments.
3. The *body* of the function, the Lisp expressions that define the function's computational behavior.

Example 2 provides a simple first function definition that allows us to examine these points in greater detail.

Example 2. Convert beats per minute to time in seconds.

- .

```
(define (bpm->seconds bpm)
  (/ 60.0 bpm))
```

- .

The code in Example 2 corresponds to the three parts of a function as follows:
1. Function name: bpm->seconds
2. Function parameter: bpm
3. Function body: (/ 60.0 bpm)

Function name
A function's name should reflect the programming task that the function implements. In our example, the name bpm->seconds was chosen because it tells the caller what the function does, namely, convert a metronome value measured in beats per minute (bpm) into time measured in seconds. Of course, other names are possible. Here are just a few alternatives that could have been used:

• metronome-to-seconds
• beats-per-minute->seconds
• metronome->seconds
• metro->secs
• bpm2secs

Input parameters
A function's input parameters are the "windows" through which the function receives input values. Each parameter can be thought of as a variable that is automatically bound to an argument value whenever the function is called. Statements inside the body of the function can then treat input values as defined variables within the *lexical scope*, or textual extent, of the function's body. Once the function finishes executing the input parameters are automatically *unbound* such that their symbols no longer reference the values that were input into the function. For example, the function definition for bpm->seconds declares a single input parameter *bpm*. When the function is called, this symbol will become a variable bound to the value specified as the argument in the function call. In the following function call:

        (bpm->seconds 60)

the *bpm* parameter will be bound to the value of 60 when the function executes. When the function returns its value the symbol *bpm* is unbound so that its association with the input value 60 no longer exists.

Function body

The *body* of a function definition consists of one or more Lisp expressions that will be evaluated in succession each time the function is called. The value of the last expression in the body determines the value of the function call. The body of the bpm->seconds definition consists of a single expression:

    (/ 60.0 bpm)

The effect of this expression is to turn an input value like 60 into time measured in seconds, as shown in Interaction 14.

Interaction 14. Converting beats per minute to time in seconds.

```
cm> (bpm->seconds 60)
1.0
cm> (bpm->seconds 120)
0.5
cm> (bpm->seconds 90)
0.6666666666666666
cm> (bpm->seconds 40)
1.5
cm>
```

Local Variables

Sometimes a function defines *local variables* within its body to store values that the function will use in its calculation. Variables can be bound anywhere in a program using the let and let* special functions:

(let (*variable* ...) *expression* ...)   [Special Form]
(let* (*variable* ...) *expression* ...)   [Special Form]

Both forms of let define variables within the lexical scope of their bodies. The first form in a let definition is a *variable binding list*. Each binding within this list is itself a list of the form:

    (*variable value*)

where *variable* is the name of the variable and *value* is its value. After the variable binding list comes one or more lisp expressions that constitute the body of the let. These expressions will be evaluated in sequential order and the last expression will become the value of the let. Example 3 shows several sample let statements:

Example 3. Three example let statements.
- -.
```
(let ()
   3)

(let ((a 10)
      (b 20))
  (* a b))

(let ((a (random 10)))
  (* a a))
```
- -.

The first let does not declare any variables and simply returns the value 3. The second let declares two variables *a* and *b* and binds them to the values 10 and 20, respectively, and returns their product. The third let binds a single variable *a* to a random number less than 10 and then returns the square of the value. Notice that in all cases the binding list *must* be specified. If no variables are bound then the bindings list is an empty list.

The body of a let behaves exactly like the body of a function definition: each expression inside the body is evaluated in sequential order and the last expression determines the value of the entire expression. Interaction 15 is an example of a let expression that establishes two variables, *a* and *b*, and executes three expressions, one after the other:

Interaction 15. A let definition with three expressions.

```
cm> (let ((a 10)
          (b (random 10)))
      (print a)
      (print b)
      (list a b (+ a b)))
10
2
(10 2 12)
cm>
```

The first statement in the body of the let prints the value of *a*, the second prints the random value of *b* and the third expression returns a list containing the value of the two variables along with their sum. All three expressions are evaluated in sequential order and the value of the last expression is returned as the value of the entire let statement. Note that it appears as if the let statement actually returned three values: 10 2 and (10 2 12). But only the last value was actually returned by the let; the first two values were printed to the window by the print statements. The last value is printed in the window by the Listener's read-eval-print loop when that list is returned as the value of the entire let expression.

The only difference between `let` and `let*` is that `let` binds variables in parallel while `let*` binds variables in *sequential* order such that the binding of one variable can depend on the value of a preceding variable in the variable binding list. The following `let*` defines two variables *key* and *oct* and returns a list containing a randomly chosen MIDI key number and the key number one octave above it. `let*` is required because the second variable, *oct*, depends on the first variable, *key*, for its value:

Interaction 16. A let* definition with a dependent variable definition.

```
cm> (let* ((key (random 116))
           (oct (+ key 12)))
      (list key oct))
(33 45)
cm>
```

In this example the *key* variable holds a randomly chosen MIDI key number less than 116. (The upper bound for the random key choice is 116 because we do not want the upper octave value to ever exceed 127, the maximum MIDI key number). The *oct* variable is defined to be 12 semitones above the randomly chosen *key*. Inside the body of the `let*` the `list` function creates a list containing the random key number and its octave. Since the list expression is the last form inside the `let` (it is also the first form) the value returned by `list` becomes the value of the entire `let` expression.

Note that the expression in Interaction 16 will need be evaluated a number of different times in order to see the effect of the random octave selection. Rather than input the same let expression over and over again we will use this opportunity to define a new function that *encapsulates* the `let` such that it can be called by name. Our new function, defined in Example 4, will be called `random-octave`.

Example 4. Encapsulation by a function definition.
- -
```
(define (random-octave)
  (let ((key (random 116)))
    (list key (+ key 12))))
```
- -

Interaction 17. Calculating random octaves with a function call.

```
cm> (random-octave)
(21 33)
cm> (random-octave)
(88 100)
cm> (random-octave)
(17 29)
cm>
```

Now that the calculation has been defined as a function our `let` expression has become a (potentially) useful compositional tool that can be called in different musical contexts and reused in different programs.

Chapter Source Code

The source code to all of the examples and interactions in this chapter can be found in the file core.cm located in the same directory as the HTML file for this chapter. The source file can be edited in a text editor or evaluated inside the Common Music application.

7

Etudes, Op. 2: Musical Math

Through and through the world is infested with quantity. To talk sense is to talk quantities. It is no use saying the nation is large — how large? It is no use saying that radium is scarce — how scarce? You cannot evade quantity. You may fly to poetry and music and quantity and number will face you in your rhythms and your octaves.

— Alfred North Whitehead

The Etudes in this chapter demonstrate how the core Lisp functions introduced in the previous chapter can be used to implement new functionality in Lisp. There are often many possible ways to implement a given function; the implementations discussed in this chapter were chosen more for their pedagogical clarity than anything else.

Op. 2, No. 1: Rhythmic Time

In our first exercise we implement a function that converts metric rhythm values into time in seconds. We will use Lisp ratios to represent metric proportions. For example, a quarter-note will be notated as 1/4, a whole note as 1, three sixteenths is 3/16, and seven twenty-third notes would be 7/23. Since the basic metric proportions are relative to a whole note (at least for simple meters) to convert a metric value to seconds simply requires that the ratio be multiplied by 4.0, the length of a whole note in seconds. For example, (* 1/4 4.0) gives 1.0 seconds per quarter-note, and (* 3/16 4.0) gives .75 seconds. Of course, every musician knows that to convert a metric proportion into seconds really requires that a *tempo factor* be specified in addition to a metric value. We will use the bpm->seconds function we defined in the last chapter for just this purpose. Example 1 includes the definition of bpm->seconds as well as our new function rhythm->seconds.

Example 1. Converting metric proportion into time in seconds.

```
-------------------------------------------------.
(define (bpm->seconds bpm)
  (/ 60.0 bpm))

(define (rhythm->seconds rhy tempo)
  (* rhy 4.0 (bpm->seconds tempo)))
-------------------------------------------------.
```

When the tempo is 60 then bpm->seconds returns 1.0 and the value returned by rhythm->seconds will be unchanged. However, a tempo of 120 produces .5 as a tempo coefficient and scales the metric values returned by rhythm->seconds in half (Interaction 1).

Interaction 1. Using the rhythm->seconds function.

```
cm> (rhythm->seconds 1/4 60)
1.0
cm> (rhythm->seconds 1/2 120)
1.0
cm> (rhythm->seconds 1/8 90)
0.3333333333333333
cm>
```

As an additional exercise, try defining a variation of this function that allows a beat value other than the whole note to serve as the basis for calculation.

Op. 2, No. 1: Transposing Hertz Frequency

In this next exercise we implement a function that transposes Hertz values by semitones, quarter tones, 13th tones, or any other equal division of the octave. In order to implement this function we must first understand something about the nature of frequency calculations. Every musician knows that an *octave* represents a doubling or halving of frequency. This means that a sequence of frequencies spaced an octave apart can be calculated from a frequency f by simple multiplication: $1f$, $2f$, $4f$, $8f$, $16f$, and so on. A process of halving the frequency will produce octaves downward: $1f$, $1/2f$, $1/4f$, $1/8f$, $1/16f$, Doubling and halving are *exponential progressions*, that is, each can be expressed as a power of 2: $2^0=1$, $2^1=2$, $2^2=4$, $2^3=8$,

2^4=16, and 2^0=1, 2^{-1}=1/2, 2^{-2}=1/4, 2^{-3}=1/8, 2^{-4}=1/16. The the Lisp function expt can be used to calculate exponential progressions in either ascending or descending order, as shown in Interaction 2.

Interaction 2. Calculating octaves as powers of 2.

```
cm> (expt 2 -2)
.25
cm> (expt 2 -1)
.5
cm> (expt 2 0)
1
cm> (expt 2 1)
2
cm> (expt 2 2)
4
cm>
```

We can see in the previous example that as the exponents progress linearly from -2 to 2 the values returned by expt progress exponentially. Since 2^0 is the unison (1) and 2^1 is the octave (2) then exponents that lie between 0 and 1 will determine frequencies within a single octave. The exact middle of an octave (tritone) must be $2^{1/2}$, 1 semitone up from f is $f * 2^{1/12}$, 3 quarter-tones down from f is $f * 2^{-3/24}$, and so on. Interaction 3 demonstrates the use of fractional exponents to calculate frequencies within one octave.

Interaction 3. Exponentiation.

```
cm> (expt 2 0)
1
cm> (expt 2 1)
2
cm> (expt 2 1/2)
1.4142135623730951
cm> (expt 2 1/12)
1.0594630943592953
cm> (expt 2 -3/24)
0.9170040432046712
cm>
```

The expt function is one of our core functions, and we can use it to define a new function that scales any hertz value by any equal tempered amount, as shown in Example 2.

Example 2. Scaling Hertz frequency values by equal tempered amounts.
- .
```
(define (scale-hz hz mul)
   (* hz (expt 2 mul)))
```
- .

The `scale-hz` function multiplies an input Hertz value by an octave scaler to transpose the value by an equal division of the octave, as shown in Interaction 4.

Interaction 4. Calculating Hertz values with scale-hz.

```
cm> (scale-hz 440 1)
880
cm> (scale-hz 440 -2)
110
cm> (scale-hz 440 1/24)
452.8929841231365
cm>
```

Op.2, No. 2: Converting MIDI Key Numbers to Hertz Frequency

In Example 3 we implement a function `keynum->hertz` to convert MIDI key numbers into equivalent Hertz frequencies in the equal tempered scale. Recall that MIDI key numbers represent positions in a 128 key virtual keyboard, where key number 0 is the lowest C (8.175 Hertz), 60 is Middle C (261.625), and 127 is the highest key (12543.853 Hz).

Example 3. Converting MIDI key numbers to Hertz frequency.
- .
```
(define lowest-freq 8.175)

(define (keynum->hertz knum)
   (* lowest-freq (expt 2 (/ knum 12)))))
```
- .

Since an octave contains 12 semitones, the octave exponent to `expt` is calculated by dividing the input key number by the number of keys in one octave.

Interaction 5. Converting MIDI key numbers to Hertz equivalents.

```
cm> (keynum->hertz 60)
261.6255653005986
cm> (keynum->hertz 69)
439.99999999999994
cm>
```

In the last expression of the preceding interaction the key number 69 returns 439.999, a value very close to, but not exactly, 440.0, the true frequency of tuning

A. This small error is due to the fact that floating point numbers are inexact quantities and we are basing our calculations on a very low C. To implement a version of `keynum->hertz` in which Middle C is key number 60 but key number 69 returns exactly 440.0 requires that the Hertz calculation be based on a low A rather than a C, and that the key number difference between A and C (3 semitones) then be added to the input key number, as shown in Example 4.

Example 4. A version of keynum->hertz based on A.

```
(define lowest-freq 6.875)

(define (keynum->hertz knum)
  (* lowest-freq (expt 2 (/ (+ knum 3) 12)))))
```

Interaction 6. Converting MIDI key numbers to Hertz equivalents.

```
cm> (keynum->hertz 60)
261.6255653005986
cm> (keynum->hertz 69)
440.0
cm>
```

Op.2, No. 3: Bounded Random Selection

Recall from the last chapter that the `random` function returns a value equal to or greater than zero but less than the upper bounds specified to the function. In this next exercise we will implement a function that generates random selection between any lower and upper boundary specified by the user. If both boundaries are integers then `pick-range` will return a discrete (integer) value, otherwise a continuous value (floating point number) that lies between the low and high bounds will be returned.

Example 5. Random selection between a low and high bounds.

```
(define (pick-range low high)
  (let ((rng (- high low)))
    (if (> rng 0)
        (+ low (random rng))
        0))))
```

The `pick-range` function converts a lower and upper bounds for random selection to a range *rng* by subtracting *low* from *high*. If the difference is greater than zero then `pick-range` selects a random value less than *rng* and adds it back to *low* so that the value returned again lies between *low* and *high*, otherwise zero is returned.

Interaction 7. Examples of pick-range.

```
cm> (pick-range 60 100)
96
cm> (pick-range -1.0 1.0)
-0.697347603174574
cm> (pick-range 440 880)
789
cm>
```

Op.2, No. 4: Random Selection from a List

Our next function randomly selects an element from a list of values that the user specifies to the function.

Example 6. Random selection from a list of values.
- -
```
(define (pick-list lst)
  (let* ((len (length lst))
         (pos (random len)))
    (list-ref lst pos)))
```
- -

The function pick-list first calculates a random position *pos* in the input list and then returns the element at that position using the list-ref accessor. The let* special function is used so that the value of *len* can be used to calculate the value of *pos*. Recall that list positions range from zero to one minus the length of the list. By specifying the length of the list as the exclusive upper bounds to random a valid position in the list is guaranteed to be chosen. The element returned by list-ref becomes the value of the function call (Interaction 8).

Interaction 8. Examples of pick-list.

```
cm> (define aeolian-mode
       '(57 59 60 62 64 65 67
            69 71 72 74 3 77 79 81))

cm> (pick-list aeolian-mode)
62
cm> (pick-list aeolian-mode)
79
cm> (pick-list aeolian-mode)
71
cm> (pick-list '(1/16 1/8 1/8 1/4))
1/4
cm>
```

Note that the last expression in Interaction 8 contains a rhythms list with twice as many 1/8th notes as 1/16ths or 1/4 notes. This is one simple way to implement *weighted random selection*, in which some outcomes have more probability of selection than others. The `random` function generates numbers in a *uniform distribution* which means that there is an equal chance of any number in the range being selected. By specifying multiple copies of an element there will be more chances that one of its instances will be chosen.

Op.2, No. 5: Chance and Probability

The function defined in Example 7 is a predicate function that determines if a randomly chosen number is within the probability factor *prob* specified by the user. If it is then the function returns true, otherwise it returns false (Example 7).

Example 7. Random selection from a list of values.

```
(define (chance? prob)
  (< (random 1.0) prob))
```

The probability factor *prob* should be a real number between 0.0 and 1.0 inclusive. If *prob* is 0.0 then there is a zero chance that the predicate will return true because the `random` function never returns a value less than zero. If *prob* is 1.0 then there is a 100% probability of `chance?` returning true because `(random 1.0)` is guaranteed to return a value less than 1.0. Interaction 9 demonstrates several calls to the `chance?` function.

Interaction 9. Examples of chance?

```
cm> (chance? 0)
#f
cm> (chance? 1)
#t
cm> (chance? .75)
#t
cm> (if (chance? .8) 'retrograde 'prime)
retrograde
cm> (if (chance? 0) 'retrograde 'prime)
prime
cm>
```

Chapter Source Code

The source code to all of the examples and interactions in this chapter can be found in the file math.cm located in the same directory as the HTML file for this chapter. The source file can be edited in a text editor or evaluated inside the Common Music application.

8

Iteration and the Loop Macro

do — a deer, a female deer
re — a drop of golden sun
mi — a name, I call myself
fa — a long long way to run!
so — a needle pulling thread
la — a note to follow *so*
ti — a drink with jam and bread
That will bring us back to ...

Oscar Hammerstein, The Sound of Music

Programming tasks often consist of actions that must be repeated over and over again. The process of repeating actions is called *iteration*, or *looping*. Lisp provides a powerful iteration facility called Loop that allows many different types of iterative tasks to be described. Loop is really more of a language for describing iterations than it is a Lisp function. In order to introduce the expressive power of Loop, we start by examining two very small music programs, both of which require iterative solutions.

Two Iteration Examples

Consider a program that transposes twelve tone rows onto specific notes in the standard scale. Assume for the moment that notes are represented by MIDI key numbers 0-127 and that a twelve tone row is simply a list of pitch class integers 0-11. Data for this program could be defined using two variables, as shown in Example 1.

Example 1. Defining a transposition offset and a twelve tone row.

```
(define my-key 60)

(define my-row '(0 3 7 11 2 5 9 1 4 6 8 10))
```

The iterative task that our transposition program must implement can be expressed in a single sentence:

> "For each pitch class *pc* in the list *my-row*, add *pc* to *my-key* and collect it into a new row."

This sentence is easily translated from English into Loop:

```
(loop for pc in my-row
      collect (+ pc my-key))
```

Interaction 1. Loop implementation of the transposition program.

```
cm> (loop for pc in my-row
          collect (+ pc my-key))
(60 63 67 71 62 65 69 61 64 66 68 70)
cm>
```

Example 1 implements our row transposition. Within the Loop expression, the *stepping* variable named *pc* was automatically mapped over the list *my-row* and set to each pitch class in the list. The function call (+ pc my-key) defines the operation applied to each pitch class to effect the transposition. The collect command tells Loop to gather each transposed value into a new list and to return that list as the value of the entire loop expression.

Our second program computes a list of Hertz frequencies from the harmonic series. The fundamental, starting harmonic number and ending harmonic number are defined in Example 2.

Example 2. Defining the fundamental and bounds for a harmonic series.

```
(define fundamental 220)

(define start-harm 1)

(define end-harm 8)
```

The iterative task that our program must implement can be expressed as follows:

> "For each harmonic number *h* from *start-harm* to *end-harm*, multiply *fundamental* by *h* and collect it into a list."

This is implemented by the Loop expression:

```
(loop for h from start-harm to end-harm
      collect (* fundamental h))
```

Interaction 2. Loop implementation of the harmonic series iteration.

```
cm> (loop for h from start-harm to end-harm
          collect (* fundamental h))
(220 440 660 880 1100 1320 1540 1760)
cm>
```

Both Interaction 1 and Interaction 2 repeat a single task, or *action*, over a range of values. The first loop iterated over elements in a list. Its action was to add a transposition offset to a pitch class. The second loop iterated over a range of integers and its task was to multiply a fundamental frequency by each harmonic number. The Loop language allowed both of these examples to be expressed in a simple and clear manner. In neither case did we have to explicitly increment stepping variables, or test when the iteration should stop, or even construct the list that was returned by the loop! The loop language took care of these chores automatically from our description of the iteration.

The Loop Facility

Loop is a *macro* that implements an English-like syntax for describing iterative tasks. This special syntax makes it very easy for a programmer to implement different types of iterations, from simple "repeat" loops to multiple tasks performed in parallel. Note that — like the special function define — the loop syntax is so natural that we may not notice the fact that its syntax actually "breaks the rules" of normal Lisp evaluation! This can be shown by analyzing what should happen when the following loop expression is evaluated:

Interaction 3. A loop that sums numbers from zero to ten.

```
cm> (loop for i to 10 sum i)
55
cm>
```

If the loop expression in Interaction 3 were treated as regular function call then Evaluation Rule 2 should signal an "unbound variable error" because the unquoted symbol for is not a defined variable. An error does not occur because loop is a macro function (Chapter 2) that defines its own evaluation strategy. Loop treats symbols like for, to and sum as *command names* rather than variables. Many introductory Lisp books and courses eschew Loop precisely because it does not follow the standard evaluation model. Unfortunately this means the student must learn other, more cumbersome methods to achieve the same effect that is more clearly expressed using Loop. This book expresses all iteration and mapping tasks using the Loop language for several important reasons:

- Loop's English-like syntax makes is very natural and easy to learn.
- Loop can express many different types of iteration.
- Loop syntax is used by the process macro introduced in Part 2 of this book.

The process iteration macro supports algorithmic generation of music. So if you can write a loop then you are ready to start composing algorithmic compositions!

Loop Syntax

A Loop expression consists of one or more *clauses*. A number of different types of clauses may appear within the scope of a single Loop expression:

- *Initialization* clauses establish starting conditions for the iteration.
- *Stepping* clauses limit the iterative process and provide *stepping variables* whose values automatically change each time through the loop.
- *Action* clauses define task actions and allow values to be returned from the loop expression.
- *Conditional* clauses allow action clauses to depend on the truth or falsity of a test.
- *Finalization* clauses execute immediately after the iteration stops.

Stepping clauses

Stepping clauses place limits on the number of times a loop executes and may also increment *stepping variables* each time through the loop. More than one stepping clause may be defined in a single Loop expression. In the case of multiple stepping clauses, the entire loop stops as soon as the first stepping clause terminates.

repeat *expr*   [Clause]

The repeat clause repeats the loop *expr* number of times.

Interaction 4. The repeat clause.

```
cm> (loop repeat 10 collect (random 100))
(9 3 93 58 23 0 79 48 27 60)
cm> (loop repeat (random 5) sum 10)
30
cm>
```

for *var* = *expr* [then *expr2*]   [Clause]

Sets variable *var* to the value of *expr* on each iteration. If an optional then clause is supplied then *expr* becomes the initial value of *var* and *expr2* becomes its value on subsequent iterations.

Interaction 5. The for clause.

```
cm> (loop repeat 5 for x = (random 100) minimize x)
12
cm> (loop repeat 5 for x = -99 then (random 10)
          collect x)
(-99 4 8 6 4)
cm>
```

for *var* [from *low*] to *end* [by *step*]   [Clause]
Increments *var* until equal to *end* and then stops iteration. If from is not specified
then *low* always defaults to 0. If by is not specified then *step* always defaults to 1.

Interaction 6. The for clause.

```
cm> (loop for i to 10 collect i)
(0 1 2 3 4 5 6 7 8 9 10)
cm> (loop for i from -1 to 2 by .5 collect i)
(-1 -0.5 0.0 0.5 1.0 1.5 2.0)
cm>
```

for *var* [from *low*] below *end* [by *step*]   [Clause]

Increments *var* while less than *end*.

Interaction 7. The below clause.

```
cm> (loop for i below 10 by 2 collect i)
(0 2 4 6 8)
cm>
```

for *var* from *top* downto *end* [by *step*]   [Clause]

Decrements *var* until equal to *end*.

Interaction 8. The downto clause.

```
cm> (loop for i from 0 downto -10 by 2 collect i)
(0 -2 -4 -6 -8 -10)
cm>
```

for *var* from *top* above *end* [by *step*]   [Clause]

Decrements *var* while greater than *end*.

Interaction 9. The above clause.

```
cm> (loop for i from 10 above 2 collect i)
(10 9 8 7 6 5 4 3)
cm>
```

for *var* in *list* [by *fn*]   [Clause]
for *var* on *list* [by *fn*]   [Clause]

The in clause maps *var* over successive elements in *list*. An optional by function increments the *list*. The on clause maps successive tails of *list*.

Interaction 10. Example list iterations.

```
cm> (define test '(a b c))

cm> (loop for v in (reverse test) collect v)
(c b a)
cm> (loop for v in test collect (list v v))
((a a) (b b) (c c))
cm> (loop for v on test collect v)
((a b c) (b c) (c))
cm>
```

Action clauses

Action clauses implement iteration tasks and return values from the loop.

do *expr* ...   [Clause]

Evaluates every *expr* on each iteration. Returns boolean false.

collect *expr*   [Clause]
append *expr*   [Clause]

The collect clause collects values of *expr* each iteration and returns the values in a list while the append clause appends the contents of *expr*, which must evaluate to a list.

sum *expr*   [Clause]
minimize *expr*   [Clause]
maximize *expr*   [Clause]
count *expr*   [Clause]
thereis *expr*   [Clause]

Return the sum, minimal and maximal values of *expr* from the loop, respectively. The count clause returns the number of times *expr* is true and thereis stops iteration and returns true from the loop as soon as *expr* is true, otherwise it returns false.

Interaction 11. Example action clauses.

```
cm> (loop repeat 2 do (print 'hi))
hi
hi
#f
cm> (loop repeat 10 collect (random 50))
(43 42 27 18 26 20 44 43 23 30)
cm> (loop repeat 10 sum (random 50))
176
cm> (loop for i below 10 count (even? i))
5
cm> (loop repeat 10 minimize (random 50))
2
cm> (loop repeat 10 maximize (random 50))
43
cm> (loop for x below 10 thereis (= x -1))
#f
cm>
```

Conditional clauses

Conditional clauses place conditions on the evaluation of action clauses or on how many times the loop will iterate.

when *test action* [and ...]	[Clause]
unless *test action* [and ...]	[Clause]
while *test* ...	[Clause]
until *test* ...	[Clause]

The when clause executes the *action* clause only if *test* is true. The optional and operator makes multiple actions dependent on a single test. The unless clause executes the *action* clause only if *test* is false. The while clause terminates iteration if *test* is false, and the until clause terminates if *test* is true.

Interaction 12. Example conditional clauses.

```
cm> (loop for i below 10 when (even? i) collect i)
(0 2 4 6 8)
cm> (loop for i below 10 unless (even? i) collect i)
(1 3 5 7 9)
cm> (loop for n = (random 10) until (even? n) collect
n)
(9 3)
cm> (loop for n = (random 10) while (even? n) collect
n)
()
cm> (loop for i below 10
          for j = (random 10)
          when (even? j) collect i and collect j)
(2 2 4 6 7 4 8 0 9 4)
cm>
```

Initialization clauses

with *var* [= *expr*] [and ...]   [Clause]

Defines *var* as a local loop variable. *var* is initialized to false unless it is explicitly
set using the optional = operator. The optional and operator allows more than one
variable to be defined by the with clause.

Interaction 13. Example initialization clause.

```
cm> (loop with hz = 220
          for h from 1 to 8
          collect (* hz h))
(220 440 660 880 1100 1320 1540 1760)
cm>
```

Finalization clauses

finally *expr*   [Clause]
(return *expr*)   [Function]

Evaluates *expr* after the iteration has stopped. The return function can be used
anywhere inside a loop to return *expr* as its value.

Interaction 14. Example finalization clause.

```
cm> (loop repeat 10
          for sum = 0 then (+ sum (random 100))
          finally (return (/ sum 10.0))))
48.6
cm>
```

Advanced loop Features

The iteration possibilities afforded by Loop are almost limitless. The following brief discussion points out two common uses of loop that involve more than one clause.

Parallel clauses

More than one stepping clause or action clause can be defined in a single loop. In the case of multiple stepping clauses the first clause that terminates will stop the entire loop.

Interaction 15. Multiple stepping clauses.

```
cm> (loop for i below 4
          for j from 100 by -10
          for k = (random 100)
          collect (list i j k))
((0 100 1) (1 90 92) (2 80 81) (3 70 2))
cm> (loop for i below 4
          collect i
          collect (expt 2 i))
(0 1 1 2 2 4 3 8)
cm>
```

Loops inside of loops

A single loop may contain other loops inside it.

Interaction 16. A loop in a loop.

```
cm> (loop for i from 0 by 10 to 20
          collect (loop repeat 4 for j from i
          collect j))
((0 1 2 3) (10 11 12 13) (20 21 22 23))
cm>
```

Chapter Source Code

The source code to all of the examples and interactions in this chapter can be found in the file loop.cm located in the same directory as the HTML file for this chapter. The source file can be edited in a text editor or evaluated inside the Common Music application.

9

Etudes, Op. 3: Iteration, Rows and Sets

In this chapter we work through examples that use iteration to implement some basic twelve-tone and set theory functions.

Op. 3, No. 1: Converting MIDI Key Numbers to Pitch Classes

In the first exercise we implement `list->pcs`, a function that converts a list of MIDI key numbers into pitch classes. A pitch class can be thought of as the "remainder" of a key number after all octave information has been "subtracted out". Since there are only 12 divisions per octave in the standard scale there are only 12 pitch classes. We will represent pitch classes using the integers 0-11. For example, all C key numbers will be pitch class 0, all F-sharps and G-flats are pitch class 6, and so on.

The Lisp function `mod` can be used to convert a key number into a pitch class. The `mod` function returns the absolute value of the remainder from the division of two integers. We can use `loop` to see the effects of `mod` on a range of numbers:

Interaction 1. Using loop to collect numbers mod 12.

```
cm> (loop for i from 60 to 72 collect (mod i 12))
(0 1 2 3 4 5 6 7 8 9 10 11 0)
```

```
cm> (loop for k from 0 downto -12 collect (mod k 12))
(0 11 10 9 8 7 6 5 4 3 2 1 0)
cm>
```

Given the mod operator our first exercise is easy to implement. We split our programming task into two small functions. The first function uses mod to convert a single key number into a pitch class. The second function converts a list of key numbers into a list of pitch classes by iterating the first function over each element in the list.

Example 1. Converting key numbers to pitch classes.

- ·

```
(define (keynum->pc k)
  (mod k 12))

(define (list->pcs knums)
  (loop for k in knums collect (keynum->pc k)))
```
- ·

list->pcs uses loop to iterate a variable k over every key number in a list of key numbers input into the function. The collect clause collects the results of keynum->pc into a new list and returns that list as the value of the loop. Since the loop expression is the last expression in the body of the function definition, the value returned by loop becomes the value of the function.

Interaction 2. Pitch classes from measure 15 of Berg's Violinkonzert.

```
cm> (define albans-notes
       '(55 58 62 66 69 72 76 80 83 85 87 89))

cm> (list->pcs albans-notes)
(7 10 2 6 9 0 4 8 11 1 3 5)
cm>
```

Op. 3, No. 2: Normalizing Pitch Classes

Note that in Interaction 2 the series of pitch classes returned by list->pcs is close to, but not the same as, a twelve-tone row. To form a twelve-tone row we would need to convert the list of pitch classes into a list of intervals, where the first interval in the row is 0, the "root" for row transpositions. We will take this opportunity to define a new function that normalizes a list of pitch classes or key numbers into a list of zero-based by subtracting the first number in the list from all the numbers in the list. Recall that the with clause is used to initialize, rather than step, a looping variable (Example 2).

Example 2. Normalizing a list of pitch classes or key numbers.

```
(define (normalize-pcs knums)
  (loop with root = (first knums)
        for k in knums
        collect (keynum->pc (- k root)))))
```

The expression with root = (first knums) directs loop to bind the
variable *root* to the first element in the input list. The key feature to remember about
a with clause is that it happens just one time, immediately before the iteration
starts. (A for clause, on the other hand, resets a variable each time through the
loop.)

Interaction 3. Normalizing pitch classes.

```
cm> (define albans-notes
        '(55 58 62 66 69 72 76 80 83 85 87 89))

cm> (normalize-pcs (list->pcs albans-notes))
(0 3 7 11 2 5 9 1 4 6 8 10)
cm>
```

Op. 3, No. 3: Matrix Operations

In Example 3 we implement four functions that perform the core manipulations for
twelve-tone composition. The function retrograde-row returns the retrograde
version (reversal) of a row. The function transpose-row shifts the row to a new
pitch class. The function invert-row inverts a twelve-tone row. The function
row->matrix returns a list of lists that represents the twelve rows of a "Prime by
Inversion" matrix. The utility function print-matrix prints a matrix so that each
row appears on its own line.

Example 3. Twelve-Tone Functions.

```
(define (retrograde-row row)
  (reverse row))

(define (transpose-row row to)
  (loop for pc in row collect (keynum->pc (+ pc to))))

(define (invert-row row)
  (loop for pc in row collect (keynum->pc (- 12 pc))))

(define (retrograde-invert-row row)
  (retrograde-row (invert-row row)))
```

```
--------------------------------------------------------.
(define (row->matrix row)
  (loop for i in (invert-row row)
        collect (transpose-row row i)))

(define (print-matrix matrix)
  (loop for row in matrix
        do (print row)))
--------------------------------------------------------.
```

The function retrograde-row is the easiest to implement, it simply calls the core function reverse to reverse the order of the input list. Notice that by defining this function we have essentially *renamed* reverse so that it better reflects our application's use of it. The function transpose-row iterates over an input row and adds an offset to each element. Notice that we filter this value through our keynum->pc function so that our result list is guaranteed to remain as pitch classes even after the addition of the offset. The function invert-row is similar to transpose-row except that it subtracts rather than adds an offset from each pitch-class in the input list. The function retrograde-invert-row is implemented simply by calling two functions we have already defined in our implementation. The last two functions operate on a matrix of twelve-tone rows. The function row->matrix computes the prime-by-inversion matrix for given a row by transposing the row to each interval in the row's inversion. Note that this function returns a list of twelve lists: the outer list represents the matrix and each sublist represents one transposition of the original row. The function print-matix can be used to display the matrix so that each row is printed on a single line. Note that — unlike all the other functions in our example — this last function is called for its *effect* (displaying the matrix) rather than for returning a value. Interaction 4 demonstrates using our functions on the row from Alban Berg's Violin Concerto.

Interaction 4. Twelve-tone matrix operations.

```
cm> (define albans-row '(0 3 7 11 2 5 9 1 4 6 8 10))

cm> (retrograde-row albans-row)
(10 8 6 4 1 9 5 2 11 7 3 0)
cm> (transpose-row albans-row 3)
(3 6 10 2 5 8 0 4 7 9 11 1)
cm> (invert-row albans-row)
(0 9 5 1 10 7 3 11 8 6 4 2)
cm> (retrograde-invert-row albans-row)
(2 4 6 8 11 3 7 10 1 5 9 0)
cm> (print-matrix (row->matrix albans-row))
(0 3 7 11 2 5 9 1 4 6 8 10)
(9 0 4 8 11 2 6 10 1 3 5 7)
(5 8 0 4 7 10 2 6 9 11 1 3)
(1 4 8 0 3 6 10 2 5 7 9 11)
```

```
(10  1  5  9  0  3  7 11  2  4  6  8)
(7  10  2  6  9  0  4  8 11  1  3  5)
(3   6 10  2  5  8  0  4  7  9 11  1)
(11  2  6 10  1  4  8  0  3  5  7  9)
(8  11  3  7 10  1  5  9  0  2  4  6)
(6   9  1  5  8 11  3  7 10  0  2  4)
(4   7 11  3  6  9  1  5  8 10  0  2)
(2   5  9  1  4  7 11  3  6  8 10  0)
cm>
```

Op. 3, No. 4: Determining Normal Order

The *normal order* of a group of notes is the most "tightly packed" permutation of its interval content. The most tightly packed permutation is the version of the set with the smallest total span. In the case of a tie, the permutation with smaller intervals leftward is the winner. For example there are four permutations of a dominant seventh chord:

Table 1. Inversions of a dominant seventh chord.

inversion	intervals
root	(0 4 7 10)
first	(0 3 6 8)
second	(0 3 5 9)
third	(0 2 6 9)

The set (0 3 6 8) is the normal order because this permutation spans only 8 semitones and is therefore the most compact.

The first step in computing the normal order of a group of notes is to define a function that accepts a list of key numbers and returns its pitch class content with no duplications. We will implement this behavior using a "scratch pad" list that represents the 12 possible pitch classes in an octave. Each of the twelve elements in the list will represent the pitch class whose number corresponds to the element's position in the list. So the 0th element in the list corresponds to pitch class 0, the element at position 1 corresponds to pitch class 1, and so on. Each element in the scratch pad list is initially set to false. A false element means that a pitch class for that position has not yet been recorded in the list. Pitch classes are recorded in the scratch pad by iterating over the input note list and — for each pitch class encountered in the input list — setting its corresponding element in the scratch pad to true. Since all elements are initially false, only pitch classes that are encountered one or more times will be set to true. Once every pitch class in the input list has been recorded, a second loop will iterate through the scratch pad list and return only those positions in the scratch pad for which a pitch class was actually recorded (Example 4).

Example 4. Determining pitch class sets.

```
(define (reduce-pcs knums)
  ;; create a scratch pad list with 12 locations to
  ;; remember the pitch classes in knums. each element
  ;; in the pad is initially false.
  (let ((pad (make-list 12)))
    ;; remember each pitch class in knums by setting
    ;; its position in the scratch pad to true.
    (loop for k in knums
          for pc = (keynum->pc k)
          do (list-set! pad pc true))
    ;; iterate over the scratch pad and return
    ;; a list of the positions where pitch classes
    ;; were recorded
    (loop for i in pad
          for j from 0
          when i collect j)))
```

The function reduce-pcs defines the local variable *pad* to hold a "scratch pad" list of 12 elements. make-list automatically sets each element in this list to false. The body of reduce-pcs consists of two loops. The first loop iterates over the input list and, for each pitch class it encounters, sets the element corresponding to that pitch class in the scratch pad to true. The loop doesn't return anything; its do clause simply invokes the function list-set! to set each element at the specified position to true.

The second loop in the body consists of three clauses. The first clause for i in pad maps the variable *i* over every value in pad. Since the pad contains only true or false values, the *i* variable is set to true only at positions where a pitch class was recorded, otherwise it remains false. The second clause for j from 0 simply steps the variable *j* in parallel with the position of *i* in the scratch pad. The third clause when i collect j collects the value of *j* only when the value of *i* is true. The loop therefore returns exactly those positions in the scratch pad at which a pitch class had been recorded. This second loop is the last form in the body of the function so its value is returned as the value of the function call.

Interaction 5. Calling reduce-pcs on two octaves of G dom7.

```
cm> (define g-dom7 '(55 59 62 65 67 71 74 77))

cm> (reduce-pcs g-dom7)
(2 5 7 11)
cm>
```

The *g-dom7* variable defines a G dominant 7th chord doubled over two octaves. reduce-pcs returns the list of pitch classes in that chord with all duplicates removed. (The pitch class 2 is D, 5 is F, 7 is G and 11 is B).

The next step is to define a function that *permutes*, or rotates, a list of pitch classes so that each of its inversions can be tested for compactness. To rotate the list to the next inversion means to move the element that is currently at the front of the list to the back of the list. In order to do this we first *destructure*, or split, the list into two separate lists. The first list will contain all but the first element, and the second list will contains only the first element. The Lisp function rest will return the first list we need:

Interaction 6. A list of all but the first element.

```
cm> (define test-set '(2 5 7 11))

cm> (rest test-set)
(5 7 11)
cm>
```

The second list must contain only one element: the pitch class that is currently at the front of the input list. The Lisp accessor first returns the first element of a list, the function list can then be used to turn that value into a list:

Interaction 7. A list of only the first element.

```
cm> (first test-set)
2
cm> (list (first test-set))
(2)
cm>
```

Given the two destructured lists in Interaction 7 and Interaction 6 we can use the Lisp function append to "glue" these lists back together in the order we want:

Interaction 8. Reordering the destructured lists.

```
cm> (append (rest test-set) (list (first test-set)))
(5 7 11 2)
cm>
```

We are now ready to implement our function that permutes a pitch class set:

Example 5. Permute pitch class set.

```
(define (permute-set set)
  (let ((front (list (first set)))
        (others (rest set)))
    (append others front)))
```

Interaction 9. Examples of set permutation.

```
cm> (permute-set test-set)
(5 7 11 2)
cm> (permute-set (permute-set test-set))
(7 11 2 5)
cm>
```

The last helper function to define is called set-weight, a function that returns a measure of how compact a set is. Rather than checking the span of each inversion and then checking "leftward packing" in case of a tie, we implement a function that returns a total measure of the compactness of a set. To do this we will use two functions that have already been introduced: the Lisp function expt and our own function normalize-pcs. Our method is quite simple: to measure the compactness of a pitch class list we will first convert the list into a normalized (zero based) set and then treat each number in the set as exponents. The power of 2 value of each exponent (interval) will then be summed together to determine the total weight. By summing exponential values a single large interval will always weigh more than smaller ones added together.

Example 6. Set permutation.

```
(define (set-weight set)
  ;; set must be normalized (zero based)
  (loop for s in set sum (expt 2 s)))
```

Interaction 10. Comparing inversion weights of a dom7.

```
cm> (set-weight '(0 4 7 10))
1169
cm> (set-weight '(0 3 6 8))
329
cm> (set-weight '(0 3 5 9))
553
cm> (set-weight '(0 2 6 9))
581
cm>
```

The `set-weight` function correctly identifies (0 3 6 8) as the most compact rotation, i.e. the normal order, of the dominant 7th chord. We are now ready to implement the actual function that calculates the normal order of group of notes (Example 7).

Example 7. Computing the normal order of a note set.
```
- - - - - - - - - - - - - - - - - - - - - - - - - - - - - - - - - - - - - - - - - - - - - -
(define (normal-order notes)
  (let ((pclist (reduce-pcs notes)))
    (loop with memory and winner
          repeat (length pclist)
          for normal = (normalize-pcs pclist)
          for weight = (set-weight normal)
          do
          (if (or (not winner)
                  (< weight memory))
            (begin (set! winner normal)
                   (set! memory weight)))
          (set! pclist (permute-set pclist))
          finally (return winner))))
- - - - - - - - - - - - - - - - - - - - - - - - - - - - - - - - - - - - - - - - - - - - - -
```

The `normal-order` function first calls our helper `reduce-pcs` to convert the input list into a list of pitch classes with all duplicate key numbers removed. The main processing loop then iterates as many times as there are pitch classes in *pclist*. The *winner* variable will hold the permutation of *pclist* with the smallest weight, i.e. the normal order of the note list. The variable *memory* will be used to "remember" the smallest weight as each inversion of *pclist* is compared to the previous one. On each iteration of the loop, the stepping variable *normal* is set to the current normalized version of *pclist* and its weight is calculated by the `set-weight` function. The `do` action clause contains two Lisp expressions: an `if` conditional statement and a `set!` assignment statement. The purpose of the assignment statement (`set! pclist (permute-set pclist)`) is to reset the *pclist* variable at the end of the loop so that when the loop repeats the variable already contains the next inversion of the set to check. The purpose of the `if` statement is to establish the very first version of *pclist* as the "winner" unless a subsequent inversion can be shown to have a smaller set weight. The *then* clause of the `if` statement actually consists of two assignment statements that are grouped into a single *then* expression using the `begin` function. (Without the surrounding begin expression the first `set!` expression would be interpreted as the *then* clause and the second `set!` expression would be considered to be an *else* clause!) The test expression: (`or (not winner) (< weight memory)`) evaluates to true if either (1) the *winner* variable has not been set (i.e. it is still false from the initial `with` clause) or (2) the current value of *weight* is less than the current value of *winner*. The `finally` clause executes at the very end of the loop, after every inversion of *pclist* has been checked. The `finally` clause uses the `return` function to return whatever version of *pclist* was saved in *winner*. Since the loop is the last statement in the body of the function, the value that the loop returns becomes the value that the function returns.

Interaction 11. Computing normal orders.

```
cm> (normal-order g-dom7)
(0 3 6 8)
cm> (normal-order '(72 64 67))
(0 4 7)
cm> (normal-order '(65 64 75 70))
(0 1 2 7)
cm>
```

Chapter Source Code

The source code to all of the examples and interactions in this chapter can be found in the file sets.cm located in the same directory as the HTML file for this chapter. The source file can be edited in a text editor or evaluated inside the Common Music application.

10

Parameterized Sound Description

Of all noises, I think music is the least disagreeable.

— Samuel Johnson

The introduction to this book identified three representation levels, or layers, that music composition applications commonly address (Figure 1).

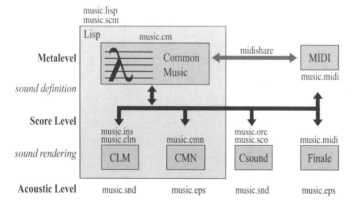

Figure 1. The composition abstraction levels

Applications that operate at the *acoustic level* record and output sound based on a digitized representation of an acoustic waveform. Computer applications in the *score level* use a symbolic encoding to represent specific attributes, or qualities, of sound. In the *metalevel*, compositional algorithms, processes and relationships are expressed. Each of these levels is a layer of abstraction that encapsulates, or hides, details in the next lower level. Figure 2 shows a single musical example depicted at the three abstraction levels. Each depiction is represented as a file containing an encoding of the example and an estimate of its size in bytes. The score and acoustic representations (Table 2 and Table 3) are generated automatically from the single metalevel construct shown in Table 1.

Table 1. Metalevel representation of a self-similar process.

sier.cm: 8 lines, 225 bytes.

```
(define (sierpinski knum ints dur depth)
  (process for i in ints
           ;; output new sound event
           output (new midi :time (now)
                        :keynum (+ knum i)
                        :duration dur :channel depth)
           when (> depth 1)
           sprout (sierpinski (+ knum i 12) ints len
                              (/ dur 3)
                              amp (- depth 1))
           wait dur))
```

Table 2. MIDI and Csound score level sound events from Table 1.

sier.mid: 250 messages, 1000 bytes.	sier.sco :117 lines, 4200 bytes.
0 <Note-On 0 25 63>	i3 0.000 1.000 34.647;
0 <Note-On 0 37 63>	i2 0.000 0.333 69.295;
0 <Note-On 0 49 63>	i1 0.000 0.111 138.591;
53 <Note-Off 0 49 127>	i1 0.111 0.111 207.652;
0 <Note-On 0 56 63>	i1 0.222 0.111 184.997;
53 <Note-Off 0 56 127>	i2 0.333 0.333 103.826;
0 <Note-On 0 54 63>	i1 0.333 0.111 207.652;
53 <Note-Off 0 37 127>	i1 0.444 0.111 311.126;
. . .	. . .

Table 3. Acoustic level waveform samples from Table 2.

sier.snd: 350,000 samples, 700,000 bytes.

```
732e 646e 0000 1c00 0000 0000 0000 0300 0000 2256
0000 0100 0000 0000 d0ff a0ff 75ff 44ff 0cff e9fe
c9fe 74fe 27fe 8dfe b1ff b100 ef00 d100 e300 0c01
1201 0c01 1c01 3f01 6801 7301 3f01 2701 c301 ff02
3504 1b05 b605 cf05 8305 9705 3b06 9006 5b06 8d06
1007 4106 d803 ff01 2d02 1803 df02 3d01 fcfe 15fd
73fc 03fd 6ffd fdfc 91fc c6fc e5fc 96fc 8bfc ...
```

The translation from the metalevel to the score level is achieved in part by representing sound *symbolically* in the metalevel, using an abstraction called a *parameterized sound event*. A sound event is a generalized description of sound information from which different score level encodings can be computed. The ability to produce different encodings of the same information is important because there are many applications in the score level that overlap in functionality but differ in the exact format they use to encode sonic information. Parameterized sound description allows the composer to represent sound in a general, consistent, and uniform manner while still being able to address the various applications and languages that define the score and synthesis composition levels.

Parameterized Sound Events

A parameterized sound event encodes sound as a collection of properties called *sound parameters*. The first step in the encoding process is to define an appropriate set of parameters that will adequately represent the characteristics of the sound that is to be encoded. Once these parameters have been determined, specific *instances* of the sound can be created by determining the set of parameter values that constitute each instance of the sound. While all sounds have a basic set of properties that event descriptions encode, the complete set of parameters for a given sound event will depend on the nature of the sound as well as on the score level synthesis algorithm that is used to produce its acoustic waveform. A useful way to think about sound parameters is that they define *dimensions* of compositional interest and coordinates for each "sound point" are expressed by values along each dimension's axis. The job for the composer, then, is to articulate interesting sound points in a multi-dimensional parameter space. Many score level applications display sound points as graphical plots. For example, notation programs map event parameters onto the traditional five-line staff of Common Practice Notation. Many MIDI sequencers provide a display style called "piano roll notation" that maps two (or more) sound parameters onto a two dimensional grid, as shown in Figure 2.

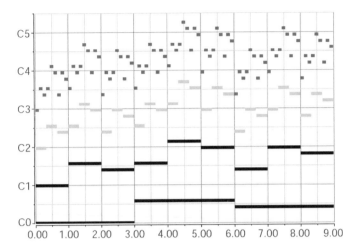

Figure 2. Piano roll graph displaying sound events from Table 2. The graph displays four sound parameters start-time, duration, frequency, and timbre (instrument).

It will be useful to remember that all the metalevel techniques that are presented in the remainder of this book must ultimately produce patterns of data organized into sound event descriptions. We begin learning about this process by defining some basic properties of sound that all events encode and then discussing some common data formats used in parameterized event description.

The Properties of Sound

When a sound source vibrates, its oscillations disturb molecules in the surrounding medium. The elastic nature of the medium causes a chain reaction to occur as the disturbance is propagated from molecule to molecule. The result is a series of *waves* that radiate outward from the sound source in all directions. These sound waves consist of compressions and rarefaction of molecules in the medium brought about by the back and forth motion of the sound source. When molecules are pushed together (compression), the pressure in that vicinity of the medium is higher than in regions still at equilibrium. Similarly, when vibration in the opposite direction pulls molecules apart (rarefaction), the pressure at that locality is less than at points in the medium still at equilibrium. This continuous, smooth change in pressure on either side of an equilibrium point has a shape that can be graphed over time (Figure 3).

Figure 3 plots a waveform as a change in pressure over time. The vertical axis displays the *amplitude* of the waveform, a measurement of the amount of energy transmitted in its compressions and rarefaction. The waveform in Figure 3 can be seen to oscillate in a very regular way. The unit of regularity in a waveform like this is called a *cycle*, and the time a cycle takes to occur is called a *period*. A wave that oscillates at a completely uniform rate such as the one in Figure 3 is called a *sine wave* and the rate of oscillation of a sine wave is called *frequency*. Frequency is typically measured in Hertz, the number of cycles per second the waveform produces.

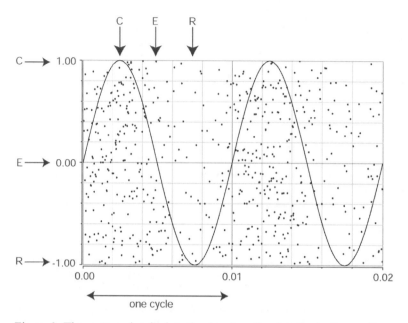

Figure 3. The scatter plot depicts the density of molecules in the medium at an instant in time. The line graph depicts pressure as a function of time. Equilibrium, compression, and rarefaction are labeled E, C and R, respectively.

Sine waves are the basic building blocks of all sound. However, most musical instruments generate *complex waveforms* rather than sine waves. A complex waveform oscillates at multiple rates (frequencies) at the same time (Figure 4).

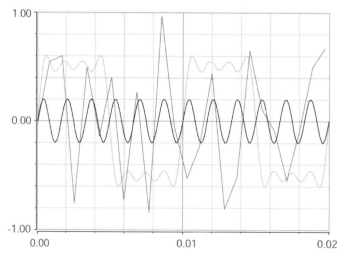

Figure 4. Plots of three different types of waves. A sine wave (small amplitude), a complex waveform containing odd harmonics (medium), and noise (large).

When these component frequencies are related by integer ratio, the sound is said to be *harmonic*. Harmonic sound is generally perceived as a single *fundamental* frequency with an associated *timbre* or tone color. Most, but not all, musical instruments produce harmonic sound. In contrast, *aperiodic* waveforms, or noise, have little or no discernible regularity in their vibration.

Sound Properties and Event Parameters

The preceding discussion of sound waves identifies some fundamental properties of sound. All sounds are comprised of one or more *frequency* components. The mixture of these components imparts a characteristic *timbre*, or tone color to the sound. Sound transmits a certain amount of *amplitude*, or energy, to our ears. All sounds also *start* and last for some *duration* of time. These five basic properties: start, duration, frequency, amplitude, and timbre are present either implicitly or explicitly in all parameterized sound event descriptions (Table 4 and 5).

Table 4. Sound event parameters for MIDI.

parameter	property	value
time	time	0.0
duration	time	0.5
keynum	frequency	60
amplitude	amplitude	64
channel	timbre	0

Table 5. Sound event parameters for FM synthesis.

parameter	property	value
time	time	0.0
duration	time	3
frequency	frequency	440
amplitude	amplitude	0.2
amplitude-env	amplitude	(1 0 .25 .1 1 0)
mratio	timbre	2
index	timbre	4
index-env	timbre	(0 0 .5 1 1 0)
degree	amplitude	0
distance	amplitude	1
reverb	timbre	.01

Of course additional sound properties could be added to the list, and properties may not correspond in a one-to-one manner with sound event parameters. For example, natural sounds have a location associated with them but this property may or may not be represented in a particular sound event. The property of timbre, on the other hand, is part of every sound but it is so complex that its specification may be spread over several parameters (Table 5), or only implicitly represented by the choice of instrument that renders the sound event description (Table 4).

Parameter Data Formats

When viewed from the perspective of sound events, the activity of music composition consists of projecting musically interesting patterns into data assigned to event parameters. But we have seen that a single sound property may be expressed differently in two sound events. Moreover, each sound event may require its parameters to be described in a particular way, by using specific formats for data. It is important, then, that description at the metalevel be flexible and interchangeable so that the composer can work with whatever data formats are most appropriate for a given situation.

Frequency formats

Over the course of centuries Western composers have developed many ways to organize and relate frequency information. Some of these methods define relationships between absolute frequency values while others describe frequency in terms of relative distances, or motion. In computer composition, some score level applications may present additional constraints on how a composer formats, or encodes frequency information. For example, the MIDI protocol insists that frequency information be encoded as integer key numbers. Notation programs, on the other hand, represent frequency in a more symbolic way that allows more than one "spelling" for a given frequency. Sound synthesis languages such as Common Lisp Music and Csound usually expect frequency to be encoded as raw Hertz values. Because there are so many ways to work with frequency, we will identify four interchangeable formats for its expression:

- in *Hertz*, or cycles per second
- as *keynum* positions in a scale
- as *note* names in a scale
- as *interval* distances between notes or key numbers

A *Hertz* value specifies frequency as the number of cycles per second of its waveform. Many synthesis languages expect frequency in Hertz because this format does not require an underlying tuning system or mode for its interpretation. In contrast to Hertz, the note and keynum formats *convert* to a frequency given the existence of some underlying scale that quantizes frequency space into discrete steps. The frequency of each scale degree depends on the tuning system that the scale employs. For example, the standard chromatic scale uses an equal tempered tuning system based on a C at 8.175 Hz with an interval of $2^{1/12}$ (100 cents) between each scale degree.

A *keynum* specifies the scale degree position of a frequency in a scale. Since a keynum is a numerical quantity like Hertz it can be used in arithmetic calculations. But unlike Hertz, keynums also encode pitch class and octave information and allow intervals to be calculated using addition and subtraction rather than multiplication and division. The MIDI protocol uses integer key numbers to identify specific tones that a Note-On MIDI message activates when it is sent to a synthesizer. Common Music extends the idea of key number to include *floating point key numbers*, such as 60.5 or 45.678, so that frequencies "in between" adjacent scale degrees in a tuning system can be specified. A floating point key number is interpreted *kkk.cc* where *kkk* is the integer key portion of the keynum and the fractional portion *.cc* is interpreted as *cc* cents above the Hertz value of *kkk*.

A *note* is a Lisp symbol that names a scale degree. Although note names can vary from scale to scale as defined by the composer, a note name generally consists of a basic class name such as a or nem, an (optional) accidental sign and an octave number. For example, a4 is the note name for 440 Hz in the standard chromatic scale, cs5 is C-sharp in the fifth octave, and nem0 is the first note in the first octave of the Pelog scale (Chapter 15). Note names are the most generally useful frequency format because they encode information about the spelling of a frequency in addition to its Hertz frequency, pitch class and octave register.

An *interval* is an integer that specifies the distance between two scale degrees. This distance can be expressed as a positive or negative number of steps or as a special *typed interval* that encodes information about an interval's spelling in addition to its size. See the Common Music dictionary for more information about typed intervals.

In a given compositional context there may be one frequency representation that has advantages over the others. The following functions provide a mapping between the frequency formats discussed above.

```
(hertz f [:in scale])                                          [Function]
(keynum f [:in scale] [:from scale] [:to scale])               [Function]
(note f [:in scale] [:from scale] [:to scale]    [Function]
[:accidental acc])
(transpose f [int] [scale])                                    [Function]
```

The functions hertz, keynum, and note all convert a frequency specification *f* into the format for which the function is named. The function transpose shifts *f* by *int* intervals while preserving the current frequency format of *f*. All four functions operate with respect to a tuning system or mode optionally specified to the function. If *scale* is not specified the functions will use the default scale stored in the system's global variable *scale*. By default, this variable holds the standard chromatic scale, whose properties are discussed in the next section of this chapter.

The hertz function returns the Hertz frequency of either a key number or note name, as shown in Interaction 1.

Interaction 1. Converting to Hertz in the standard chromatic scale.

```
cm> *scale*
#<tuning "chromatic-scale">
cm> (hertz 'a4)
440.0
cm> (hertz 69)
440.0
cm> (hertz '(a4 c5 e))
(440.0 523.251 659.255)
cm>
```

The keynum function returns the key number of a Hertz value or note name. Hertz values always produce floating point key numbers, in which the fractional value represents cents above the integer keynum, as shown in Interaction 2.

Interaction 2. Converting to key numbers.

```
cm> (keynum 'a4)
69
cm> (keynum 440 :hz)
69.0
cm> (keynum '(440 550 660) :hz)
(69.0 72.863 76.019)
cm>
```

The note function returns the note name of a key number or Hertz value.

Interaction 3. Converting to notes.

```
cm> (note 69)
a4
cm> (note 440 :hz)
a4
cm> (note '(69 72 76))
(a4 c5 e5)
cm>
```

The transpose function shifts notes or key numbers by an interval amount. If a note and typed interval are specified then the transposition will reflect the interval's spelling, as shown in Interaction 4.

Interaction 4. Transposing notes and key numbers.

```
cm> (transpose 69 6)
75
cm> (transpose 'a4 6)
ef5
cm> (transpose 'a4 (interval 'aug 4))
ds5
cm> (transpose '(a4 c5 e) (interval 'aug -2))
(gf4 bff4 df5)
cm>
```

The previous interactions point out several features common to all four functions:

- In order to distinguish a Hertz number from a keynum number a Hertz value must be "tagged" by including the keyword :hertz or :hz just after the value.
- Lists may be specified as well as single values. Lists allow sets, rows and chords to be processed in a single operation.
- A note in a note list may provide an octave number or not. If not, its octave number will default to the last specified octave number in the list, or the 4th octave (middle-C octave) if no number is specified.

The standard chromatic scale
The frequency functions documented in the previous section all operate with respect to an underlying tuning system or mode. If no mode or tuning is specified the functions use the system's default tuning object stored in the global variable *scale*. This scale is initially set to the standard chromatic scale but can be reset by the user. The standard chromatic scale is implemented with 11 octaves of note entries. The first octave in the scale is numbered -1; the Middle-C octave is 4 and the highest octave number is 10. Middle-C (written C4) is keynum 60 and has a frequency of 261.625 Hz. There is no upper octave limit for key numbers or Hertz values.

Note names in the standard chromatic scale
A note in the standard chromatic scale consists of a pitch class letter, an optional accidental and an octave number:

Table 6. Note spellings in the standard chromatic scale.

name	accidental	octave
c, d, e, f, g, a, b	ff, f, n, s, ss	-1 to 10

Note entries include all natural (n), sharp (s), flat (f), double-sharp (ss) and double-flat (ff) spellings. The symbol r means rest.

Interaction 5. Note names in the chromatic scale.

```
cm> (keynum 'c4)
60
cm> (keynum 'dff4)
60
cm> (keynum 'bs3)
60
cm> (note 'c4 :accidental 's)
bs3
cm> (note 261.625 :hz :accidental 'ff)
dff4
cm> (keynum 'c-1)
0
cm> (hertz 'b10)
31608.531
cm>
```

Key numbers in the standard chromatic scale
Key numbers in the standard chromatic scale may be expressed as integers or floating point numbers. A floating point key number is interpreted *kkk.cc* where *kkk* is the integer keynum and *cc* is cents above the Hertz value of *kkk*. For example, 60.5 means 50 cents (quarter tone) above the frequency of keynum 60, or 269.291 Hz.

Interaction 6. Key numbers in the chromatic scale.

```
cm> (keynum 439 :hz)
68.96
cm> (hertz 69)
440.0
cm> (hertz 69.5)
452.892
cm> (note 69.5)
bf4
cm>
```

Intervals in the standard chromatic scale
Intervals measure distances between scale degrees. In the standard chromatic scale this measurement can be expressed in terms of simple integer half steps or by using a specially encoded *typed interval* that includes the quality and spelling of an interval along with its size.

Time formats

A number of different time formats are commonly found in computer composition: seconds, milliseconds, "ticks", and metric proportions scaled by a tempo factor. The basic format for time in Common Music is seconds. Time values can be expressed as Lisp integers, ratios and floats. The function `rhythm` converts proportional and symbolic metric values to time in seconds.

(rhythm *rhy* [*tempo*] [*beat*])   [Function]

The `rhythm` function converts a metric value *rhy* to time in seconds. *rhy* can be a ratio, a rhythmic symbol (Table 7) or a list of the same. *Tempo* provides the optional metronome speed and defaults to 60. *Beat* specifies the metronome's pulse and defaults to .25, or quarter note. Global default metronome and beat values can be established by setting the system's `*tempo*` and `*beat*` variables, respectively.

Table 7. Table of Metric Symbols.

letter	value	letter	value
m	maxima	q	quarter
l	longa	e	eighth
b	brevis	s	sixteenth
w	whole	t	thirty-second
h	half	x	sixty-fourth

A rhythmic symbol consists of a metric letter from Table 7 that may be optionally preceded by a division letter: t for triplet or q for quintuplet, and optionally followed by any number of dots. Rhythmic symbols also support addition, subtraction and multiplication. The following table displays some representative rhythmic symbols.

Table 8. Examples of rhythmic symbols.

quarter	q
triplet quarter	tq
dotted-eight	e.
triplet dotted sixteenth	ts.
triple dotted half	h...
quintuplet whole	qw
sixteenth plus triplet quarter	s+tq
whole minus triplet sixteenth	w-ts
whole times 4	w*4

Interaction 7. Examples of using the rhythm function.

```
cm> (rhythm 'q)
1.0
cm> (rhythm 1/4 120.0)
.5
cm> (rhythm 'w+q )
5.0
cm> (define *tempo* 120.0)

cm> (rhythm '(q th e.. x) )
(0.5 0.6666666666666666 0.4375 0.03125)
cm>
```

Amplitude formats

Amplitude as a sound property is more difficult to come to terms with than frequency, partly because the word is used with different meanings (loudness, intensity, pressure, and so on) and partly because its perception depends on a number of factors, including the frequency of the sound (the Fletcher-Munson curves) and as the listener's distance from the sound source. When computers and amplifiers are involved the situation becomes even more complex because amplitude can be electronically boosted or reduced at any number of points along a signal's path such that the intensity level that reaches our ears may have little to do with the value specified in the computer score! Acoustic amplitude is usually measured by pressure, or a *sound intensity level* (SIL) as Watts per meter squared. Intensity levels are defined from 10^{-12}, the threshold of hearing, to 10^0, the threshold of pain. Since 12 orders of magnitude is an enormous range of values, SIL is typically plotted using the logarithmic *Decibel scale*, or dB (Table 9).

Table 9. Comparison of dynamic scale to SIL. (Backus)

Dynamic level	Intensity (w/m2)	I/Ir	SIL (dB)
ffff (pain)	10^0	10^{12}	120
fff	10^{-2}	10^{10}	100
ff	10^{-3}	10^9	90
f	10^{-4}	10^8	80
mf	10^{-5}	10^7	70
mp	10^{-6}	10^6	60
p	10^{-7}	10^5	50
pp	10^{-8}	10^4	40
ppp	10^{-9}	10^3	30
pppp (threshold Ir)	10^{-12}	10^0	0

Unfortunately, dB values do not really indicate how "loud" a sound seems to the listener, which is generally what composers are interested in. Composers typically express amplitude in terms of a "psychological scale" represented by symbolic *dynamic levels* whose meanings correspond only very loosely to the measured intensity levels in Table 9. Since amplitude measurement is so variable, sound synthesis languages often represent amplitude as a *normalized* value between 0.0 and 1.0, where 0.0 means silence and 1.0 means a fully saturated signal. The MIDI protocol represents amplitude values using a "key velocity" scale defined between 0 and 127, where 0 is silence and 127 is maximum. Most of the examples in this book use the normalized representation of amplitude (0.0-1.0) so that amplitude values may be easily computed or controlled by envelopes and other scaling operations.

Composers who would like to work with the musical dynamic scale can use Common Music's amplitude function to convert symbolic amplitude levels into numerical values within a specified range:

(amplitude *amp* [*softest*] [*loudest*] [*power*]) [Function]

This function converts the logical amplitude *amp* into a value between *softest* and *loudest* according to the *power* curve. A logical amplitude is a number between 0.0 and 1.0 or one of the amplitude symbols shown in Table 10:

Table 10. Table of logical amplitude levels.

0.0	0.1	0.2	0.3	0.4	0.5	0.6	0.7	0.8	0.9	1.0
niente	pppp	ppp	pp	p	mp	mf	f	ff	fff	ffff

The values of *softest*, *loudest* and *power* default to the value of the global variables *softest* *loudest* and *power*. The default power value of 1.0 cause a linear increase as the logical amplitude moves from 0.0 to 1.0, as shown in Interaction 8.

Interaction 8. The amplitude function.

```
cm> (amplitude 'mp)
.5
cm> (amplitude 'mp 0 127)
63.5
cm> (amplitude .5 0 1 4)
0.0625
cm>
```

Timbre

Timbre is such a complex sound property that there is no specific set of parameters or data formats that control its specification. Synthesis languages like Csound and CLM permit the composer to define the digital instruments that produce sound; these instruments are a strong determinant of the overall spectrum. A single sound event for one of these digital instruments may contain a number of parameters that provide precise control over the timbral evolution of the sound, by controlling the mix of overtones, or applying time varying envelopes to oscillators and so on. In comparison to synthesis languages, the MIDI protocol provides very little in the way of direct control over the timbral evolution of a sound. The MIDI channel parameter and the program change message provide the most direct means to control timbre in the synthesizers since they determine what MIDI instruments receive the note data on each channel.

Chapter Source Code

The source code to all of the examples and interactions in this chapter can be found in the file sound.cm located in the same directory as the HTML file for this chapter. The source file can be edited in a text editor or evaluated inside the Common Music application.

11

Metastructure for Composition

In Chapter 3 we learned that the property list is one way to represent the characteristics of an object we want to model. Example 1 shows how two different sounds might be represented as property lists.

Example 1. Tone descriptions represented as property lists.

```
(define piano-tone
   '(pitch 440 duration 1/4 loudness mf))

(define viola-tone
   '(pitch 440 duration 1/4 loudness mf))
```

Assume for the moment that the composer would like to define a function called play-tones to generate sound from descriptions such as those shown in Example 1. To the composer the two definitions represent very different things. But from Lisp's point of view the two lists contain the exact same information and are literally equal to one another:

Interaction 1. Lisp cannot distinguish between the two tones.

```
cm> (equal? piano-tone viola-tone)
#t
cm>
```

Since both lists contain the same information and neither list declares what *type* of sound it represents, it will be impossible for play-tones to produce a piano tone from the first description and a viola tone from the second. One possible solution to this problem might be to add a *type symbol* to the front of each list that "declares" what type of tone each list represents:

Example 2. Adding type symbols to the front of each sound description.

- .
```
(define sounds
   '((piano-tone pitch 440 duration 1/4 loudness mf)
     (viola-tone pitch 440 duration 1/4 loudness mf)
     (metal-crash duration 2 loudness ff)))
```
- .

Given a list of sound descriptions such as those shown in Example 2 the composer could then design the play-tones function to check the symbol in the first position of each tone description to determine the action appropriate to synthesize the sound encoded in the rest of the list. The addition of a type symbol to the front of each list is a form of *application datatyping*, in which a programmer defines the type and format of data that will be processed by the application. Adding type symbols to property lists was actually used by early Lisp researchers as a means of classifying the data that was processed by their programs. Most computer programs that model the real world or assist human activity in some way are faced with the need to represent various objects and behavior that make up the application's domain. The classification scheme used by the early researchers was a primitive way of doing and it had several serious limitations:

- While it is possible to have Piano-Tones and Viola-Tones, there is no way to express the fact that both tones might be *specializations* of a more general type of data called (for example) a Tone and distinguishable from, say, another type of sound called a Noise. The more general types Tone and Noise are completely absent from the representation.
- For each new type of Tone, the composer is required to add more conditional checks and type-specific behavior to the play-tones function. This function definition will soon become an unmanageable programming task as the number of different sounds in the composition increases.
- To the underlying language the data are still just lists. It is not possible to *optimize* the representation in any way.

During the 1980's Lisp adopted a powerful new methodology for modeling real world applications. This methodology is called *object-oriented programming*. In object oriented programming a domain of interest is modeled, or represented, in

terms of *classes*, *instances* and *methods* that belong to an *object system*. The Common Music application is an example of a software system that represents its data and behavior using an object system. In the case of Common Music, the application domain is musical composition and the object modeling involves the representation of compositional structure and its behavior during sound generation. Before turning our attention to the specifics of Common Music's representation, we first look at some general characteristics of object oriented design.

Objects, Classes, Instances and Slots

An object system is a mechanism for defining the characteristics of data and the behavior of functions that operate on that data in an application program. An *object* is a software unit that represents something about the domain being modeled. Most object systems distinguish between two types of objects, classes and instances. A *class* is an object that describes the general characteristics of the data being modeled. These characteristics are sometimes referred to as the *properties*, *slots* or *instance variables* of the class. When a class is defined it can be declared to be a *subclass*, or specialization, of another, more general, class called a *superclass*. The superclass-to-subclass relationship says that every slot defined in the superclass is *inherited*, or automatically present, in the subclass. A subclass may also declare additional slots not found in the superclass. An *instance* is a specific, unique member of a class. Instance objects are the actual data that an object-oriented program manipulates.

Creating Instances

Data that an object-oriented program manipulates is *instantiated*, or created, from class descriptions. When an instance is created it receives all of the slots defined by its class together with whatever *default values* the class declares for its slots. A slot's default value can be overridden by specifying a value for that slot when the instance is created. Objects can be created and their slots initialized to specific values using the macro function new:

(new *class* [:slot *value*] ...)   [Macro]

new creates an instance from a specification of its class and initial slot values. *Class* is the class name (symbol) of the instance to create. Any number of *slot initializations* may be specified following the class. Each slot initialization is a pair: a keyword slot name followed by its value in the new instance. A keyword is a symbol that is prefixed with a colon. For example, creating an instance of the midi event class with its time slot set to .5 would look like:

     (new midi :time .5)

where the symbol midi is the name of the class, :time is the keyword slot to set and .5 is its value in the new instance.

Interaction 2. Creating midi instances with new.

```
cm> (new midi)
#i(midi keynum 60 duration 0.5 amplitude 64 channel 0)
cm> (new midi :keynum 90 :time .5 :duration 3)
#i(midi time .5 keynum 90 duration 3 amplitude 64
        channel 0)
cm>
```

Common Music normally prints sound events using a specially formatted display:
        #i(*class slot value ...*)
The special prefix #i tells the user that an instance is being shown. The instance is displayed as a list containing the name of the instance's class followed by all its slots and values. This printing feature is a convenient way to inspect the various characteristics of a sound. The #i prefix tells you that you are looking at an instance object, not a list.

Lisp Note:
        An #i expression may appear in upper case letters and the order of slots may vary in different Lisp implementations.

The Common Music Class Taxonomy

There are three broad classifications of objects within the hierarchy defined by Common Music (Figure 1).
• *Events* define the characteristics of musical sounds the composer works with.
• *Containers* group musical data together to form larger units of structure.
• *Processes* implement procedural descriptions of music.

Event classes
An event is an object that represents a sound of some kind. Common Music allows the composer complete control over the definition of sound events but several specialized classes have already been defined for use with this book. The midi event class is the sound description that we will be concerned with in the next few chapters.

The midi event class
The midi event is a parameterized sound description suitable for working with MIDI synthesizers, sequencing programs, and notation programs that display MIDI data using traditional music notation.

midi supports the following slot initializations:
:time *number*
        Sets the start time of the event in the score.
:keynum {*keynum* | *note*}
        Frequency expressed as a keynum or note. (See Chapter 15)

:duration *number*
> The duration of the event in seconds.

:amplitude *number*
> A logical amplitude 0.0 < 1.0 or an integer velocity 0 to 127. Defaults to 64.

:channel *integer*
> A MIDI channel number 0-15. Defaults to channel 0.

Container classes

Container classes support the aggregation of musical material. The seq, pattern, and io classes all implement different strategies for managing the objects they contain.

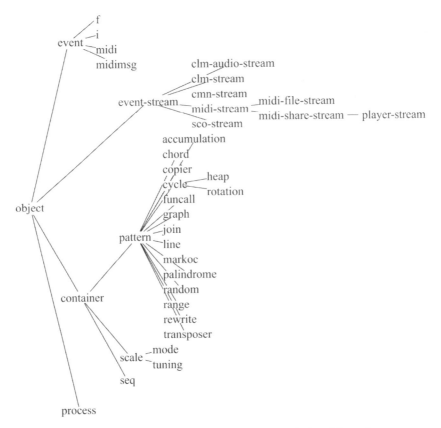

Figure 1. A graph of Common Music's superclass->subclass hierarchy.

The seq container class

A seq is a nameable object that implements musical sequencing. These objects are stored as a time ordered list of *subobjects*. The subobject list may contain events, processes, and other sequences. When sequences are generated the start times of the subobjects are always calculated relative to the start time of the seq itself.

seq supports the following slot initializations:

:time *number*

>Sets the start time of the midi event in the score.

:name {*symbol* | *string*}

>Sets then name of the object to the *symbol* or *string*.

:subobjects *list*

>A list of subobjects.

Interaction 3. Creating a seq object.

```
cm> (new seq :name 'test :time 10
          :subobjects
          (loop for i below 4
                collect (new midi :time i)))
#<seq: "test">
cm> (object-time #&test)
10
cm> (object-name #&test)
"stuff"
cm> (subobjects #&test)
(#i(midi time 0 keynum 60 duration 0.5 amplitude 64
          channel 0)
 #i(midi time 1 keynum 60 duration 0.5 amplitude 64
          channel 0)
 #i(midi time 2 keynum 60 duration 0.5 amplitude 64
          channel 0)
 #i(midi time 3 keynum 60 duration 0.5 amplitude 64
          channel 0))
cm>
```

Common Music defines a specialized printing method for containers that displays the name of the container when the object is printed in the Listener window. A container that has no name is displayed according to whatever method the Lisp implementation provides.

The special prefix #& "fetches" a container given its name. This feature saves the composer from having to define a variable just to store the object when it is created.

There are a number of accessor functions that are appropriate to use with events and containers. Consult the entry for seq in the Common Music Dictionary for more information.

Event stream classes

The `event-stream` class is the superclass for musical scores. Most scores are stored as different types of files on the computer's hard drive. Functions that perform input or output to scores accept either `event-stream` instances or strings that identify their file on the disk. Filenames specified to input or output functions must always includ a file name extension. This extension determines the type of event stream to be created. Common Music defines stream class for the following file extensions.

Table 1. File extensions and score types.

extensions	score class
.mid, .midi	`midi-file-stream` for MIDI
.sco	`sco-file-stream` for Csound
.aiff, .wav, .snd	`audio-file-stream` for Common Lisp Music
.clm	`clm-file-stream` for Common Lisp Music
.cmn, .eps	`cmn-file-stream` for Common Music Notation

Midi scores

MIDI scores supports output to Level 0 MIDI files and input from either Level 0 or Level 1 MIDI files. Level 0 means that the data in the MIDI file constitutes a single *track*, or time line of MIDI events. Level 1 MIDI files contain multiple tracks of data. The `midi-file-stream` class is automatically chosen when you specify a file with a .mid or .midi extension.

`midi-file-stream` supports the following slot initializations:
`:versions` {*number* | *true*}
>   Causes a new version of the file to be created each time output occurs. The version name is based on the name of the file and the version count, which is initialized to *number* and incremented each time output occurs. A boolean true value for `:versions` is the same as 1.

`:tempo` *number*
>   The MIDI tempo of the file. Defaults to 60 bpm.

`:divisions` *integer*
>   The number of MIDI divisions per quarter note. Defaults to 96.

`:timesig` (*numerator denominator*)
>   The time signature for the file. Defaults to (4 4). The time signature list may contain up to four values: (numerator denominator clocks-per-quarter 32nds).

:channel-tuning {*false* | *true* | *1-16* | *list*}

> The default value of :channel-tuning is false, which means that floating point key numbers are rounded to the nearest MIDI integer keynum as they are sent to a MIDI file or port. See Chapter 15 and consult the Common Music Dictionary for more information on :channel-tuning.

:pitch-bend-width *integer*

> Declares the pitch bend width in semitones of the synthesizer. This value is used to calculate pitch bend values for microtonal frequency resolution. The default value is 2, which means that the synthesizer uses a maximum pitch bend range of one whole step up and down (2 semitones).

Pattern classes

The pattern class is the root class for defining musical patterns. Pattern-based composition is the topic of Chapter 20.

Processes

A process is a special type of Lisp function that implements the procedural description of music. Processes are introduced in Chapter 13.

Defining New Classes

The class hierarchy shown in Figure 1 is only an approximation of the classes defined in Common Music. Composers who work with sound synthesis languages will typically want to define their own customized sound events as appropriate for the digital instruments they are working with the sound synthesis language they are using. Common Music provides a macro called defobject for defining new classes of objects and for specializing existing classes. These classes are automatically integrated into Common Music's score generation protocol. For more information on defobject see Chapter 24 and consult the Common Music Dictionary.

Chapter Source Code

The source code to all of the examples and interactions in this chapter can be found in the file objects.cm located in the same directory as the HTML file for this chapter. The source file can be edited in a text editor or evaluated inside the Common Music application.

12

Etudes, Op. 4: Score Generation

In *Etudes*, Op.4 we work thorough a series of examples that demonstrate how to generate scores using MIDI events, lists and sequences.

Op. 4, No. 1: The Current Working Directory.

Most of the examples in this book generate scores that are saved in MIDI files on the computer's hard drive. Although is always possible to provide a fully specified pathname when a score is saved to the disk, the examples in this book only specify the names and extensions of output files. A file that does not contain a directory component in its pathname will be written to Common Music's current "working directory". The working directory can be displayed and set using the following two functions:

(pwd)   [Function]
(cd [*dir*])   [Function]

The function pwd (print working directory) returns the string name of the current working directory. The function cd (change directory) changes the working directory. If cd is called without its optional directory argument it sets the current working directory to whatever the operating system defines as the user's "home directory". The directory specified to cd should be a string that ends with the directory character appropriate for the host operating system. For Linux, OS X and Windows use "/". For MacOS use ":" as the directory delimiter.

Before attempting to generate any scores, first make sure that Lisp's working directory is set to the directory that you would like to save score output to. Note that you must have "write permission" in order to save files to it.

Interaction 1. Using the pwd and cd functions.

```
cm> (pwd)
"/home/hkt/"
cm> (cd "/tmp/")
"/tmp/"
cm> (pwd)
"/tmp/"
cm>
```

Op. 4, No. 2: The events Function

The main score output processing function is called events. This function can be used to output events, sequences, processes and lists of these to a destination such as a file or port.

(events *objects score* [*ahead*] ...)   [Function]

The events function is the main entry point for generating scores. *Objects* can a single object or a list of objects. *Score* can be a score or a filename. *Ahead* is an optional start time offset for *objects* in the score. If *ahead* is a single number it is applied to all the *objects*. If *ahead* is a list of numbers then each number is matched in left to right order with the corresponding object in *objects*. Following the optional offset may come any number of *keyword value* initializations suitable to *score*. events returns the name of the score as its value.

In our first example we output a single MIDI event to a MIDI score file. Before generating the file we use the pwd function to tell us what the current working directory is. If you do not have write permission in the directory that is returned by pwd then you can use cd to change to an appropriate output directory:

Interaction 2. Generating a MIDI event to a MIDI file.

```
cm> (define one (new midi :time 0
                    :keynum 60 :duration 2))

cm> (events one "myscore.mid")
"myscore.mid"
cm> (midi-file-print "myscore.mid")
File: myscore.mid
Format: 0
Tracks: 1
Division: 480

Track 0, length 20
        0 #<Tempo Change 1000 ms>
        0 #<Note-On 0 60 64>
      960 #<Note-Off 0 60 127>
"myscore.mid"
cm>
```

Op. 4, No. 3: Listening to MIDI Files

In this next exercise we listen to our score. Score files can be played from inside Common Music if there is an appropriate player defined for your operating system and audio/MIDI setup. The following MIDI file players can be used:

OSX:

        (osx-play-midi-file *file*)   [Function]

        plays a MIDI file using the QuickTime Player application.

Linux:

        (oss-play-midi-file *file*)   [Function]

        plays a MIDI file using the OSS utility /usr/bin/playmidi.

MacOS:

        (mac-play-midi-file *file*)   [Function]

        plays a MIDI file using the QuickTime Player application.

Windows:

        (win-play-midi-file *file*)   [Function]

        plays a MIDI file using the Windows Media Player application.

These functions can be called by hand or set as *output hooks* that automatically play score files after they are generated. In Interaction 3 we call the function by hand to listen to the score.

Interaction 3. Listening to a MIDI file on OSX.

```
cm> (osx-play-midi-file "myscore.mid")
"myscore.mid"
cm>
```

Op. 4, No. 4: File Versions and Automatic Playback

It is possible to generate different versions of the same basic score and automatically play each version after it has been generated by the events function. If *file versioning* is activated, the file name specified to events serves as a "base name" for creating numbered versions of the same score. For example, if the name of the score is "myscore.mid" and file versioning is activated, then successive calls to events will produce a sequence of files named "myscore-1.mid", "myscore-2.mid", "myscore-3.mid", and so on. Versioning ensures that no score will be accidentally overwritten by the events function if it generates the same score again. Versioning is also a convenient way to compare different "takes" of a score as it is incrementally developed. Almost all of the file names that appear in this book reflect file versioning. This means that as you work through the examples and perform your own experiments, the file names that you see returned by the events function will not exactly match the file names printed in this book.

The function that activates and deactivates file versioning for MIDI scores is called set-midi-file-versions!:

(set-midi-file-versions! *bool*)   [Function]

Specifying true to set-midi-file-versions! enables file versioning for MIDI scores, specifying false turns file versioning off.

Automatic playback for MIDI files can be activated by setting an *output hook* that Common Music calls after the score is complete to play the new file. (The term "hook" describes a Lisp function that is associated with an automatic action.)

(set-midi-output-hook! *fn*)   [Function]

Set-midi-output-hook! establishes the function *fn* as a hook that called on MIDI files after they are generated by events. The hook function is passed the pathname (string) of the file and any additional hook arguments the user sets in the file. To remove an existing output hook specify false in place of a function. In order to set a hook you must specify the actual function, not just its name. The special Lisp prefix #' "fetches" a function object given its name. In this next example we activate file versioning for MIDI files, and set an output hook for automatic score playback.

Interaction 4. Activating file versioning and setting an output hook for automatic playback.

```
cm> (set-midi-file-versions! true)

cm> (set-midi-output-hook! #'osx-play-midi-file)
```

Since these functions are used for an effect rather than for a value they do not return anything back to the Listener window for printing.

Op. 4, No. 5: Generating a score from Multiple Events

Multiple events can be generated to a score by specifying a list of objects to the events function. In this next example we use a loop to define a list of MIDI notes.

Example 1. Definition of a list of events.

```
(define up
    (loop for key from 60 to 72
          for beg from 0 by .1
          collect (new midi :time beg
                            :keynum key
                            :duration 1)))
```

Once the list is defined it can be passed to the events function to create a score.

Interaction 5. Generating a score from a list of events.

```
cm> (events up "myscore.mid")
"myscore-1.mid"
cm>
```

➙nm/12/snd/myscore-1.mid

In Interaction 5 the variable *up* is defined to hold a list of midi events. The list is created using a loop that iterates two stepping variables. The first variable *key* is looped over every key number from 60 (Middle-C) to the octave above. The second variable *beg* starts at time 0 and is incremented by .1 seconds on each. Note that an upper bound for this second iteration clause is not necessary because the first iteration clause already defines the scope of the iteration. For each value of *key* and *beg* the loop collects a new MIDI event. The overall effect is to generate a rapid, chromatic "strum" over one octave. This is the first example in the book that demonstrates a *procedural* description of musical structure. Try redefining the *up* variable using a loop that iterates over different values for *beg* and *key*.

Op. 4, No. 5: Mixing Objects

What if we would like to hear two simultaneous strums, one up and one down? A situation like this requires that two musical gestures "overlap" in the score. This is most naturally achieved by mixing the "parallel" output from two or more sequences together. Before defining these objects we first generalize our loop into a function that creates either an ascending or descending chromatic strum at a specified rate, amplitude and duration:

Example 2. Create a list of midi events between two key numbers.

```
(define (strums key1 key2 rate dur amp)
  (let ((step (if (< key2 key1) -1 1))
        (diff (abs (- key1 key2))))
    (loop repeat (+ diff 1)
          for key from key1 by step
          for beg from 0 by rate
          collect (new midi :time beg
                            :duration dur
                            :amplitude amp
                            :keynum key))))
```

The strums function creates either upward or downward strums between a starting *key1* and an ending *key2*. The direction of the iteration is controlled by the variable *step*. The value of *step* is determined by an if expression that tests to see if the ending key is lower that the starting key or not. If it is then -1 is returned and the iteration proceeds downward from *key1*. If *key2* is greater than *key1* then the iteration ascends from *key1* by 1. The variable *diff* holds the number of chromatic steps between the two keys. The abs function is used get the absolute value of the difference since the difference will be negative if *key2* is less than *key1*. The loop then repeats *diff+1* times so that the last note will actually be the value of *key2*. The rest of the loop is similar to the first example. In this next interaction we look at the output from a call to strums to see the list it computes. pprint displays the list in a "pretty format" that is easy to read in the Listener window.)

Interaction 6. Generating strum data.

```
cm> (pprint (strums 60 61 .1 1 .2))
(#i(midi time 0 keynum 60 duration 1 amplitude 0.2
channel 0)
 #i(midi time 0.1 keynum 61 duration 1 amplitude 0.2
channel 0))
cm>
```

In Interaction 7 we create two seq objects to hold different strums and then mix them together to form the output score. The list function is used to make a list around the sequences "up" and "down" so that they can both be passed as the first argument to the events function. The special prefix #& is used to "fetch" each container from its name.

Interaction 7. Creating two strum sequences.

```
cm> (new seq :name 'ups
        :subobjects (strums 48 60 .1 1 .4))
#<seq "ups">
cm> (new seq :name 'downs
        :subobjects (strums 84 72 .1 1 .2))
#<seq "downs">
cm> (events (list #&ups #&downs) "myscore.mid")
"myscore-2.mid"
cm>
```

→ nm/12/snd/myscore-2.mid

Op. 4, No. 6: Start Time Offsets

Our final example demonstrates the effect of specifying start time offsets to the events function. If offsets are provided they should appear directly after the score argument in the events call. In the first interaction of Interaction 8 the onset of both strums is delayed by 5 seconds in the score. In the second interaction each strum receives a different offset, 0 for the up strum and .5 for the down. The last input schedules four instances of the strums at different times.

Interaction 8. The effect of start time offsets.

```
cm> (events (list #&ups #&downs) "myscore.mid" 5)
"myscore-3.mid"
cm> (events (list #&ups #&downs) "myscore.mid"
            '(0 .5))
"myscore-4.mid"
cm> (events (list #&ups #&downs #&ups #&downs )
            "myscore.mid"
            '(0 .5 1 1.5))
"myscore-5.mid"
cm>
```

→ nm/12/snd/myscore-3.mid
→ nm/12/snd/myscore-4.mid
→ nm/12/snd/myscore-5.mid

Chapter Source Code

The source code to all of the examples and interactions in this chapter can be found in the file scores.cm located in the same directory as the HTML file for this chapter. The source file can be edited in a text editor or evaluated inside the Common Music application.

13

Algorithms and Processes

An algorithm must be seen to be believed, and the best way to learn about what an algorithm is all about is to try it.

— Donald Knuth, *The Art of Computer Programming*

In this chapter we begin to explore the procedural description of musical scores, an activity that is sometimes referred to as *algorithmic composition*. In this style of composition the composer writes a program to compute music. This program provides a level of abstraction above the score that allows the composer to explore techniques for music composition that otherwise would be difficult or impossible to achieve. But the use of algorithms to create music also raises some artistic issues that should be kept in mind as you progress through the remaining chapters of this book:

- What is the relationship between a composer and a computed score? If the composer cannot predict what notes will be contained in the score should he or she claim authorship of the composition?
- When an algorithm creates a score is it really composing, does it mimic composition or neither? If a person cannot tell the difference by listening to the score or by studying it, does it matter?

- Should a listener try to appreciate algorithmic constructions aesthetically apart from their sound?
- What happens when a computer program creates the best piece on the concert? Should the audience clap?

Before turning our attention to some specifics of algorithmic composition we first define what an algorithm is and how it relates to the generation of musical material. In The Art of Computer Programming (Knuth), Donald Knuth defines an *algorithm* as a set of steps, or rules, with five basic properties:

- An algorithm must start and stop. The rules an algorithm applies must also conclude in a reasonable amount of time. What "reasonable" is depends on the nature of the algorithm, but in no case can an algorithm take an infinite amount of time to complete its task. Knuth calls this property the *finiteness* of an algorithm.
- The actions that an algorithm performs cannot be open to multiple interpretations; each step must be precise and unambiguous. Knuth terms this quality *definiteness*. An algorithm cannot iterate a "bunch" of times. The number of times must be precisely expressed, for example 2, 1000000, or a randomly chosen number.
- An algorithm starts its computation from an initial state. This state may be expressed as input arguments to the algorithm.
- An algorithm must produce a result with a specific relation to the inputs.
- The steps an algorithm takes must be sufficiently simple that they could be expressed "on paper"; these steps must make sense for the quantities used. Knuth terms this property *effectiveness*.

These points can be illustrated using the strum procedure presented in Chapter 10 and shown again here in Example 1 under a slightly different name.

Example 1. The strum1 definition.

```
(define (strum1 key1 key2 rate dur amp)
  (let ((step (if (< key2 key1) -1 1))
        (diff (abs (- key2 key1))))

    (loop repeat (+ diff 1)
          for key from key1 by step
          for beg from 0 by rate
          collect (new midi :time beg
                           :duration dur
                           :amplitude amp
                           :keynum key))))
```

The strum1 function adheres to Knuth's five characteristics as follows:
1. Strum1 is finite because it iterates a specific number of times. The loop's repeat clause expresses this finiteness quite succinctly.
2. Strum1 is definite because it consists of Lisp expressions in which every quantity and relation is well defined.

3. Strum1 has five input parameters that determine the initial state of the algorithm.
4. Strum1 produces a result, the list of musical events it returns to the caller.
5. Strum1 is effective because it is able to compute its result from its inputs and rules.

As we can see from Example 1, functions provide a natural mechanism for expressing algorithms. When an algorithm is implemented as a Lisp function it is no longer just a series of steps or rules — it is a concrete Lisp object that be manipulated and processed like all other data in the language. This means that it is possible to test and judge an algorithm as entity in its own right. The criteria for judging an algorithm might include its effectiveness, speed, complexity, or even elegance.

Musical Processes

All of the algorithms we will explore in this book are implemented as Lisp functions. One special type of function, called a *process*, will be used more than any other tool to express procedural composition. A process is a Common Music function that computes musical structure (sound events, sequences, even other processes) *dynamically*, during the time it takes for the events function to generate a score. A process really represents the evolution of a compositional idea over time. Processes execute in such a way that many different processes may run in parallel. Each process can be thought of as an iteration that creates a single time line through a score. This time line may co-exist with other time lines that also span the same score. These parallel processes are all managed by controlling software called a *scheduler*.

The scheduler
A scheduler is like a conductor — its job is to insure that the musical objects under its control are evaluated in a systematic order and at their correct times within a score. Scheduling is initiated by the events function when it is called with a list of objects to evaluate. The scheduler generates a time ordered series of sound events from these objects by maintaining a *priority queue* for their time ordered evaluation. The priority of each object is determined by the value of its time slot. (If two objects have the exact same score time then the object that was placed in the queue first has more evaluation priority than the other object at that same time.) The scheduler evaluates an object by first removing it from the head of the queue, and then processing it in some manner appropriate to the object and score being generated. Evaluating one object may result in the same object or new objects being inserted into the scheduling queue with new priority times. The scheduler continues to evaluate the objects in its queue until no more objects remain to be processed. At that point score generation is complete, the scheduler stops, and the score is saved.

Process evaluation
Each time a process function is evaluated by the scheduler its program code executes. While there is no restriction on what a process function does, typical actions include:

- creating musical events and sending them to the score.
- creating new structures (events, sequences and processes) and adding them to the priority queue.
- determining if the process should run again and, if so, determining what its next priority time will be.

Sequence evaluation

The scheduler evaluates a seq object by enqueing all of its subobjects into the scheduling queue. The priority time of the sequence is added to the priority time of each subobject inserted in the queue.

Event handling

When the scheduler evaluates a musical event it sends a parameterized sound description of that event to the score that is being created. The nature of this sound description depends both on the type of event and the type of score being processed. For example, a MIDI event that is sent to a MIDI score results in a number of MIDI byte messages being written to a file on the disk. A MIDI event that is sent to a seq results in the event itself being inserted into the seq's list of subobjects.

Defining Musical Processes

A process function is created using the process macro function. A process definition looks almost identical to a loop definition except that its action clauses implement scheduling and score actions rather than loop actions. The major difference between loop and process is that the loop macro returns values to the caller while the process macro returns a *function* to evaluate inside the scheduler.

Functions as process wrappers

In this book we will always define processes inside of Lisp functions and then call the functions to create processes. A function that contains a process definition can be thought of as a "wrapper" that permits the process to access all the parameter and variable values that exist when the function is called. This is called *encapsulation* and it has several important consequences:

- An encapsulated process definition is a named, reusable abstraction. Its function wrapper can be called any number of times to create new instances of the process it encapsulates.
- If the wrapper function is passed arguments, different versions of the same process description can be created simply by calling the function with different input values. This provides a very powerful "template" mechanism that can produce variations on the process without any extra work.

In all cases we will avoid storing processes in global variables. A process only "lives" inside the scheduler, once the scheduler has finished all of the processes inside it are of no more use. If a process is stored in a global variable then that variable will have to be set to a new process function each time it is used. This is much more work than simply calling a function.

Before actually learning the specifics of the process macro we will look first at two example process descriptions.

Converting strum1 into a process
We start with an example that converts the strum1 function (Example 1) to return a process rather than of a list of events.

Example 2. Converting the strum algorithm into a process description.

```
(define (strum2 key1 key2 rate dur amp)
  (let ((step (if (< key2 key1) -1 1))
        (diff (abs (- key2 key1))))
    (process repeat (+ diff 1)
             for key from key1 by step
             for beg from 0 by rate
             output (new midi :time beg
                             :duration dur
                             :amplitude amp
                             :keynum key))))
```

The definition of strum2 is almost the same as strum1 except for three simple modifications:
- The name of the function has been changed.
- process appears in place of loop.
- An output action appears in place of the collect action.

Interaction 1 demonstrates the use of strum2 to generate a score.

Interaction 1. Using the strum2 process.

```
cm> (events (strum2 48 60 .1 1 .4) "strum.mid")
"strum-1.mid"
cm>
```

→ nm/13/snd/strum-1.mid

Using now and wait
In Example 3 we rewrite strum2 to better reflect the dynamic nature of processes. The strum3 process differs from strum2 only in the way that time is handled. In strum2 the start time of each event is determined by *beg*, which stepped from 0 by the *rate* specified to the function. This caused the time of each generated event to change but the time of the process itself remained unchanged. But strum3 presents the opposite strategy: the time of the *process* is incremented and each MIDI event is then output at the current time of the process. The function now returns the current priority time of the scheduler. The wait action causes the scheduler to reinsert the current process back into the scheduling queue at *rate* seconds later than its current time.

Example 3. A process with changing run times.
- -

```
(define (strum3 key1 key2 rate dur amp)
  (let ((step (if (< key2 key1) -1 1))
        (diff (abs (- key2 key1))))
    (process repeat (+ diff 1)
             for key from key1 by step
             for beg = (now)
             output (new midi :time beg
                            :duration dur
                            :amplitude amp
                            :keynum key)
             wait rate)))
```
- -

In Interaction 2 we listen to two different versions of the strum3 process.

Interaction 2. Listening to strum3.

```
cm> (events (strum3 84 72 .1 1 .4) "strum.mid")
"strum-2.mid"
cm> (events (list (strum3 48 60 .1 1 .4)
                  (strum3 84 72 .1 1 .2))
            "strum.mid")
"strum-3.mid"
cm>
```

→ nm/13/snd/strum-2.mid
→ nm/13/snd/strum-3.mid

Note that in all three strum functions we did not need to create lists of events or define seq objects to hold separate musical time lines. Processes can produce the same effects dynamically, while the score is being generated, without the overhead of allocating sequences and lists ahead of time. This also means that the actions taken by processes can evolve over time, on the fly, in response to dynamic conditions in the score.

The process Macro

The process macro supports the description of iterative musical processes using the same basic syntax as the loop macro introduced in Chapter 8. While both process and loop perform iteration they are not equivalent constructs. A loop executes immediately and returns values back to the caller. A process, on the other hand, does not iterate immediately — it returns a special type of function that is then *scheduled* to iterate and generate music at a later time.

A process iteration is defined as a series of clauses that differ from loop only in the type of actions that they implement. In particular, the process macro defines a set of actions that are specific to music composition and only these clauses are documented below. The other types of clauses — iteration, conditional, and finalization — are identical to those provided by loop. See Chapter 8 for the explanation of these clauses.

Process action clauses
Process action clauses implement score and scheduler tasks. Unlike loop actions, process actions never return values.

```
output event [score]                                           [Clause]
wait delta                                                     [Clause]
sprout object [at ahead]                                       [Clause]
do expr ...                                                    [Clause]
set var = value                                               [Clause]
each var {in ... | from ...} [as ...] action                  [Clause]
```

The output clause sends *event* to *score*, which defaults to the score specified to the events function. Wait sets the next priority run time of the process to *delta* seconds later. The sprout clause adds *object* to scheduling queue. (One *object* or a list of objects may be sprouted.) An optional at specifies a future *ahead* time. If at is not supplied then *object* is inserted into the scheduling queue at the current process time. The do clause evaluates one or more Lisp expressions and is equivalent to the same clause in loop. The set clause sets a variable *var* to *value* but does not actually define *var* inside the process. Use set to set variables that are established outside the lexical scope of the process but are set inside it.

The each clause defines an iteration over the *action* clause. It supports the same stepping clauses that the for iteration clause supports. The difference between for and each is that the former defines a process iteration while each defines an iterative action inside the process.

Process Examples

We now look at several process definitions that demonstrate different process action clauses. The first few examples require several of the chance and 12-tone functions implemented in Chapter 7 and Chapter 8. These are shown again here in Example 4.

Example 4. Helper Functions from Chapter 6 and 8.

```
- - - - - - - - - - - - - - - - - - - - - - - - - - - - - - - - - - - - - - -
(define (chance? prob)
  (< (random 1.0) prob))

(define (keynum->pc k)
  (mod k 12))

(define (retrograde-row row)
  (reverse row))

(define (transpose-row row to)
  (loop for pc in row
        collect (keynum->pc (+ pc to))))

(define (invert-row row)
  (loop for pc in row
        collect (keynum->pc (- 12 pc))))
- - - - - - - - - - - - - - - - - - - - - - - - - - - - - - - - - - - - - - -
```

A simple row process

In the first example we implement a simple process to play twelve-tone rows.

Example 5. Basic row playing.

```
- - - - - - - - - - - - - - - - - - - - - - - - - - - - - - - - - - - - - - -
(define row1 '(0 1 6 7 10 11 5 4 3 9 2 8))
(define row2 (invert-row row1))
(define row3 (retrograde-row row1))
(define row4 (retrograde-row row2))

(define (ttone1 reps row key beat amp)
  (process with len = (length row)
           repeat reps
           for i from 0
           for p = (mod i len)
           for pc = (list-ref row p) ; i mod 12
           for k = (+ key pc)
           output (new midi :time (now)
                           :duration (* beat 2)
                           :keynum k
                           :amplitude amp)
           wait beat))
- - - - - - - - - - - - - - - - - - - - - - - - - - - - - - - - - - - - - - -
```

The ttone1 process plays *reps* number of events given a *row* of pitch classes, a *key* number offset, a rhythmic *beat* and an *amp* loudness factor. The stepping variable *i* is a counter that increases by 1 each time the process runs. The variable *pc* is set to the current pitch class at position *p* in *row*. Recall that list-ref returns an element from a list at a specified index and that the first element in a list is always at index 0 and the last element is at index *len-1*. Our index into *row* is determined by taking the mod 12 value of *i*. Although this length is always 12 in our examples we have avoided specifying the value 12 directly so that it is possible to listen to pitch class lists with more or fewer than twelve elements. The `mod` calculation insures that our index *p* will always cycle over valid list positions from 0 to 11 as *i* continually increases by 1. The key number *k* for the current event is calculated by adding the value of the pitch class *pc* to the *key* offset that was input into the function. The duration of each event is set to twice the value of *beat* so that a legato effect is produced no matter what value of *beat* is specified to `ttone1`.

Interaction 3. Listening to ttone1

```
cm> (events (ttone1 36 row1 60 .2 .5)
            "ttone.mid")
"ttone-1.mid"
cm>
```

➙ nm/13/snd/ttone-1.mid

Variation 1

In this next example we make simple variation of `ttone1` that plays a "pointillistic" version of a row.

Example 6. A pointillistic row.

```
- - - - - - - - - - - - - - - - - - - - - - - - - - - - - - - - - - - - - - -
(define (ttone2 len row key beat amp)
  (process repeat len
           for i from 0
           for pc = (list-ref row (mod i 12))
           for n = (if (chance? .5)
                       (+ key 12)
                       (- key 12))
           for k = (+ n pc)
           output (new midi :time (now)
                           :duration (* beat 2)
                           :keynum k
                           :amplitude amp)
           wait beat))
- - - - - - - - - - - - - - - - - - - - - - - - - - - - - - - - - - - - - - -
```

The main difference between this example and the preceding one is that ttone2 determines a key number *k* by randomly choosing between values one octave up or down from the *key* number input into the function. This has the effect of randomizing the register of the row so that it does not sound quite so mechanical when the row repeats over the course of the process. The transposition value *n* is chosen by calling the chance? function we defined in Chapter 7. The expression (if (chance? .5) (+ key 12) (- key 12)) says that 50% of the time *n* will be *key+12* and 50% of the time it will be *key-12*.

Interaction 4. Listening to ttone2.

```
cm> (events (ttone2 36 row1 60 .2 .5)
            "ttone.mid")
"ttone-2.mid"
cm>
```

→ nm/13/snd/ttone-2.mid

Variation 2
The next variation improves on the preceding one by implementing different wait times and controlling the amount of random pointillism that is applied to the row.

Example 7. A pointillistic row with random waits.

```
- - - - - - - - - - - - - - - - - - - - - - - - - - - - - - - - - - - - - - -
(define (ttone3 len row key beat amp)
  (process repeat len
           for i from 0
           for pc = (list-ref row (mod i 12))
           for w = (* beat (random 4))
           for n = (if (= w 0)
                       (if (chance? .5)
- - - - - - - - - - - - - - - - - - - - - - - - - - - - - - - - - - - - - - -
```

```
                              (+ key 12)
                              (- key 12)))
                         key)
                for k = (+ n pc)
                output (new midi :time (now)
                                :duration (* beat 2)
                                :keynum k
                                :amplitude amp)
                wait w))
```

In Example 7 the *w* stepping variable is set to a random multiple of *beat*. Recall that the expression (random 4) generates random integers 0 to 3. This means the wait value *w* will be either 0 (when random returns 0), *beat* (when random returns 1), *2*beat* or *3*beat*. A zero wait value causes the next run time of the process to be the same as its current time in the score. This means that the events generated over separate iterations will sound simultaneously in the score. The last improvement ttone3 makes is to transpose the key number only in the case of simultaneous notes. This has the effect of preserving some "registeral integrity" of the row's melodic contour while still providing variety.

Interaction 5. Listening to ttone3

```
cm> (events (list (ttone3 36 row1 40 .2 .5)
                  (ttone3 36 row1 60 .2 .5))
            "ttone.mid"
            '(0 4))
"ttone-3.mid"
cm>
```

→ nm/13/snd/ttone-3.mid

Variation 3

In our final twelve-tone example we modify the process definition to improve sound characteristics if that simultaneous instances of the process are running.

Example 8. Defining sections and instrumentation.

```
(define (ttone4 dur row key beat amp chan)
  (process while (< (now) dur)
           for i from 0
           for pc = (list-ref row (mod i 12))
           for r = (* beat (random 4))
           for n = (if (= r 0)
                       (if (chance? .5)
                           (+ key 12)
                           (- key 12))
                       key)
```

```
              for k = (+ n pc)
              output (new midi :time (now)
                               :duration (* beat 2)
                               :keynum k
                               :amplitude amp
                               :channel chan)
              wait r))
```

The `ttone4` process makes two small modifications that greatly improve the musicality of the output. The first modification is the addition of the new *chan* parameter to the function so that the process outputs to a specific MIDI channel specified by the composer. MIDI channels control which instruments in the synthesizer receive Note On and Note Off messages. When you work with MIDI channels, remember that indexing always starts from 0 in Lisp so MIDI channels in Common Music are numbered from 0 to 15.

The second modification to the process alters the way in which the algorithm controls iteration. In all of the preceding examples the processes iterate a specified number of times. In this version, the process iterates for a specified *duration* of time, regardless of how may iterations the process executes. The conditional clause

```
        while (< (now) dur)
```

says to run the process as long as the current time of the process is less than the duration specified to the function. As soon as this condition is false the scheduler automatically stops the process.

We now listen to three contrapuntal voices of the same basic process definition, where each version has a different row form, register, instrument, start time and duration in the score. All three processes stop generating events at the same time in the score. Before playing the example be sure to select different MIDI instruments on the first three channels of your synthesizer. Listen to several versions of the example to observe the large scale effects that random selection has on each process.

Interaction 6. Playing a little 12-tone etude.

```
cm> (events (list (ttone4 16 row1 40 .2 .5 0)
                  (ttone4 12 row2 60 .2 .5 1)
                  (ttone4 8 row3 80 .2 .5 2))
            "ttone.mid"
            '(0 4 8))
"ttone-4.mid"
cm>
```

→ nm/13/snd/ttone-4.mid

Ghosts

As a final example of algorithmic process definition we look at a more involved definition called ghosts, written by Tobias Kunze. In addition to its interesting musical properties ghosts also provides examples of most of the action clauses supported by the process macro. The definition of ghosts requires several "helper functions" introduced in Chapter 7. The definitions of these auxiliary functions are shown again here in Example 9.

Example 9. Helper functions for ghosts.

```
(define (pick-list lst)
  (let* ((len (length lst))
         (pos (random len)))
    (list-ref lst pos)))

(define (pick-range low high)
  (let ((rng (- high low)))
    (if (> rng 0)
      (+ low (random rng))
      0)))

(define (bpm->seconds bpm)
  (/ 60.0 bpm))

(define (rhythm->seconds rhy tempo)
  (* rhy 4.0 (bpm->seconds tempo)))
```

The ghosts process gets its name from the fact that a short, randomly generated melody serves as the basis for computing other bits of dependent structure that echo the melody in different ways at larger temporal levels in the piece. ghosts generates the following gestures, each of which depends on certain tests applied to the main melody:

• Temporally stretched versions of some melodic tones are repeated high above the main melody.
• Percussive thumps in the low register sometimes accompany the main melody.
• Distant strums accompany the high stretched melody at even larger time scales.

Before looking at the main process we first define the functions that create the dependent gestures used in ghosts.

Example 10. Defining gestures for ghosts.

```
(define (hitone knum at)
  ;; create a long tone two octave above knum
  (new midi :time at
       :keynum (+ knum 24)
       :duration at
       :amplitude .5))
```

```
(define (thump knum at)
  ;; make two percussive events below knum
  (list (new midi :time at
             :keynum (- knum 18)
             :duration .05 :amplitude .4)
        (new midi :time at
             :keynum (- knum 23)
             :duration .05 :amplitude .4)))

(define (riff knum rhy)
  ;; generate an upward strum of notes
  (let ((rate (rhythm->seconds (/ rhy 4) 60)))
    (process repeat 5
             for k from (+ 39 (mod knum 13)) by 13
             output
             (new midi :time (now) :keynum k
                  :amplitude .3 :duration 10)
             wait rate)))
```
- -

The hitone function creates a single midi event two octaves (twenty-four semitones) above the *knum* specified to the function. The *at* parameter serves as both the start time of the new midi event as well as its duration! The effect of this is to create longer and longer high tones as the ghost process increments over time.

The thump function returns a list of two midi notes, each with a very short duration. *Knum* is the current main melody note and *at* is the time at which the thump events are to occur in the score. The key number of the first thump event is (- knum 18) — an octave and a tritone lower than the main melody note; the second event is a perfect fourth above that. Since these transpositions are a fixed relationship, the thump events will follow the general melodic contour of the main melody notes to which they are attached.

The riff function defines a process that outputs five rapid events in an upward arc. *Knum* is the current main melody note and *rhy* is its metric rhythm value. riff converts this metric rhythm into a wait value that is four times faster then the main melody rhythm. The first event that riff plays is a transposition of the main melody key number shifted to lie somewhere within the octave above key number 39 (E-flat in the second octave). Each of the remaining four events will have a key number one minor-9th above the previous event.

We can listen to the gestures of thump and riff in isolation before proceeding to the main ghosts process definition:

Interaction 7. A sample thump and strum.

```
cm> (events (hitone 60 0) "thump.mid")
"thump-1.mid"
cm> (events (thump 60 0) "thump.mid")
"thump-2.mid"
```

```
cm> (events (riff 60 1/8) "riff.mid")
"riff-1.mid"
cm>
```

→ nm/13/snd/thump-1.mid
→ nm/13/snd/thump-2.mid
→ nm/13/snd/riff-1.mid

The ghosts process generates a main melody in the middle register of the MIDI keyboard and then *sprouts* dependent structure above and below the main melody based on tests it applies to the melodic material. Recall that a sprout clause inserts objects into the scheduling queue at a future time. By using sprout instead of output the dependent structures that ghosts generates reflect current conditions of the process that are actually heard at a much later point in the score.

Example 11. The ghosts process.

- .

```
(define (ghosts)
  (process repeat 12
           for here = (now)
           for ahead = (* (+ here .5) 2)
           for main = (pick-range 53 77)
           for high? = (>= main 65)
           for amp = (if high? .6 .4)
           for rhy = (pick-list '(1/16 1/8 3/16))
           ;; output main melody
           output (new midi :time here
                            :keynum main
                            :duration
                            (rhythm->seconds rhy 60 )
                            :amplitude amp)
           when high?
           sprout (hitone main ahead)
           and sprout (riff main rhy) at (* ahead 2)
           when (= rhy 3/16)
           sprout (thump main (+ here .5))
           wait (rhythm->seconds rhy 60 )))
```

- .

The *here* variable holds the current score time returned by now. *Ahead* is a future time twice the value of one-half second later than the current time in the score. In other words, as *here* increases each time the process runs the value of *ahead* is roughly twice as far in the future. *Main* is the main key number of the melody randomly set to any key number within a two octave range above key number 53 (F below Middle C). The *high?* variable is set to either true or false based on a test of the *main* key number. Recall that arithmetic relations like = are functions that return either true or false. The expression (>= main 65) returns boolean true if the *main* key number is greater than or equal to 65 otherwise it returns false. So the *high?* variable will be true if the main key number was selected from the upper octave in the key number range, otherwise *high?* will be false. If *high?* is true then the main melody is played with at an amplitude of .6 otherwise it is played at the softer level of .4.

The last stepping clause sets the rhythm *rhy* of main melody to a random choice of either a sixteenth, eighth or dotted-eighth value.

The first action that `ghosts` performs is to output a main melody `midi` event at the current time in the score. The next clause is a *conditional* clause that executes two sprout actions only if the *high?* variable is true. The conditional clause is reduced to one line here to show its important clausal features:

when *high?* sprout (hitone ...) and sprout (riff ...)

A when clause performs a test and evaluates one or more dependent action clauses only if the test is true. The `and` conjunction joins action clauses together that depend on a single test. The conditional clause in `ghosts` has the effect of generating a high melodic tone 24 semitones above the main tone and a riff gesture only if the current *main* tone lies within the upper octave of its register.

The next clause in the process is another conditional clause but this time with only one dependent action:

when (= *high* 3/16) sprout (thump ...)

The effect of this clause is to only create a thump gesture if the current value of *rhy* is 3/16, i.e. a dotted-eighth value.

The last clause in `ghosts` is a `wait` action clause that increments the priority time of the process by the current rhythmic value of *rhy* converted to seconds. Since there is no `and` conjunction preceding this `wait` it is independent of the preceding conditional clause, which means that the `wait` is evaluated every time the process runs.

We are now ready to listen to `ghosts`. Generate the score a number of different times to hear how the non-random dependent gestures track the randomly generated main melody.

Interaction 8. Listening to `ghosts`.

```
cm> (events (ghosts ) "ghosts.mid")
"ghosts-1.mid"
cm> (events (ghosts ) "ghosts.mid")
"ghosts-2.mid"
cm>
```

→ nm/13/snd/ghosts-1.mid
→ nm/13/snd/ghosts-2.mid

Chapter Source Code

The source code to all of the examples and interactions in this chapter can be found in the file processes.cm located in the same directory as the HTML file for this chapter. The source file can be edited in a text editor or evaluated inside the Common Music application.

References

Knuth, D.E. (1981). *The Art of Computer Programming*. Reading: Addison-Wesley.

14

Etudes, Op. 5: Steve Reich's *Piano Phase*

In *Etudes* Op. 5 we model some of the basic algorithmic features of Steve Reich's composition *Piano Phase*. The reprinted score and directions to *Piano Phase* can be found on page 554 of Tonal Harmony, by Kosta and Payne. (Kosta). The purpose of this Etude is not to recreate a complete and faithful rendition of Reich's composition, but rather, to try to understand some of the issues involved with his notion of *phasing*, and to see how these issues might be represented in the metalevel. Once our chapter implementation is complete the reader may use it to experiment with different phasing materials and to extend and enhance its functionality.

The Composition

Steve Reich's *Piano Phase* is a composition for two pianists that repeats a single group of notes — called the *trope* in this Etude — over and over again for the entire length of the composition. The piece is laid out in a series of sections; the exact length of each section (measured in repetitions of the trope) is left up to the performers. The first pianist plays the trope at a constant tempo for the duration of the composition. After several repetitions of the material the second pianist joins at the unison and remains "in phase" for several repetitions of the trope. At this point

the second pianist gradually speeds up until he or she is playing the trope one note ahead of the first performer. Once this has occurred, the second pianist resumes a constant tempo so that both performers play in lock step again but now one note out of phase. The entire process is repeated again and again until the second performer has finally moved ahead through all of the notes in the trope. In the final section of the composition both performers are once again playing in unison at an identical constant rate.

The Implementation

Our implementation of *Piano Phase* will provide the basic looping and phasing features of the piece without random section lengths or a slowly increasing tempo. Our first exercise will be to define the musical process that represents Piano 1.

Opus 5, No. 1: Piano 1

Example 1. Helper functions and Piano 1.

```
(define phasing-trope
   (keynum '(e4 fs b cs5 d fs4 e cs5 b4 fs d5 cs5)))
(define phasing-pulse 1/24)
(define phasing-tempo 72)

(define (bpm->seconds bpm)
   (/ 60.0 bpm))

(define (rhythm->seconds rhy tempo)
   (* rhy 4.0 (bpm->seconds tempo)))

(define (piano1 trope amp chan)
   (let* ((tlen (length trope))
          (cycs tlen)
          (rate (rhythm->seconds phasing-pulse
                                 phasing-tempo)))
     (process repeat (* tlen cycs)
              for i from 0
              for x = (mod i tlen)
              for k = (list-ref trope x)
              output (new midi :time (now)
                          :keynum k
                          :duration (* rate 1.5)
                          :amplitude amp
                          :channel chan)
              wait rate)))
```

Since the first pianist plays the trope without any change for the length of the composition the basic process definition for piano1 is rather straightforward, as shown in Example 1. The piano1 process repeats a *trope* of key numbers for as many times as there are key numbers in the trope. The total number of events that the process plays is equal the trope's length *tlen* times *cycs*, the number of times the trope is repeated. The variable *i* counts each event that the process plays. The variable *x* is the index of the current key number to play in the trope and it is set to *i* mod *tlen* so that *x* continually cycles from zero to *tlen*-1 as *i* increases by one each time the process runs. The *rate* at which the process plays is determined by multiplying the global pulse value *phasing-pulse* by the global tempo factor *phasing-tempo*.

In Interaction 1 we listen to several repetitions of the trope played by piano1.

Interaction 1. Listening to 12 repetitions of phasing-trope.

```
cm> (events (piano1 phasing-trope .5 0) "reich.mid")
"reich-1.mid"
cm>
```

↪ nm/14/snd/reich-1.mid

Opus 5, No. 2: Piano 2

The function that represents the second performer is responsible for producing the regular pattern of phasing that occurs throughout the piece. The phasing pattern consists of two parts. The first part maintains a constant rate of events at the identical speed as piano1. The second part of the pattern is slightly faster, which causes piano2 to slowly move one note ahead of piano1. At this point the phasing pattern starts over with the constant rate again. The phasing pattern will be computed from a *tempo curve*, a list of tempo coefficients that produce a dynamically changing rate in the piano2 process. The coefficients in the first half of the tempo curve will consists of 1's (which cause the rate of the process to remain constant) and the coefficients in the second half of the tempo curve will consist of values slightly less than 1 — these smaller coefficients cause the value of *rate* to become shorter, thereby increasing the speed at which the piano2 process plays the trope.

The phasing coefficients can be represented as the ratio *p/n* where *p* is the number of pulses the phasing takes and *n* is the number of events to play in that time. For example, a *p/n* of 16/17 would mean to play 17 notes in the time of 16 pulses. If we assume that each half of the phasing equals one repetition of the trope, then the *p/n* ratio for our version of Piano Phase would be 12/13, where 12 is the length of Reich's trope and *n* is one more than that value. That extra *n* value is the note that the performer moves ahead by. We now implement a function that creates a tempo curve (Example 2).

Example 2. The phasing-tempo-curve definition.

```
(define (phasing-tempo-curve tlen stay move)
  (let* ((p (* tlen move))
         (n (+ 1 (* tlen move)))
         (l1 (loop repeat (* tlen stay)
                   collect 1))
         (l2 (loop repeat (+ 1 (* tlen move))
                   collect (/ p n))))
    (append l1 l2)))
```

phasing-tempo-curve returns a list of tempo coefficients for scaling the rate of events that piano2 produces. *Tlen* is the length of the trope. *Stay* is the number of repetitions of the trope in which piano2 is synchronized with piano1. *Move* is the number of repetitions of the trope during which piano2 plays faster than piano1. The *p* and *n* values are calculated from these repetition factors times the length of the trope. The *l1* variable holds the list of tempo values for the constant half of the phasing pattern in which the coefficients are all 1. The *l2* variable holds the list of the *p/n* tempo values for the second half of the phasing that produces the faster tempo. Since piano2 must move ahead by one note, the second half of the tempo curve list contains 1 more element than the first half. The entire tempo curve is created by appending the two halves of the pattern together to form one large list that is returned as the value of the function. We can test the tempo curve function with input values to see what it produces (Interaction 2).

Interaction 2. Creating a tempo curve list.

```
cm> (phasing-tempo-curve 3 1 1)
(1 1 1 0.75 0.75 0.75 0.75)
cm>
```

The first half of the tempo curve contains three 1's which add up to 3 beats. The second half of the tempo curve list contains four .75 values which also add up to 3 beats. The total duration of the phasing sequence is 6 beats, so this tempo curve process would play seven events in the same time that a constant process at tempo 1 played 6. Given our tempo curve function we are now ready to implement piano2 (Example 3).

Example 3. The piano2 process.

```
(define (piano2 trope stay move amp chan)
  (let* ((tlen (length trope))
         (cycs tlen)
         (coda (* stay tlen))    ; ends with unison
         (curve (phasing-tempo-curve tlen stay move))
         (clen (length curve))
```

```
            (rate (rhythm->seconds phasing-pulse
                                   phasing-tempo))))
   (process repeat (+ (* clen cycs) coda)
            for i from 0
            for k = (list-ref trope (mod i tlen))
            for c = (list-ref curve (mod i clen))
            output (new midi :time (now)
                             :keynum k
                             :duration (* rate 1.5)
                             :amplitude amp
                             :channel chan)
            wait (* rate c))))
```

Trope is the list of key numbers to play. *Stay* and *move* are the two parts of the phasing pattern — *stay* is the number of repetitions of *trope* during which piano2 remains at the constant tempo, *move* is the number of repetitions of *trope* during which the tempo is increased. *Tlen* and *cycs* are exactly the same as in piano1. *Coda* is the number of events to play at the very end of the piece, after *cycs* number of pattern cycles has occurred and the entire process has moved through all the notes of the trope. The extra *coda* amount allows both pianos to conclude the piece by playing the constant portion of the pattern in unison again, just as the piece began. *Curve* is the tempo curve and *clen* is its length, which is also the total number of notes in the phasing pattern.

The body of the process definition is very much like piano1, except that piano2 gets its current tempo coefficient *c* from the tempo curve. This coefficient is then used to scale the *rate* value in the wait clause.

Interaction 3. Listening to repeats of the phase pattern.

```
cm> (events (piano2 phasing-trope 1 1 .5 0)
            "reich.mid")
"reich-2.mid"
cm>
```

→ nm/14/snd/reich-2.mid

Opus 5, No. 3: the final version
All that remains in our Etude is to define a wrapper function called piano-phase that creates both processes together (Example 4). We will also reimplement our piano1 function so that it also accepts the *stay* and *move* repetition factors that determine the length of the phasing pattern. The *stay* and *move* parameters will allow us to experiment with different phasing proportions without having to redefine the functions for each experiment (Example 4).

Example 4. The final version of piano1 and the pphase function.

```
- - - - - - - - - - - - - - - - - - - - - - - - - - - - - - - - - - - - - - - - - -
(define (piano1 trope stay move amp chan)
  (let* ((tlen (length trope))
         (cycl tlen)
         (reps (* tlen (+ stay move) cycl))
         (coda (* stay tlen))
         (rate (rhythm->seconds phasing-pulse
                                phasing-tempo)))
     (process repeat (+ reps coda)
              for i from 0
              for x = (mod i tlen)
              for k = (list-ref trope x)
              output (new midi :time (now)
                          :keynum k
                          :duration (* rate 1.5)
                          :amplitude amp
                          :channel chan)
              wait rate)))

(define (pphase trope stay move amp)
   (list (piano1 trope stay move amp 0)
         (piano2 trope stay move amp 1)))
- - - - - - - - - - - - - - - - - - - - - - - - - - - - - - - - - - - - - - - - - -
```

Before listening to the phasing examples make sure that you have piano sounds selected on the first two channels of your synthesizer. The first input expression in Interaction 4 creates a score with *stay* and *move* both set to 1. This produces a very short version of the piece (about 40 seconds) in which the short phasing sections sound more like cross rhythms than they do actual phasing. The second score keeps *stay* at 1 repetition but increases *move* to 8, which allows the phasing sections to evolve at a more realistic rate of eight cycles of the trope. This second version of the piece lasts 3 minutes.

Interaction 4. Listening to pphase.

```
cm> (events (pphase phasing-trope 1 1 .5) "reich.mid")
"reich-3.mid"
cm> (events (pphase phasing-trope 1 8 .5) "reich.mid")
"reich-4.mid"
cm>
```

→ nm/14/snd/reich-3.mid
→ nm/14/snd/reich-4.mid

Try experimenting with phasing using shorter or longer tropes as well as different *stay* and *move* values.

Chapter Source Code

The source code to all of the examples and interactions in this chapter can be found in the file reich.cm located in the same directory as the HTML file for this chapter. The source file can be edited in a text editor or evaluated inside the Common Music application.

References

Kosta, S., & Payne, D. (2000). *Tonal Harmony*. Boston: McGraw Hill.

15

Microtonality, Tunings and Modes

There is still a lot of good music waiting to be written in C major.

— Arnold Schönberg

One of the most liberating aspects about using a computer to compose music is that non-traditional "frequency space" can be explored in different ways without having to address the limitations of physical instruments or human performers. This sort of experimentation may involve working with raw, untempered Hertz values, just harmonic ratios, microtonal inflections, or "alternate" tuning systems, which we define very broadly to mean any tuning system other than the standard 12-tone equal tempered scale. But working with an expanded frequency space using MIDI synthesizers will quickly expose MIDI's strong bias towards the popular music tradition and the Western tonal system in general. Nowhere is this bias more pronounced than in the implementation of *key number* frequency control, which quantizes an infinite number of frequencies into just 128 scale degrees that represent the Western keyboard instrument. As a result, composers working outside the popular, mainstream tradition (or even outside the popular keyboard tradition!) must find ways to overcome the tendency of MIDI to generate sounds based on the standard twelve note division of the equal-tempered chromatic scale.

MIDI and Microtonal Tuning

There are two basic methods for producing microtonal sound on a MIDI synthesizer. The first method is to retune the synthesizer "by hand" and then activate the retuned sounds using normal integer key numbers. The advantage with this approach is that the stream of messages between the computer and synthesizer does not change, i.e. nothing extra needs to be done in order to produce microtones. But there are some disadvantages with this method as well:

- since tuning methods vary with each synthesizer they cannot be explained in a general way
- specific retunings may not be supported by a given synthesizer
- retuning the synthesizer may affect all the sounds in the synthesizer
- retuning may be difficult or time consuming to do by hand

A second, alternate approach for producing microtones on a MIDI synthesizer is to include specific retuning instructions in the stream of messages that is sent to the synthesizer. We will refer to this type of tuning as *channel tuning* because it only affects sounds on specific channels of the synthesizer. The MIDI instructions that produce these microtonal frequency adjustments are called *pitch bend messages*. The effect of these messages can be heard by moving the synthesizer's pitch bend wheel up or down while a tone is sounding. The result is a smooth glissando moving upward or downward from the original frequency. On most synthesizers the maximum pitch bend width is set to a major second on either side of a given key. This width is important to know because the tuning instructions sent to the synthesizer are defined as a "percentage" of this value. If the maximum pitch bend value on your synthesizer is not a major second, consult the explanation of :pitch-bend-width in the Common Music dictionary.

Channel Tuning

Channel tuning produces microtonal inflections by calculating specific pitch bend adjustments to retune the closest integer key number to a desired frequency. The pitch bend instruction is sent to the synthesizer immediately before the integer key number is sent so that when the sound starts it is already tuned to the correct frequency. The advantages that channel tuning has over retuning the synthesizer by hand is that the process happens dynamically and can produce almost any untempered frequency, not just those the composer initializes in the sequencer beforehand. The disadvantage with channel tuning is that MIDI pitch bends are will affect *all* sounds on a particular MIDI channel, not just specific key numbers. This means that if a sound is currently playing on the same channel to which a pitch bend is sent, the existing sound will be affected as well as the tone for which the pitch bend is intended. The basic strategy for channel tuning, then, is to send bend and key number pairs to channels that are currently silent. This generally requires that the composer reserves some range of channels for the software to use as its "pool" of available channels for retuning.

Note-by-note tuning

There are several different strategies for managing this pool of tuning channels. In *note-by-note tuning* each pitch bend and key number pair is sent to the next available channel in the pool. The selection of this channel can be made either by maintaining a queue of available "open" channels (channels that are not currently sounding a note) or simply by cycling thorough a sufficiently large number of channels such that no overlapping notes in any channel will be produced. Both the queuing and cycling methods then send an exact microtonal pitch bend adjustment for the next note. The disadvantage with both methods is that it is possible to run out of available channels if there are too many overlapping durations in the MIDI data.

Equal division tuning

An alternate method for implementing channel tuning is to quantize microtones to a sufficiently small division of the semitone such that one gets "close enough" to the desired microtonal inflection. These divisions are then "spread" over a fixed range of channels pretuned to the desired quantization step. Since pitch bends do not need to be sent on each note they cannot incorrectly affect overlapping sounds. The disadvantage, of course, is that the quantization size may be too "coarse" to sufficiently approximate the microtonal inflections. But the minimum possible quantization step size in Common Music is 6.25 cents, very close to the smallest perceivable change in frequency by humans. Only experimentation can determine the best channel tuning strategy for a given situation. If quantization is not an issue — for example the microtones are equal tempered, or the texture is sufficiently dense so that it does not matter — then the quantization is inherently more efficient and less problematic than the note-by-note method.

Channel tuning in Common Music

Common Music supports both note-by-note and equal division styles of channel tuning. Either method can be specified using the :channel-tuning keyword argument to the events function. Most of the examples in this chapter quantize each semitone into 9 equal divisions, or approximately 11 cents per quantization step. This tuning will use only the first nine channels of the synthesizer to avoid the drum channel that is hardwired on many synthesizers. You should experiment with different forms of channel tuning to compare the results. The documentation on MIDI files in the Common Music Dictionary contains complete information on the :channel-tuning initialization. This documentation should be reviewed before beginning to work with the examples.

Listening to the Harmonic Series

In Chapter 10 we learned that many musical instruments produce complex waves whose frequencies are related by the *harmonic series* (Figure 1). Recall that the harmonic series can be generated from any frequency f by simple multiplication: $f*1$, $f*2$, $f*3...f*n$. A loop can be used to generate this series based on any fundamental f:

Interaction 1. Computing a harmonic series based on 100 Hz.

```
cm> (loop with f = 100 for h from 1 to 12
          collect (* f h))
(100 200 300 400 500 600 700 800 900 1000 1100 1200)
cm>
```

Similarly, we can also define a process to play any segment of the harmonic series between a lower and upper harmonic number:

Example 1. Playing the harmonic series.
- .
```
(define (play-harms frq low high rate)
  (process for h from low to high
           for f = (* frq (/ h low))
           for k = (keynum f :hz)
           output (new midi :time (now)
                       :keynum k
                       :duration (* rate .9))
           wait rate))
```
- .

The play-harms process produces tones in the harmonic series between a *low* and *high* harmonic number based on a low frequency *frq*. The frequency *f* of each harmonic *h* is determined by multiplying *frq* by the ratio *h/low* such that the series starts with *frq* as the *low* harmonic. The keynum function is used to produce a floating point MIDI key number *k* for each calculated Hertz value *f*. (The :hz keyword after *h* in the argument list tells keynum that *f* is a Hertz number.)

We can now listen to the harmonic series using several different channel tuning methods (Example 2).

Interaction 2. Playing the harmonic series.

```
cm> (events (play-harms 440 8 16 .4) "micro.mid"
            :channel-tuning true)
"micro-1.mid"
cm> (events (play-harms 440 8 16 .4) "micro.mid"
            :channel-tuning 108)
"micro-2.mid"
cm> (events (play-harms 440 8 16 .4) "micro.mid"
            :channel-tuning false)
"micro-3.mid"
cm>
```

➙ nm/15/snd/micro-1.mid
➙ nm/15/snd/micro-2.mid
➙ nm/15/snd/micro-3.mid

The last expression in Interaction 2 "turns off" channel tuning. As an alternate method for canceling pitch bend effect one could also define a process that sends a series of level 0 pitch bends to every channel to reset the synthesizer to its "normal" state, as shown in Example 2.

Example 2. Clearing pitchbends.

```
(define (clearbends )
   (process for c below 16
            output (new midimsg :time (now)
                        :msg (make-pitch-bend c 0))))
```

One of the most interesting properties of the harmonic series is its fractal nature: each prime number in the series introduces a new (non-doubled) tone that then becomes a new "fundamental" for generating another harmonic series. For example, the third harmonic in Interaction 1 at 300 Hz is the first frequency in the series that is not a doubling (octave) of the fundamental and it generates its own series: 300, 600, 900, 1200. Similarly, the 5th harmonic generates the series 500, 1000, 1500, and so on.

Another interesting aspect of the harmonic series is that its harmonic "density" rises with the harmonic number. Since the harmonic series is linear but octaves are powers of two, there are more and more harmonics per octave as the series rises: the first octave in the series contains 1 frequency, the second 2, the third 4, the fourth 8 and so on. This increasing harmonic density does not produce much harshness in the timbre of physical instruments because the amplitudes of the higher harmonics tend to fall off rapidly with the harmonic number. This means that the effect of the higher harmonics quickly becomes *masked* by the louder, more widely spaced frequencies lower in the spectrum (Figure 1).

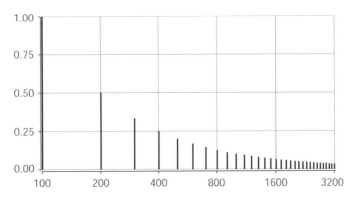

Figure 1. The first 32 harmonics in the harmonic series based on a fundamental of 100 Hz. The amplitude of each harmonic has been calculated as the reciprocal of the harmonic number, or *1/h*.

But using the computer we can listen to the relationships between higher harmonics by defining a process that plays multiple octaves in the series "wrapped" to fit within a single octave:

Example 3. Playing the harmonic series.

- -

```
(define (play-harms2 octs)
  (process with hz = (hertz 'c3)
           for h from 1 to (* 12 octs)
           for k = (keynum (* h hz) :hz)
           output (new midi time (now)
                       duration 1.0
                       amplitude (between 0.4 0.6)
                       keynum (+ 48 (mod k 12)))
           wait .15))
```

- -

The play-harms2 process plays the harmonic series based on the hertz value C3 in the standard chromatic scale. The series is produced modulo the octave (12 semitones) so that consecutive octaves in the series start over again on the same bottom tone. Notice that each time the octave starts over the number of divisions in the octave doubles.

Interaction 3. Playing four octaves of a normalized harmonic series.

```
cm> (events (play-harms2 4) "harms.mid"
            :channel-tuning 108)
"harms-1.mid"
cm> (events (clearbends ) "clearbends.mid")
"clearbends-1.mid"
cm>
```

→ nm/15/snd/harms-1.mid
→ nm/15/snd/clearbends-1.mid

Intervals in the harmonic series
Since each ascending octave in the series contains more frequencies, it stands to reason that the intervals between consecutive harmonics in the series decrease as the harmonic number increases. Musically speaking, these intervals are a difference — the space between two tones. But physically speaking, an interval is a proportion, or ratio, between two frequencies. Ascending or descending intervals between any two tones in the harmonic series can be determined by the ratio of their harmonics numbers. The order in which the ratio is expressed does not matter — if the ratio is larger than 1 then an ascending interval is described, if the ratio is less than 1 then the interval is downward. For example, a 3/2 ratio produces is a perfect fifth up and 2/3 is a perfect fifth down. The 3/2 perfect fifth is called a *just interval* because it is found in the harmonic series, i.e. it is a ratio of two whole numbers. In contrast, the ratio for an equal-tempered perfect 5th is $2^{7/12}$, or 1.4983070768766815, which is

very close, but not equal, to 3/2. Ratios for some common just musical intervals are shown in Table 1.

Table 1. Ratio and cent values of common just intervals.

Interval	ratio	cents	interval	ratio	cents
unison	1/1	0	perfect 5th	3/2	702
minor 2nd	16/15	112	minor 6th	8/5	814
major 2nd	9/8	204	major 6th	5/3	884
minor 3rd	6/5	316	minor 7th	9/5	1018
major 3rd	5/4	386	major 7th	15/8	1088
perfect 4th	4/3	498	octave	2/1	1200
tritone	45/32	590			

Interval math

Since intervals are ratios they must be "added" using multiplication and division rather than addition and subtraction. For example, to *add* the intervals of a just fifth and fourth, multiply their ratios together:

$$(3/2 * 4/3) = 12/6 = 2/1$$

Similarly, the "subtraction" of minor third from an octave requires division:

$$(2/1 / 6/5) = (2/1 * 5/6) = 10/6 = 5/3$$

To "invert" a perfect fifth means to take its reciprocal by dividing into 1.

$$(1/1 / 3/2) = (1/1 * 2/3) = 2/3$$

To find the "complement" of a ratio, multiply the smaller of the numerator or denominator by 2. If the numerator is smaller then multiply by 2/1, if the denominator is smaller multiply by 1/2. For example, to find the complement of 3/2 multiply by 1/2 to produce the perfect fourth:

$$(3/2 * 1/2) = 3/4 = 4/3$$

A just major sixth is the complement of a minor third:

$$(5/6 * 2/1) = 10/6 = 5/3 = 3/5$$

Cents

One problem with using ratios to describe intervals is that the size of a ratio can be non-intuitive. For example, which is larger: 256/243 or 9/8? The *cent* scale is an alternate method for describing the distance between two frequencies. By definition, there are 100 cents in a tempered semitone and 1200 cents per octave. This means that one cent is 1/1200 of an octave — an imperceptibly small change in frequency. The smallest frequency difference humans can perceive is approximately 5 cents, so the cent unit is more than adequate for describing minute changes in frequency. Unlike ratios, cent values are linear and can be combined using simple addition and subtraction. For example, the size of just perfect fifth can be determined by adding the cent values of a just major third and a just minor third: 316+386=702 cents. Common Music provides two functions that convert between cents and ratio scalers:

```
(cents->scaler cents)                                      [Function]
(scaler->cents ratio)                                      [Function]
```

The `cents->scaler` function converts *cents* into the scaler value $2^{cents/1200}$ while the `scaler->cents` function performs the reverse calculation $1200*\log_2 ratio$.

Interaction 4. Converting cents to scaler values.

```
cm> (cents->scaler 1200)
2.0
cm> (scaler->cents 3/2)
702
cm> (scaler->cents 5/4)
386
cm> (scaler->cents 6/5)
316
cm> (cents->scaler 700)
1.4983070768766815
cm>
```

Listening to microtonal intervals

We can define functions that create MIDI events that play and compare microtonal intervals:

Example 4. Playing microtonal intervals.

```
- - - - - - - - - - - - - - - - - - - - - - - - - - - - - - - - - - - - - - - -.
(define (midi-ratio at note ratio dur)
  (let ((fkey (keynum (* (hertz note) ratio) :hz)))
    (list (new midi :time at :keynum note :duration dur)
          (new midi :time at :keynum fkey
                  :duration dur))))

(define (compare-ratios note rat1 rat2 dur)
  (append (midi-ratio 0 note rat1 dur)
          (midi-ratio (+ dur .5) note rat2 dur)))

(define ct8 (list true 1 9))
- - - - - - - - - - - - - - - - - - - - - - - - - - - - - - - - - - - - - - - -.
```

The `midi-ratio` function returns two MIDI events whose key numbers are *ratio* interval apart. The first event in the list plays the specified *note* in the standard chromatic scale. The second event plays a tone at *fkey* calculated to be *ratio* distance above or below *note*. This value is determined by multiplying the hertz value of *note* by *ratio* and then converting the value to a floating point key number in the chromatic scale.

The second function `compare-ratios` allows us to compare two different intervals. This function simply appends the results of two calls to `midi-ratio`. The second interval will be played .5 seconds after the first interval ends. The `ct8` variable is a `:channel-tuning` value for producing note-by-note tuning using channels 1-8. Channel 0 remains free of pitch bends so that the first tone of each interval will be tuned to the standard chromatic scale.

Interaction 5. Playing and comparing ratios.

```
cm> (events (midi-ratio 0 'c4 5/4 3) "rat.mid"
            :channel-tuning true)
"rat-1.mid"
cm> (events (compare-ratios 'c4 5/4 (expt 2 4/12) 3)
            "rat.mid" :channel-tuning ct8)
"rat-2.mid"
cm>
```

→ nm/15/snd/rat-1.mid
→ nm/15/snd/rat-2.mid

The first input produces a just major third. The second example compares the just major third with the equal tempered major third, or $2^{4/12}$. The just major third is noticeably smaller at 386 cents — 24 cents less than the equal tempered version.

Scales and Temperament

A musical scale quantizes infinite frequency space into a finite number of steps, called *scale degrees*. Scale degrees serve as the raw material for a composition and are generally ordered low to high within a given scale. The term *temperament* refers to the precise relationships between the ordered degrees in a scale, and a *tuning system*, describes a formal method for tempering each scale degree.

Scales and tunings in common music

A scale in Common Music is an object that defines an order series of scale degrees. Each scale degree is represented by an integer position in the scale called a *keynum*, a hertz value, and possibly one or more *note names* associated with each degree. The term *scale* in Common Music actually applies to two different types of objects. A `tuning` is a scale that defines the precise frequencies for between scale degrees. A `mode` defines a transposable subset of a `tuning`. Modes are discussed in a later section of this chapter.

tuning   [Class]

A `tuning` is a scale with Hertz frequencies defined for each scale degree. Scale degrees may also have note names associated with them.

`tuning` supports the following slot initializations:

`:name` {*string* | *symbol*}

> An optional name for the tuning.

`:lowest` *number*

> The lowest Hertz value defined in the scale. Defaults to 8.175, which is C-1 in the standard chromatic scale.

`:cents` *list*

> One octave of the tuning specified as a list of cent values. Fewer or more than 12 degrees may be specified and an "octave" does not have to equal 1200 cents. If the cent values in *list* start with 0 and are in increasing order they specify the cent difference from the lowest degree to each degree above it. In this case the last value in *list* determines the octave width of the scale. If *list* does not begin with 0 then the cents values describe the distances between adjacent steps. In this case the octave width is set to the sum of the cent steps. To define a tuning with note names, specify each step as a list: (*cent* {*note*}*) where *cent* is the cent value followed by one or more *note* declarations. Each *note* declaration may consist of symbol *note* or a list (*note* &key `:accidental`) where the value of `:accidental` is the portion of *note* that represents the accidental. For example, the 8th step in the definition of the standard chromatic scale is:

```
(100 (af :accidental f)
     (gs :accidental s))
```

`:ratios` *list*

> Exactly like `cents` except that the tuning values are specified as ratios (direct frequency scalers) rather than as cent values.

`:octaves` {*number* | *list*}

> The number of octaves defined in the scale. Defaults to 10. The value can be a number or a list of two values (*start end*) where *start* is the first octave number and *end* is the last octave number. Specify false if the tuning has no octaves.

`:keynum-offset` *integer*

> An integer offset added to all keynums values returned by `keynum`. Defaults to 0.

`:default-octave` *integer*

> The default octave for notes without octave numbers. Defaults to the 4th octave.

Tuning Systems

In the remaining sections of this chapter we present some examples of tuning systems that demonstrate different approaches to temperament. There is really no way to adequately cover the full breadth and variety of different tuning systems in a single chapter. However, the Web is an excellent resource for gathering descriptions of tuning systems; many of these descriptions provide ratios or cent specifications and can be easily implemented by tuning objects in Common Music. Use Google to search for "Alternate Tuning" and "Tuning Systems" for a good candidate list to start exploring!

Before presenting some example tunings we will first define a process to play them. This process will "preview" the scale degrees of a tuning in ascending, descending, and random order. This will allow us to hear the tonal material of the scale in several different contexts.

Example 5. A process to play tuning examples.

```
(define (play-tuning tuning low high rate amp)
  (let* ((rise (loop for i from low below high
                    collect i))
         (fall (loop for i downfrom high downto low
                    collect i))
         (ran1 (shuffle (rest rise)))
         (ran2 (shuffle (rest rise)))
         (coda (loop for i from low to high collect i))
         (all (append rise fall ran1 ran2 coda)))
    (process for k in all
             for x = (keynum k :from tuning)
             output (new midi :time (now)
                         :keynum x
                         :amplitude amp
                         :duration (* rate .95))
             wait rate)))
```

The play-tuning process previews the scale degrees of *tuning* between a *low* and *high* key number. The variables *rise* and *fall* contain the ascending and descending patterns, while *ran1* and *ran2* hold randomized versions of this material. Common Music's shuffle function randomly reorders lists of data, and is discussed in Chapter 18. The *coda* segment of the melodic material again ascends from *low* to *high*. *All* holds the entire list of key numbers to play and is created by appending all of the sublists together to form a single long list of key numbers. The variable *x* holds a key number converted from the tuning to an equivalent value in the standard chromatic scale. The :from argument to keynum converts an integer key number from the specified tuning object into an equivalent floating point key number in the standard chromatic scale.

The harmonic scale
We can treat any segment of the harmonic series as a scale by defining a function that converts harmonic numbers into ratios. These ratios can then be used as the value of the :ratios initialization when the tuning is created (Example 6).

Example 6. Converting harmonic numbers to ratios.

```
(define (harms->ratios low high)
  (loop for h from low to high collect (/ h low)))

(new tuning :name 'jmaj
     :ratios (harms->ratios 8 16))

(new tuning :name 'jmin
     :ratios (harms->ratios 9 18))
```

In the first scale we use an eight note segment of the harmonic series from the 8th to the 16th partial to give us a just "major scale" that we name Jmag. The second scale (Jmin) defines a nine tone octave based on the 9th partial with a just minor third between the 1st and 3rd scale degrees. Both tunings are based on a low C at 8.125 Hz. Since there are eight tones per octave in Jmag and nine in Jmin, Middle C is key number 40 in Jmaj and key number 45 in Jmin.

Interaction 6. A process to play microtonal examples.

```
cm> (hertz 40 :in #&jmaj)
261.6255653005986
cm> (hertz 45 :in #&jmin)
261.6255653005986
cm> (keynum 40 :from #&jmaj)
60.0
cm> (keynum 41 :from #&jmaj)
62.039100017307746
cm> (events (play-tuning #&jmaj 40 56 .25 .6)
            "hscale.mid" :channel-tuning 9)
"hscale-1.mid"
cm> (events (play-tuning #&jmin 45 63 .25 .6)
            "hscale.mid" :channel-tuning 9)
"hscale-2.mid"
cm>
```

→nm/15/snd/hscale-1.mid
→nm/15/snd/hscale-2.mid

Pythagorean tuning

The Pythagorean scale, named after the Greek philosopher Pythagoras of Samos, was the primary tuning system used in Western music for about 2000 years. Pythagoras noticed that a pleasing scale could be built using a 3/2 ratio as the interval between each tone. Rather than work with steps that are all 3/2 apart, the ratios in the Pythagorean scale are "normalized" to lie within a single octave. This is accomplished by reducing any ratio greater than 2 (the octave) by 1/2 such that the value again fits within a single octave. For example, the first tone in the scale (call it

C) has a ratio of 1/1 = 1. The second tone G is (1 * 3/2) = 3/2; the third tone D is (3/2 * 3/2 * 1/2) = 9/8; A is (9/8 * 3/2) = 27/16, and so on. The tones are then ordered low to high to form an ascending step wise pattern based on C. The missing F can be calculated from C using 4/3, the interval complement of 3/2. Table 2 shows the ratios of the seven-tone Pythagorean Diatonic Scale:

Table 2. Step ratios in the diatonic Pythagorean scale.

C	D	E	F	G	A	B	C
1	9/8	81/64	4/3	3/2	27/16	243/128	2

Given our set of ratios we can create a tuning to implement the Pythagorean diatonic scale:

Example 7. Tuning definition for the Pythagorean Diatonic Scale

```
(new tuning :name 'pyth-d
     :ratios '(1 9/8 81/64  4/3  3/2  27/16 243/128 2))
```

The tuning named Pith-d in Example 7 defines seven tones per octave based on a low C at 8.175 Hz. Since there are 7 notes per octave, Middle C is key number 35 in pyth-d, and D4 (key number 62 in the chromatic scale) is key number 36.

Interaction 7. Converting key numbers to and from a tuning.

```
cm> (keynum 60 :to #&pyth-d)
35
cm> (keynum 36 :from #&pyth-d)
62.039100017307746
cm>
```

We now listen to the sound of the Pythagorean diatonic scale. The key numbers specified to play-tuning are in the coordinates of the pyth-d tuning system; the process then converts these to floating point equivalents in the standard scale.

Interaction 8. Playing the Pythagorean diatonic scale.

```
cm> (events (play-tuning #&pyth-d 35 49 .3 .7)
            "pyth.mid" :channel-tuning 108)
"pyth-1.mid"
cm>
```

➜ nm/15/snd/pyth-1.mid

The Pythagorean chromatic scale

If we continue the 3/2 ratio series from Table 2 we can eventually generate all 12 pitches in the *cycle of 5ths* (Table 3):

Table 3. Fifth ratios in the chromatic Pythagorean scale.

F	$3/2^{-1}$	2/3	F#	$3/2^6$	729/64
C	$3/2^0$	1	C#	$3/2^7$	2187/128
G	$3/2^1$	3/2	G#	$3/2^8$	6561/256
D	$3/2^2$	9/4	D#	$3/2^9$	19683/512
A	$3/2^3$	27/8	A#	$3/2^{10}$	59049/1024
E	$3/2^4$	81/16	E#/F	$3/2^{11}$	177147/2048
B	$3/2^5$	243/32	B#/C	$3/2^{12}$	531441/4096

The cycle of 5ths tells us that after a series of 12 5ths we should end up on a power of two, i.e. an octave doubling of our original frequency. In other words, if the cycle of 5ths is really a cycle then $3/2^{12}$ must equal to 2^7. As we can plainly see in Interaction 9, this is not true!

Interaction 9. The Big Lie.

```
cm> (expt 3/2 12)
531441/4096
cm> (expt 2 7)
128
cm> (= 531441/4096 128)
#f
cm> (/ 531441/4096 128.0)
1.0136432647705078
cm> (scaler->cents 1.0136432647705078)
23
cm>
```

The difference between $3/2^{12}$ and 2^7 is 1.746337890625 or 23 cents. So the "cycle of fifths" is fiction, at least if one uses the 3/2 fifths that nature gives us! The 23 cent difference between the octaves and fifths is called the *Pythagorean comma* and it is one of the central issues that designers faced as they worked on the tuning systems that followed the Pythagorean Scale. The discrepancy between the cycle of fifths and octaves means that it is mathematically impossible to design a tuning system in which all intervals are just while still remaining true to the octave.

There are other "problems" lurking in the Pythagorean tuning as well. While fifths and whole steps are just, both the major and minor thirds are out of tune. The Pythagorean major third is 81/64 (408 cents), 22 cents wider then the just major third, and the Pythagorean minor third 32/27 (294 cents) is 22 cents smaller than the just minor third. This 22 cent difference between Pythagorean and just thirds is called the *syntonic comma*. Half steps in the Pythagorean scale have a different problem. Notice that the ratio between E (81/64) and F (4/3) is (4/5*64/81=256/243, or 90 cents but the ratio between F and F-sharp is 2187/2048, or 114 cents. This means that the chromatic Pythagorean scale has two versions of the half step: 90 cents and 114 cents!

Interaction 10. Comparing major thirds, minor thirds and minor seconds.

```
cm> (events (compare-ratios 'c4 5/4 81/64 3)
            "maj3.mid" :channel-tuning '(#t 1 3))
"maj3-1.mid"
cm> (events (compare-ratios 'c4 6/5 32/27 3)
            "min3.mid"
            :channel-tuning '(#t 1 3))
"min3-1.mid"
cm> (events (compare-ratios 'c4 256/243 2187/2048 3)
            "min2.mid"
            :channel-tuning '(#t 1 3))
"min2-1.mid"
cm>
```

→ nm/15/snd/maj3-1.mid
→ nm/15/snd/min3-1.mid
→ nm/15/snd/min2-1.mid

We now define a version of the Pythagorean chromatic scale whose degrees are expressed by the cent measurements between its minor seconds:

Example 8. Pythagorean chromatic scale.
- -
```
(new tuning :name 'pyth-c
     :cents '(114 90 90 114 90 114 90 114 90 90 114 90))
```
- -

Interaction 11. Listening to the Pythagorean chromatic scale.

```
cm> (events (play-tuning #&pyth-c 60 84 .3 .7)
            "pyth.mid" :channel-tuning 108)
"pyth-2.mid"
cm>
```

→ nm/15/snd/pyth-2.mid

Equal temperament
In the Pythagorean scale fifths and whole steps are just but thirds are badly out of tune. As the role of the third became more important in Western music, composers

searched for alternate tuning methods to replace the Pythagorean system. Different tunings arose, in part, because there are different ways to deal with the comma differences exhibited in the Pythagorean scale. *Quarter Comma Meantone Tuning* distributes the syntonic comma equally over four 5ths: C, G, D and A, which then allows the thirds within the fifths to remain just. But of course, each fifth at 696.5 cents is now out of tune, 1/4 syntonic comma (22/4 cents) flatter than the just fifth. Quarter Comma Meantone Tuning allows closely related keys to sound in tune while distant keys are badly out of tune. In *Just Tuning*, a series of stacked major and minor triads are justly tuned but more distantly related triads are out of tune. *12-tone equal temperament* takes a different approach altogether. Rather than keeping some ratios just at the expense of others, equal temperament distributes the syntonic comma equally over all 12 fifths, thereby reducing each just fifth by 2 cents to 700 cents. This means that in equal temperament there are no just intervals at all, but all intervals are affected by only a very small amount. In Chapter 7 we learned that another way to think about equal temperament is as a system that divides the octave into n equal half steps with a ratio size of $2^{1/n}$ between each step. In the case of the standard chromatic scale n is 12 and the step ratio is $2^{1/12}$, or 1.0594630943592953. But of course there is nothing magical about 12 steps, as we can see in Example 9 it is just as easy to design tuning systems with more or fewer steps, or to base an equal temperament on an "octave" that is not a power of two.

Example 9. Alternate equal tempered scales.

```
(new tuning :name '5-tone
     :cents (loop repeat 5 collect (/  1200 5)))

(new tuning :name '24-tone
     :cents (loop repeat 24 collect 50))

(new tuning :name 'bohlen-pierce
     :ratios (loop for i to 13
                   collect (expt 3.0 (/ i 13))))
```

The 5-tone equal tempered scale is a very rough approximation of the Javanese Slendro scale, which has no single exact tuning. 24-tone implements quarter tone tuning. The Bohlen-Pierce scale is a 13-step scale with an octave ratio of 3/1 rather than 2/1. In other words, the "octave" for the Bohlen-Pierce scale is the octave-plus-a-fifth interval between the first and third harmonics in the harmonic series. There are also justly tuned chromatic and diatonic versions of the Bohlen-Pierce scale. For more information on this scale, consult Current Directions in Computer Music Research (Pierce).

Pelog

Pelog is a 7-tone, non-octave scale characteristic of Javanese gamelan music. The degrees in the Pelog scale are named but there is no single relationship defined between them. Instead, each gamelan is tuned to its own version of Pelog. The two

"octave" version shown in Example 10 was taken from Harvard Dictionary of Music
(Hood) .

Example 10. A two octave version of the Pelog scale.

```
(new tuning :name 'pelog
     :lowest 220.0
     :octaves #f
     :cents '((0     nem0)
             (125   barang0)
             (266   bem0)
             (563   gulu0)
             (676   dada0)
             (800   pelog0)
             (965   lima0)

             (1220  nem1)
             (1360  barang1)
             (1503  bem1)
             (1778  gulu1)
             (1905  dada1)
             (2021  pelog1)
             (2225  lima1)

             (2447  nem2))))
```

La Monte Young's Well Tuned Piano
La Monte Young's piano composition *The Well Tuned Piano* is based on a 12-tone,
justly tuned scale that features the "flat" 7th partial in its design. A complete
description of the scale can be found in La Monte Young's The Well-Tuned Piano
(Gann) by Kyle Gann. Young's scale (Table 4) is a *seven limit* tuning, which means
that ratios defining the scale degrees contain no prime numbers greater than seven.

Table 4. Step ratios in Young's scale.

Eb	E	F	F#	G#	G	A
1/1	567/512	9/8	147/128	1323/1024	21/16	189/128

Bb	B	C#	C	D	Eb	
3/2	49/32	441/256	7/4	63/32	2	

This tuning has a number of interesting features. First, it contains a wide variety of
interval sizes, ranging from the smallest, a 27 cents half-step between E and F, up to
204 cents, the just major second between E-flat and F. The scale's steps are also
grouped into a pentatonic clustering around E-flat, F, G, B-flat and C in the standard

chromatic scale. Another interesting feature of the scale is its use of the "flat" seventh harmonic to define its consonant third relation. Young's tuning uses a 9/7 major third between E and G-sharp, G and B, A and C-sharp, D and F-sharp, and a 7/6 minor third between F-sharp and A, B and D, and C-sharp and E. Another unusual feature is that its G-sharp is lower than its G, and C-sharp is is lower than C! These pairs of tones were reordered to create 3/2 perfect fifths between the F-sharp, C-sharp and G-sharp spellings.

Example 11. Young's scale.

```
- - - - - - - - - - - - - - - - - - - - - - - - - - - - - - - - - - - - - - - - - - -.
(new tuning :name 'young
     :ratios '((1 ef)
               (567/512 e)
               (9/8 f)
               (147/128 fs)
               (1323/1024 gs)
               (21/16 g)
               (189/128 a)
               (3/2 bf)
               (49/32 b)
               (441/256 cs)
               (7/4 c)
               (63/32 d)
               2)
     :octaves '(-1 10)
     :lowest (* (hertz 'a-1) 128/189))
- - - - - - - - - - - - - - - - - - - - - - - - - - - - - - - - - - - - - - - - - - -.
```

Young's scale is based on an E-flat that is actually closer to D in the standard chromatic scale. But the sixth scale degree, A, is tuned to exactly 440.0 Hz, which means that the scale's lowest E-flat can be calculated by multiplying the lowest A in the standard chromatic scale by 128/189, the reciprocal of the sixth degree's ratio. The scale degree ratios in Example 11 are listed in monotonically increasing order, which means that the symbols that define the G-sharp and C-sharp note names appear before their natural versions. The last ratio in the list is 2, which establishes the octave ratio without defining a redundant note name.

Interaction 12. Values in Young's scale.

```
cm> (note 0 :in #&young)
ef-1
cm> (hertz 'a4 :in #&young)
440.0
cm> (keynum 'c4 :in #&young)
70
cm>
```

The following musical examples, implemented by Michael Klingbeil, demonstrate Young's tuning.

Example 12. A process to preview Young's scale.

```
- - - - - - - - - - - - - - - - - - - - - - - - - - - - - - - - - - - - - - - - - .
(define (arp-chord notes rate dur amp)
  ;; arpeggiate a list of notes.
  (process with transp = 0
           for n in notes
           for k = (keynum n :from #&young)
           output (new midi :time (now)
                       :keynum (+ transp k)
                       :duration dur
                       :amplitude amp)
           wait rate))
- - - - - - - - - - - - - - - - - - - - - - - - - - - - - - - - - - - - - - - - - .
```

The following two examples demonstrate the basic scaler and intervalic relations in Young's scale.

Example 13. Scale and septimal interval relations.

```
- - - - - - - - - - - - - - - - - - - - - - - - - - - - - - - - - - - - - - - - - .
(define youngs-scale
  '(ef4 e4 f4 fs4 gs4 g4 a4 bf4 b4 cs5 c5 d5 ef5))
(define sept-7th '(ef4 c5))
(define sept-min-3rds '(e4 gs4 f4 g4 a4 cs5))
(define sept-maj-3rds '(fs4 a4 b4 d5 cs5 e5 c5 f5))
- - - - - - - - - - - - - - - - - - - - - - - - - - - - - - - - - - - - - - - - - .
```

Interaction 13. Listening to the scale and intervals.

```
cm> (events (arp-chord youngs-scale 0.4 2 .6)
            "young.mid" :channel-tuning (list true 0 8))
"young-1.mid"
cm> (events (play-tuning #&young 48 96 .15 .5)
            "young.mid")
"young-2.mid"
cm> (events (arp-chord sept-7th 0 3 .6)
            "young.mid")
"young-3.mid"
cm> (events (arp-chord sept-min-3rds 0 2 .6)
            "young.mid")
"young-4.mid"
cm> (events (arp-chord sept-maj-3rds 0 2 .6)
            "young.mid")
"young-5.mid"
cm>
```

➙ nm/15/snd/young-1.mid

→ nm/15/snd/young-2.mid
→ nm/15/snd/young-3.mid
→ nm/15/snd/young-4.mid
→ nm/15/snd/young-5.mid

Example 14 defines some representative sonorities that Young uses in The Well Tuned Piano.

Example 14. Chords from The Well Tuned Piano.

```
(define opening-chord
   '(ef3 bf3 c4 ef4 f4 bf4))
(define magic-chord
   '(e3 fs3 a3 b3 d4 e4 g4 a4))
(define gamelan-chord
   '(fs3 a3 c4 e4))
(define tamiar-dream-chord
   '(b2 d3 g3 a3 b3 d4 g4 a4))
(define lost-lake-chord
  '(g2 b2 d3 fs3 g3 a3))
(define brook-chord
   '(bf3 c4 ef4 f4 g4 bf4 c5 ef5 f5 bf5))
(define pool-chord
   '(ef3 f3 fs3 bf3 c4 ef4 f4 bf4))
```

Interaction 14 demonstrates the Opening Chord, Magic Chord, Gamelan Chord, Tamiar Dream Chord, 89/89 Lost Ancestral Lake Region, The Brook, and The Pool chords:

Interaction 14. Sonorities from The Well Tempered Piano.

```
cm> (events (arp-chord opening-chord 0.25 3 .6)
            "young.mid" :channel-tuning (list true 0 8))
"young-6.mid"
cm> (events (arp-chord magic-chord 0.25 3 .6)
            "young.mid")
"young-7.mid"
cm> (events (arp-chord gamelan-chord 0.25 3 .6)
            "young.mid")
"young-8.mid"
cm> (events (arp-chord tamiar-dream-chord 0.25 3 .6)
            "young.mid")
"young-9.mid"
cm> (events (arp-chord lost-lake-chord 0.25 3 .6)
            "young.mid")
"young-10.mid"
```

```
cm> (events (arp-chord brook-chord .15 5 .6)
           "young.mid")
"young-11.mid"
cm> (events (arp-chord pool-chord .15 5 .6)
           "young.mid")
"young-12.mid"
cm>
```

→ nm/15/snd/young-6.mid
→ nm/15/snd/young-7.mid
→ nm/15/snd/young-8.mid
→ nm/15/snd/young-9.mid
→ nm/15/snd/young-10.mid
→ nm/15/snd/young-11.mid
→ nm/15/snd/young-12.mid

Modes

A mode in Common Music is a scale that defines a transposable subset of a tuning. Adjacent degrees in the mode may be non-contiguous in the tuning.

mode   [Class]

mode supports the following slot initializations:
:name {*string* | *symbol*}
> An optional name for the mode.

:tonic *note*
> Sets the tonic note name of the mode. Defaults to the first note in the steps specification, or C if the steps are described as intervals.

:scale *tuning*
> Sets the tuning system for the scale. Notes in the mode must also be notes in the tuning. Defaults to the standard chromatic scale.

:steps {*notes* | *intervals*}
> One octave of the mode specified as a list of notes or list of intervals between notes. If steps is a list of notes the tonic (transposition offset) of the mode is automatically set to the note class of the first note in the list. If the steps are specified as a list of intervals the transposition is set to C. A mode can be transposed to a new tonic using the transpose function.

Functions like hertz, keynum, note and transpose accept modes as well as tunings as scale inputs:

Interaction 15. Transposing modes.

```
cm> (new mode :name 'dorian :steps '(d e f g a b c d))
#<mode:"dorian" (on d)>
cm> (keynum 'd4 :in #&dorian)
35
cm> (loop for i from 35 to 42
           collect (note i :in #&dorian))
(d4 e4 f4 g4 a4 b4 c5 d5)
cm> (transpose #&dorian 'cs)
#<mode:""dorian" (on cs)>
cm> (loop for i from 35 to 42
           collect (note i :in #&dorian))
(cs4 ds4 e4 fs4 gs4 as4 b4 cs5)
cm>
```

To demonstrate the use of modes we define a process that harmonizes random chords on Messiaen's Modes of Limited Transposition.

Example 15. Messiaen's Modes of Limited Transposition.
```
- - - - - - - - - - - - - - - - - - - - - - - - - - - - - - - - - - - - - - - - - -·
(new mode :name 'mode1 :steps '(c d e fs gs bf c))
(new mode :name 'mode2 :steps '(c df ef e fs g a bf c))
(new mode :name 'mode3
          :steps '(c d ef e fs g af bf b c))
(new mode :name 'mode4 :steps '(c df d f fs g af b c))
(new mode :name 'mode5 :steps '(c df f fs g b c))
(new mode :name 'mode6 :steps '(c d ef fs gs as b c))
(new mode :name 'mode7
          :steps '(c df d ef f fs g af a b c))

(define chords '((0 2 4 5) (0 1 3 5) (0 2 3 4)))

(define (messiaen mode start end rate)
  (let ((num (length chords)))
    (process for m from start to end
             for c = (list-ref chords (random num))
             for l = (note (transpose c m) :in mode)
             each n in l
             output (new midi :time (now)
                              :keynum n
                              :duration (* rate 2))
             wait (odds .15 (* rate .5) rate))))
- - - - - - - - - - - - - - - - - - - - - - - - - - - - - - - - - - - - - - - - - -·
```

The `messiaen` process selects chords at random from a list of possible chord templates defined in the global variable *chords*. Each chord template is a list of intervals that will be transposed to specific key numbers in the *mode* specified to the process. The `wait` expression uses Common Music's `odds` function to randomly produce "added value" rhythms that are characteristic of much of Messiaen's music.

Interaction 16. Listening to Messiaen's Modes

```
cm> (events (messiaen #&mode2 35 50 .4)
            "messiaen.mid")
"messiaen-1.mid"
cm> (events (messiaen #&mode6 35 50 .4)
            "messiaen.mid")
"messiaen-2.mid"
cm>
```

→ nm/15/snd/messiaen-1.mid
→ nm/15/snd/messiaen-2.mid

Chapter Source Code

The source code to all of the examples and interactions in this chapter can be found in the file scales.cm located in the same directory as the HTML file for this chapter. The source file can be edited in a text editor or evaluated inside the Common Music application.

References

Mathews, M. & Pierce, J. (1989). The Bohlen-Pierce Scale. In Mathews V., & Pierce, J. (Eds.), *Current Direction in Computer Music Research* (pp.165-174). Cambridge: The MIT Press.
Hood, M. (1972).Java. In Apel, W. (Ed.), *Harvard Dictionary of Music* (pp.435). Boston: Harvard University Press.
Gann, K. (1993). La Monte Young's The Well-Tuned Piano. *Perspectives of New Music, 31(1),* 134-162.

16

Mapping

A mapping is between two things: it is the life of the argument, linking and identifying and relating. The life of music may have some relationship to this concept as well: how else would music be able to teach itself, unless there were a process at work that made connections, showed similarities, identified differences, and conveyed their significance?

— Edward Rothstein, Emblems Of Mind: The Inner Life of Music and Mathematics

Proportion, juxtaposition and balance between musical ideas are fundamental relationships in music, and transformations that affect these properties permeate the craft of composition. *Scaling* and *offsetting* are two simple yet powerful ideas that composers use to transform musical ideas. In this chapter we examine some computer techniques related to scaling and offsetting and demonstrate how they can be used to control the procedural description of parameterized sound data.

Scaling and Offsetting

As its name suggests, *scaling* a quantity means to change its size, or magnitude, by multiplication. In the visual domain, scaling causes an object to appear bigger or smaller without altering its origin with respect to the visual field. In music composition, the idea of scaling can be observed in our system of mensural rhythmic proportions, augmentation and diminution, in the harmonic series and tuning systems, and in amplitude shapes such as the crescendo and decrescendo. *Offsetting* a quantity means to add a value to it. Offsetting affects the origin of something along an axis of interest. Offsetting can be observed in music in semitonal transposition, and in the 12-tone system. Rhythmic effects such as syncopation and the added values of Messiaen are also "offset effects", as is the sequencing of motives and intervallic patterns.

Mapping

Throughout history composers have been interested in projecting extra-musical ideas into sound. Dufay's famous isorhythmic motet *Nuper Rosarum Flores* was composed using the architectural ratios of the dome in the Santa Maria del Fiore cathedral in Florence. These ratios were transformed into musical proportions for his motet commissioned for the cathedral's opening in 1436. See Charles Warren's Brunelleschi's Dome and Dufay's motet (Warren) for more information. In the twentieth-century, Charles Dodge's famous work *The Earth's Magnetic Field* is based on measurements of the Earth's yearly average magnetic activity that are projected onto a set of pitches to create an eight minute piece. The general term for this type of transformation is called *mapping*. Mapping means to relate, or project, values from one domain of interest into another. We will implement a simple mapping function called `rescale` that uses only scaling and offsetting to transform values from one coordinate system into another.

The Rescale Function

The `rescale` function implements a simple, general tool for effecting transformations by scaling and offsetting (Example 1).

Example 1. Common Music's rescale function.

```
(define (rescale x old-min old-max new-min new-max)
  ;; scale the size of x by the proportion of ranges
  ;; then shift into the new coordinate system.
  (let ((old-range (- old-max old-min))
        (new-range (- new-max new-min))
        (old-size (- x old-min)))
    (+ (* (/ new-range old-range)
          old-size)
       new-min)))
```

The simplicity of `rescale` belies its expressive power — we will have opportunities to use this function many times throughout the remainder of this book to reformulate values from one range into another, or to translate a value from one parameter into a value for another, or to map non-musical data into musical parameter space. The `rescale` function is actually defined by Common Music but is presented here in Example 1 to show how its scaling and offsetting can be implemented.

The `rescale` function takes a value *x* that lies within the inclusive boundaries *old-min* to *old-max* and returns a value equivalent to *x* that lies between the boundaries *new-min* to *new-max*. The values *x*, *old-min* and *old-max* are first converted to proportional quantities by subtracting out the *old-min* offset. The local variable *old-range* is the difference between *old-max* and *old-min*, while *new-range* is the same between *new-max* to *new-min*. The body of the function is a single nested expression containing division, multiplication and addition terms. Division and multiplication are inverse scaling operations and addition is offsetting. The expression (`/ old-range new-range`) is the ratio of the magnitudes of the two ranges. This ratio scales *old-size*, the magnitude of the value *x*. If *new-range* is larger than *old-range* then the multiplication will increase *old-size*. If *new-range* is smaller than *old-range* then *old-size* will decrease by the same proportion. The outermost addition in the expression offsets the rescaled *old-size* by *new-min*, the minimum value of the new coordinate system, to shift the new quantity back within the y boundaries specified to the function. A few sample interactions will suffice to show how the function operates:

Interaction 1. Examples of rescale.

```
cm> (rescale 5 0 10 10 20)
15
cm> (rescale 5 0 10 0 40)
20
cm> (rescale 5 0 10 100 200)
150
cm> (rescale 5 0 10 -200 0)
-100
cm> (rescale 2 0 10 200 100)
180
cm>
```

The first two interactions demonstrate offsetting and scaling in isolation. The first expression shifts, or offsets, the value 5 (which lies half way between old boundaries 0 and 10) to the value 15, which lies half-way between the new boundaries 10 and 20. The second interaction scales the value 5 to a value four times as large. The remaining three interactions combine scaling and offsetting. The third interaction rescales 5 to lie halfway between the boundaries 100 and 200. The fourth interaction transforms 5 to lie within negative boundaries. The last interaction inverts 5 within the new boundaries by reversing the *new-max* and *new-min* values.

Points on a curve to find?

We now use the `rescale` function to define a musical process that maps values of the `sin` function, which range from -1 to 1, onto a range of MIDI key numbers.

Example 2. Playing MIDI notes along a sine curve.

```
(define (play-sine len cycs key1 key2 rhy dur amp)
  (let ((maxx (- len 1))
        (maxr (* 2 pi cycs)))
    (process for x from 0 to maxx
             ;; rescale i to radians
             for r = (rescale x 0 maxx 0 maxr)
             ;; calc sine value -1 to 1 of r
             for a = (sin r)
             ;; rescale sin to keynum
             for k = (rescale a -1 1 key1 key2)
             output
             (new midi :time (now)
                  :keynum k
                  :amplitude amp
                  :duration dur)
             wait rhy)))
```

play-sine plays MIDI events as discrete points along *cycs* cycles of a "sinewave". We learned in Chapter 10 that a sinewave describes a smooth oscillation between a minimum and a maximum amplitude over time. Points along this smoothly changing shape can be calculated using the trigonometric function sin. The sin function computes the ratio of the hypotenuse to the opposite side of an angle as it sweeps around the unit circle (Figure 1.) The angular input to sin is expressed in term of *radians*, not degrees. Radians are just another way to measure angles, by definition there are *2pi* radians in 360°.

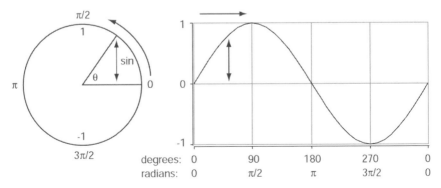

Figure 1. The sine function.

As the angle sweeps from 0 to 2pi radians (0-360°) the value of sin produces one oscillation between -1 and 1. At 0 radians sin is 0, at pi/2 radians (90°) it is 1, at pi radians (180°) it is 0 again, and at 3pi/2 radians (270°) it is -1. The cycle repeats itself every 2pi radians (360°), which is same as 0.

The Play-sine process uses rescale to map a counter *i* onto an equivalent radian value *r* and to map values of sin onto key numbers. *Len* is the total number of events that play-sine creates, and *cycs* is the number of cycles of the "sine wave" produced over *len* events. Since there are 2*pi radians in one cycle of a sine wave, the maximum radian value *maxr* is *2*pi*cycs* radians over *cycs* cycles of the sine wave. Each time the process runs, *r* is set to the current radian value determined by rescaling the *x* counter into radians. The current sine amplitude value *a* is then calculated and converted to the current key number *k* using the rescale function again.

Interaction 2. Listening to play-sine.

```
cm> (events (play-sine 80 4 20 100 .1 .1 .6)
            "sine.mid")
"sine-1.mid"
cm> (events (list (play-sine 80 4 20 100 .1 .1 .6)
                  (play-sine 60 5.7 50 80 .1 .1 .6))
            "sine.mid"
            '(0 2))
"sine-2.mid"
cm>
```

➙ nm/16/snd/sine-1.mid
➙ nm/16/snd/sine-2.mid

In the next example we define a variation of the play-sine process that calculates MIDI notes along the sine curve based on the current time of the process. This version allows us to listen to different densities of events along the curve.

Example 3. Variation of sine wave process.
- .
```
(define (play-sine2 end cycs rate keymin keymax
                    ampmin ampmax)
  (process for r = (rescale (now) 0 end 0 (* 2 pi cycs))
           for a = (sin r)
           while (< (now) end)
           output (new midi :time (now)
                       :keynum
                       (rescale a -1 1 keymin keymax)
                       ;; invert sine shape for amp
                       :amplitude
                       (rescale a -1 1 ampmax ampmin))
           wait rate))
```
- .

End is the stopping time for the algorithm and *rate* is the speed between MIDI events in seconds. *Cycs* is the total number of cycles to produce: as *cycs* increases for a given *rate* there will be fewer and fewer events per cycle of the sine curve. The process uses the `rescale` function to control amplitude using the same `sin` values that control key numbers.

Interaction 3. Listening to play-sine2.

```
cm> (events (play-sine2 10 6 .1 20 70 .1 .9)
"sine.mid")
"sine-3.mid"
cm> (events (play-sine2 10 6 .5 20 70 .1 .9)
"sine.mid")
"sine-4.mid"
cm>
```

→ nm/16/snd/sine-3.mid
→ nm/16/snd/sine-4.mid

Linear Interpolation

The mathematical operation that `rescale` performs is called *linear interpolation*. The x on which the equivalence is based is called the "independent" variable and the output value that `rescale` calculates is called the "dependent", or y, variable. We can use a loop to collect pairs of x and y interpolation values into a list:

Interaction 4. X and y interpolation pairs.

```
cm> (loop for x in '(0 .2 .4 .6 .8 1)
          for y = (rescale x 0 1 100 200)
          collect x collect y)
(0 100 0.2 120.0 0.4 140.0 0.6 160.0 0.8 180.0 1 200)
cm> (loop for x in '(0 .25 .5 .75 1)
          for y = (rescale x 0 1 440 220)
          collect x collect y)
(0 440 0.25 385.0 0.5 330.0 0.75 275.0 1 220)
cm>
```

The linear relationship between these values can be displayed by graphing the x and y pairs. The independent x value ranges along the horizontal, or x axis, and the dependent y values range over the vertical, or y axis (Figure 2).

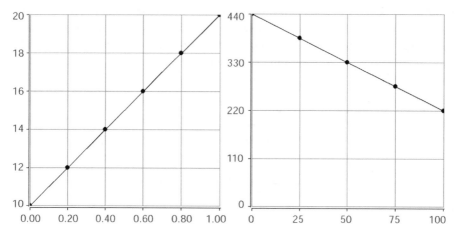

Figure 2. Graphic display of x and y pairs in Example 2.

The points in the plot mark the positions of values along both axes. We can see in both graphs that linear interpolation produces values on a straight line between a minimum and maximum value and that the *slope* of the line may be upward or downward.

Envelopes

The list of *x* and *y* pairs in Interaction 4 form a data structure called an *envelope*. Each pair of values defines a single *coordinate* or point, in the envelope. The *x* values in the envelope must be specified in monotonically increasing order to insure that only one unique *y* value can exist for every unique *x* value. The *y* values in the envelope are not ordered, they may range anywhere within the minimum and maximum y axis values (Interaction 5 and Figure 3).

Interaction 5. x and y interpolation pairs.

```
cm> (loop for x in '(0 .2 .4 .6 .8 1)
          for y = (between 40 80)
          collect x collect y)
(0 50 20 83 40 59 60 66 80 51 100 66)
cm>
```

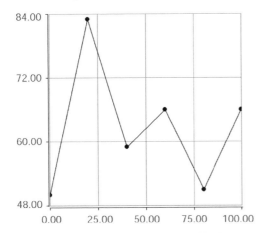

Figure 3. Graphic display of x and y pairs in Example 2.

Common Music provides two functions that perform interpolation with envelopes:

```
(interp x x1 y1 x2 y2 ...)                              [Function]
(interpl x env [:scale s] [:offset o] [:base b])        [Function]
```

Both functions perform linear interpolation over a series of point specifications. The first argument to both functions is the independent *x* value to interpolate. The other arguments to `interp` are the sequences of coordinate pairs that define the shape of the envelope. In contrast, the `interpl` function takes an *envelope list* as its second argument. The two calls shown in Interaction 6 are equivalent.

Interaction 6. interp and interpl

```
cm> (interp .5 0 0 1 100)
50
cm> (interpl .5 '(0 0 1 100))
50
cm>
```

The `interpl` function also supports a set of optional *keyword arguments* after the envelope specification. Recall from Chapter 3 that a keyword argument is expressed as a pair: the keyword name of the argument followed by its value (Interaction 7).

Interaction 7. Passing keyword arguments to the interpl function.

```
cm> (interpl 0.5 '(0 0 1 1) :scale 100)
50.0
cm> (interpl 0.5 '(0 0 1 1) :offset 100)
100.5
```

```
cm> (interpl 0.5 '(0 0 1 1) :scale 100 :offset 100)
150
cm>
```

The next example demonstrates how `interp` can be used to control parameter values in a musical process. The process interpolates amplitude and tempo values using two `interp` expressions. Each interpolation divides the total length of the process into two segments on either side of a randomly chosen midpoint *mid* between 20 and 80 percent of the total length of the process. Each interpolation produces increasing values over the first segment and decreasing values over the second.

Example 4. Interpolating amplitude values from event number.

```
(define (play-interp len rate key1 key2
                     mintem maxtem minamp maxamp)
  (let* ((end (- len 1))
         (mid (+ (* .2 len) (random (* .6 len)))))
    (process for x from 0 to end
             for a = (interp x 0 minamp mid maxamp
                             end minamp)
             for c = (interp x 0 mintem mid maxtem
                             end mintem)
             output (new midi :time (now)
                              :keynum (+ key1 (random key2))
                              :amplitude a
                              :duration (* rate 1.5 c))
             wait (* rate c))))
```

In Interaction 8 we use a loop to sprout six versions of the process, each with a start time .5 seconds later than the preceding one.

Interaction 8. Listening to play-interpl

```
cm> (events (loop for k
                  in (keynum '(c6 f5 bf4 ef af3 df))
                  for s from 0 by .5
                  collect (play-interp 40 .2 k (+ k 7)
                                       1 .6 .4 .8))
            "interp.mid")
"interp-1.mid"
cm>
```

→nm/16/snd/interp-1.mid

Normalized envelopes

The envelope is a very simple yet powerful data structure in computer composition because the "shape" it defines can be scaled and offset in control the evolution of one or more sound parameters (Example 5 and Figure 4). A *normalized* envelope is an envelope whose *xy* coordinates are defined within the range 0 to 1. Normalized envelopes express proportion, or shape, rather than absolute values. Composers often define global variables to hold the most common envelopes they work with. Some sample normalized envelope definitions are shown in Example 5 and their shapes are graphed in Figure 4.

Example 5. Common envelope shapes.

```
(define ramp-up '(0 0 1 1))
(define ramp-down '(1 0 0 1))
(define tri-env '(0 0 .5 1 1 0))
(define mid-env '(0 0 .25 1 .75 1 1 0))
(define exp-down '(0 1 .25 1/4 .5 1/16 .75 1/32 1 0))
(define exp-up '(0 0 .25 1/32 .5 1/16 .75 1/4 1 1))
```

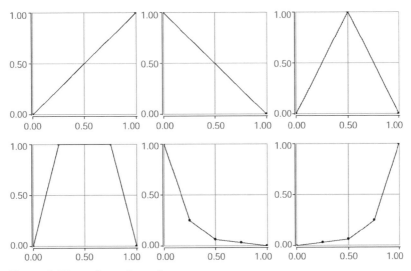

Figure 4. Plots of envelope shapes.

To use a normalized envelope the *y* output value must be rescaled and offset to lies within the appropriate range for a given parameter. The `interp1` function can perform both of these actions in a single function call (Example 6 and Interaction 9).

Example 6. Applying normalized shapes to a process.

```
(define (shaper len env rate ampscale ampoff keyscale
                keyoff)
   (let ((last (- len 1)))
```

```
(process for i below len
         for x = (/ i last)
         for a = (interpl x env :scale ampscale
                                :offset ampoff)
         for k = (interpl x env :scale keyscale
                                :offset keyoff)
         output (new midi :time (now)
                          :duration rate
                          :keynum k
                          :amplitude a)
         wait rate)))
```

Interaction 9. Calling shaper with different envelopes.

```
cm> (events (shaper 20 tri-env .15 .7 .05 16 48)
            "shaper.mid")
"shaper-1.mid"
cm> (events (shaper 20 exp-down .15 .5 .2 20 30)
            "shaper.mid")
"shaper-2.mid"
cm>
```

↪ nm/16/snd/shaper-1.mid
↪ nm/16/snd/shaper-2.mid

Exponential Scaling

Linear interpolation is a wonderful tool, it provides a simple and general way to control sound parameters as a function of some variable whose domain may not be directly related to the parameter in question. However, there are times when the "straight line" effect produced by linear interpolation may be inappropriate. For example, changes in tempo and amplitude often sound more natural if they are produced by *exponential scaling* rather than linear interpolation. Values generated by exponential scaling lie on a power curve rather than on a straight line. The :base keyword argument to interpl can be used to produce interpolation along a power curve. If :base is 1 (the default) then linear interpolation results. If :base is greater than 1 the interpolated values lie on a convex curve for positive slopes, or concave curves if it is less than 1 (Figure 5.) The more :base deviates from 1 the steeper the power curve between points.

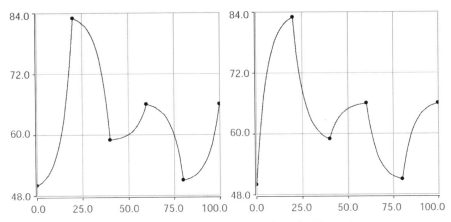

Figure 5. Exponential interpolation using the envelope in Figure 3.

Common Music provides several additional functions for working with exponential scaling.

(expl *x* [:y0 *n*] [:y1 *num*] [:base *num*])   [Function]
(explsegs *len sum base*)   [Function]

The expl function returns an exponential value between :y0 and :y1 for the given *x* value that must range from 0 to 1. Explsegs returns a list of *len* number of exponentially scaled segments that add up to *sum*. The :base arguments to these functions are the same as for interpl. explsegs allows the composer to "chop up" a quantity into a specified number of exponentially related segments. The next example defines a process called ballfall whose tempo and key numbers are controlled by a list of exponential values produced by explsegs.

Example 7. Exponential curve for falling ball.
```
(define (ballfall drops end curve key amp)
  (let* ((all (explsegs drops end curve))
         (max (first all))
         (low (hertz key)))
    (process for d in all
             for e = (random (expt 2.0 (/ d max)))
             for k = (keynum (* low e) :hz)
             for a = (rescale d 0 max .1 amp)
             output (new midi time (now)
                         :duration d
                         :keynum k
                         :amplitude a)
             wait d)))
```

Drops are the number of times the ball bounces and *end* is the time it takes to decay. *Curve* controls the steepness of the power curve. Since the longest drop occurs at the beginning the curve value should always be less than 1 for this process. *Key* is the lowest key number the ball will play and *amp* is the maximum amplitude. The variable *all* is set to the list of exponential values returned by `explsegs`. Since *curve* is less than 1 the first value in this list is the maximum drop value *max*. The process iterates for each drop value *d* in *all*. On each iteration, the variable *e* is set to a random value between 1 and 2 based on the proportion of the current drop *d* to the longest drop *max*. This means that as the process iterates, the range for successive random values of *e* diminishes from 2.0 to a value approaching 1.0 (Figure 6.) This value is then used to transpose the *low* frequency to somewhere within an octave and *k* is set to the key number of that Hertz frequency.

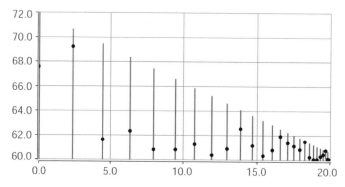

Figure 6. X axis plots start time, y axis plots range and value of random key number (for *drop=25, end=20, curve=1/20*).

The amplitude variable *a* is determined by rescaling the current drop value to a value between .1 and the maximum amplitude specified to the process.

Interaction 10. Exponential curve for tempo and key number.

```
cm> (events (ballfall 40 10 1/256 60 .8) "ball.mid")
"ball-1.mid"
cm> (events (ballfall 100 15 1/150 40 .8) "ball.mid")
"ball-2.mid"
cm>
```

➡ nm/16/snd/ball-1.mid
➡ nm/16/snd/ball-2.mid

Self-Similar Scaling and Recursion

Scaling and offsetting can be combined to produce patterns that consist entirely of a single shape that is projected in identical proportions at smaller and smaller magnitudes. This kind of pattern is called a *self-similar*, or *fractal* pattern. Self-similarity can be found not just in visual patterns, but in musical ones as well. For example, the intervals in the chromatic scale are derived from a single ratio of $2^{1/12}$. An equal-tempered melody sounds the same when transposed to different octaves even though the actual Hertz frequency values between the tones are not equivalent.

One simple way to create a self-similar pattern is to apply the same set of rules (i.e. an algorithm) over and over again at different levels of magnitude until the pattern has been generated to a sufficient resolution. Self-similarity is most naturally implemented using a *recursive* function definition. A recursive function is a function that calls itself to solve successively simplified versions of a problem. In order to illustrate self-similarity and recursion we will create a function that simply "chops up" a quantity into self-similar segments at smaller and smaller magnitudes and then returns a list of all the segments that it calculates. For example if an input of 8 were chopped into 2 segments over 4 levels of magnitude the algorithm would return the list:

> (8 4 2 1 1 2 1 1 4 2 1 1 2 1 1)

which corresponds to the levels and proportions in Table 1.

Table 1. Levels and proportions of a self-similar organization.

Level 1	8							
Level 2	4				4			
Level 3	2		2		2		2	
Level 4	1	1	1	1	1	1	1	1

The `sschop` function Example 8 is a recursive algorithm that calls itself to reproduce its rules at different levels of magnitude. Its recursive nature means that `sschop` reflects self-similarity in its definition as well as in the results it returns.

Example 8. Self-similar segments of a line.
- -

```
(define (sschop value segments levels)
  (if (< levels 1)
      '()
      (let* ((nextval (/ value segments))
             (nextlev (- levels 1))
             (chopped (loop repeat segments
                            append
                            (sschop nextval segments
                                    nextlev))))
        (list* value chopped))))
```
- -

The function `sschop` takes three inputs: a *value* to chop, the number of *segments* to chop *value* into, and the number of magnitude *levels* to chop over. The function returns a list of chopped values. The body of `sschop` consists of a single `if` expression. If the value of *levels* is less than 1 then `sschop` returns an empty list

(Interaction 11). If *levels* is greater than zero then sschop calculates a list of values to return. These values consist of the current value added to the front of a list containing all the successive levels of chopped values at proportionally smaller sizes. The let* establishes three variables. *Nextval* is the proportionally smaller next value, computed by dividing the current *value* by the number of segments in each level. *Nextlev* is set to *level-1*. *Chopped* holds the list of segments that constitute all the values under *nextlev*. This value is computed by a loop that iterates *segments* number of times and appends the results of a recursive call to *sschop* at the next smaller size with *levels* reduced by one. Since *sschop* always returns a list, the append clause is used to concatenate each sublist into one large list. The list* function then adds *value* to the front of this list so that the current level's value is in front of all of its recursively generated segments. Interaction 11 shows several sample calls to sschop that demonstrate its self-similar nature.

Interaction 11. Calling sschop.

```
cm> (sschop 440 2 0)
()
cm> (sschop 440 2 3)
(440 220 110 110 220 110 110)
cm> (sschop 36 3 3)
(36 12 4 4 4 12 4 4 4 12 4 4 4)
cm>
```

Sierpinski's triangle
Sierpinksi's Triangle is a famous two-dimensional fractal (Figure 7). The rules to create Sierpinski's triangle are simple:
1. Start with a triangle.
2. Draw a smaller triangle in the middle of the larger triangle with the points of the smaller triangle on the midpoints of the larger triangle's sides. This partitions the large triangle into 4 smaller triangles: a middle triangle and the triangles at each of the corners of the larger triangle.
3. Leave the middle triangle empty.
4. Visit each of the corner triangles in the larger triangle and repeat the rules starting with step 1 but now using each of these smaller triangles as the starting triangle.
5. Repeat for as many levels as you want: the result is Sierpinski's Triangle.

Figure 7. Four levels of Sierpinski's Triangle.

We will now transform our `sschop` algorithm into a musical process that generates a self-similar melody as an "homage" to Sierpinski's Triangle. Our algorithm will use the basic method described in `sshop` to generate its self-similar melody from a set of three tones, where each tone represents the side of a triangle.

Example 9. Sierpinski's Melody

```
- - - - - - - - - - - - - - - - - - - - - - - - - - - - - - - - - - - - - - - - - -
(define (sierpinski tone melody levels dur amp )
  (let ((len (length melody)))
    (process for i in melody
             for k = (transpose tone i)
             ;; play current tone in melody
             output (new midi :time (now) :duration dur
                         :amplitude amp :keynum k
                         :channel 0)
             when (> levels 1)
             ;; sprout melody on tone at next level
             sprout (sierpinski (transpose k 12)
                                melody
                                (- levels 1)
                                (/ dur len)
                                amp)
             wait dur)))
- - - - - - - - - - - - - - - - - - - - - - - - - - - - - - - - - - - - - - - - - -
```

The `sierpinski` process reproduces a melodic shape based on successive degrees and octaves of itself. *Tone* is the current melodic tone to play, *melody* is a list of intervals representing the melody, *level* is the number of levels of the melody to produce, and *dur* and *amp* are the tone's duration and amplitude, respectively. The variable *len* is set to the number of intervals in the *melody*. The process first outputs the current *tone*. If *levels* is greater then 1 then the process sprouts a recursive process to generate the next melodic level. The next level's tone is calculated by transposing the current tone in the melody up one octave. The duration for each tone becomes the current level's duration divided by the number of intervals in the melody. Thus, the entire melody in the next level will occupy the same amount of time as the current tone in the current level (Figure 8).

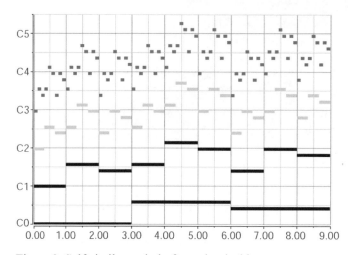

Figure 8. Self-similar melody from sierpinski.

The value for *levels* is decremented by 1 , which will cause the recursive generation to finally stop when this value reaches 0.

Interaction 12. Listening to sierpinski.

```
cm> (events (sierpinski 'a0 '(0 7 5 ) 4 3 .5)
"sier.mid")
"sier-1.mid"
cm> (events (sierpinski 'a0 '(0 -1 2 13) 5 24 .5)
"sier.mid")
"sier-2.mid"
cm>
```

➡ nm/16/snd/sier-1.mid
➡ nm/16/snd/sier-2.mid

Specify levels and melody with care! The number of events the `sierpinski` process generates is exponentially related to the length m of the melody and the number of levels l:

$$m \cdot \sum_{i=0}^{l-1} m^i$$

Accordingly, the first events call in Interaction 12 generates 120 events and the second produces 1364.

Chapter Source Code

The source code to all of the examples and interactions in this chapter can be found in the file mapping.cm located in the same directory as the HTML file for this chapter. The source file can be edited in a text editor or evaluated inside the Common Music application.

References

Warren, C. (1973). Brunelleschi's Dome and Dufay's motet. *Music Quarterly, 59,* 92-105.

17

Etudes, Op. 6: Sonification of Chaos

Thru all the tumult and the strife,
I hear that music ringing.
It sounds and echoes in my soul;
How can I keep from singing?

— Quaker, *Worship Comes Alive*

Sonification means to use an acoustic signal to make information inherent in a collection of data audible (see the on-line report Sonification Report: Status of the Field and Research Agenda at http://www.icad.org/websiteV2.0/References/nsf.html (Kramer) by Gregory Kramer for an overview of research in this area.) Sonification is to the ear what graphic plotting is to the eye — a way to understand relationships that would otherwise be difficult or impossible to perceive. Our ears are very keen instruments that can detect subtle, multidimensional changes in sound space. We have probably all had the experience of diagnosing a problem with a car by listening to minute variations of the sound it produces. Sonification can yield information about regularity, overall shape, grouping, transitions, and deviations in the data presented in an acoustic signal. *Parameter mapping* is one of the most common ways to implement sonification. By projecting data onto frequency, amplitude and timbre over time, many dimensions of data can be perceived and related simultaneously. In this Etude we apply the mapping techniques presented in Chapter 16 to data sets generated by several chaotic functions. The text and examples in this Etude were written by Tobias Kunze for a workshop on algorithmic composition held at CCRMA, Stanford University. Our aims in the Etude are twofold: to understand how mapping can be implemented given a set of non-musical equations, and to demonstrate how sonification can reveal the behavior of non-musical functions. The term *deterministic chaos* refers to the behavior of systems that are not random but are nevertheless unpredictable in nature. The physical world is filled with complex dynamic processes (like turbulence and weather) that are deterministic but whose behavior is nevertheless impossible to predict. There are several features that characterize these systems. First, chaotic systems are highly sensitive to initial conditions — in one starting arrangement their elements produces periodicity; in another, closely proximate arrangement, complete unpredictability ensues. Chaotic systems are *nonlinear*, which means that changes in one element do not produce a like, or equivalent change in others. This means the cause and effect relationships are not proportional in a chaotic system, so that two functions for a single equation may evolve in a similar way but then suddenly diverge along very different paths (Figure 3). The *butterfly effect* observed first by the meteorologist Edward Lorenz encapsulates the sensitivity and nonlinear nature of these systems quite well: a butterfly flaps its wings in Tokyo and it rains in New York.

Op. 6 No. 1, The Logistic Map

The *logistic map* is a simple example of a discrete dynamical system that actually names a whole family of iterative functions described by the Logistic Equation:

$$f_{n+1} = cf_n(1-f_n); \quad \text{for } 0.0 \leq c \leq 4.0$$

Each real value of c in the equation yields a different dynamic behavior and hence a different function.

Background

The logistic map models population growth in a basic *activator-inhibitor* system. Although population growth rates are constant in an ideal environment, actual growth rates are not due to limited resources such as food and water and natural catastrophe. If resources are limited, the growth rate slows down as a population increases and eventually reaches a limit or *attractor* at which point the population is at its maximum capacity for the environment. The S-shaped curve of population growth in such an environment is known as the *logistic curve* (Figure 1).

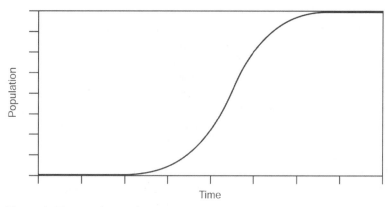

Figure 1. Expected growth curve.

Resource limitations may be viewed as "passive" inhibitors, that is, they only slow down population growth. However, most environments also involve "active" inhibitors, such as floods and epidemics, which reduce a population or at times cause extinction. Whether populations in such an environment approach a maximum, die out or tend to converge towards a number in between these extremes is hard to predict, since most systems with active inhibitors behave in a chaotic manner. Each function of the *logistic map* may serve as an algebraic model of such a chaotic environment.

Activation and inhibition
As a model for the development of populations (and similar processes), the logistic map may be broken down into activating and inhibiting terms, related by a function R with a weighting constant c applied to one of the terms: $f=(c * activator)$ $RInhibitor$. R happens to be the multiplication operator in the logistic map (Figure 2) although other possibilities are imaginable.

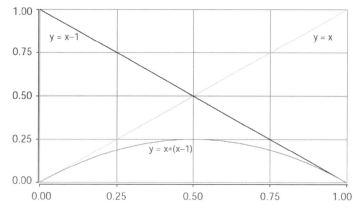

Figure 2. Activator term x (rise) and inhibitor term 1-x (fall) and their product (curve) of the logistic map.

Chaos and the butterfly effect

In contrast to the many random processes which produce *indeterministic* behavior, the logistic map is strictly deterministic. For instance, we can iterate a given function of the logistic map *n* times to determine its *nth* value. The *nth* value of the function is determined solely by the initial value, f_0 and the function constant *c*. But exactly how the *nth* value is determined by the initial conditions is hard to predict. Figure 3 displays two functions with only minimally altered initial states. But after an initial phase of almost parallel evolution this difference leads to totally different behavior between the processes. Moreover, it is almost impossible to predict the exact iteration at which the two functions take on different behavior.

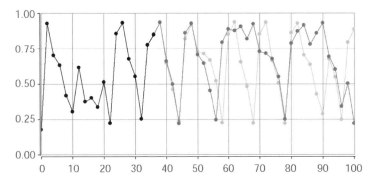

Figure 3. Development of the logistic function for f_0=.95 and f_0=.949999999 for *c*=3.75 in both cases. This minimal variation of the initial value yields dramatically different sequences for *n>30*.

Bifurcation

The behavior of the logistic map does not depend only on the value of f_0 alone but also on the constant *c*. In fact, for numerous values of *c*, *f0* does not matter much at all since the function will eventually converge. Most obviously, setting *c*=0 yields zero values for all values of f_n for *n>0*. (Figure 4). Similar behavior results for all values of *c<~3.0*. At this point, the map converges to several attractors again, depending on the value of the initial f_0. It converges first to 2 attractors, then to 4, 8, 16, and so on until it reaches chaotic behavior. (This repeated doubling within families of functions such as the logistic map has been first noted and extensively studied by the physicist Mitchell J. Feigenbaum.) Interestingly, the sequence of functions of the logistic map traverse several states of temporary tranquility on their way to sheer chaotic behavior. Thus, f_n is actually a family of functions of the form $y(s,c) = c * y * (1 - y)$, with seed values $s = \{0.0005, 0.001 \ldots 1.0\}$. Although the logistic map may give radically different numerical sequences for any two functions of the same family (functions with equal *c* but differing seed value *s*) the distribution pattern of a family after *i* iterations and the histogram of any of its functions up to the *i*th iteration approach the same attractor.

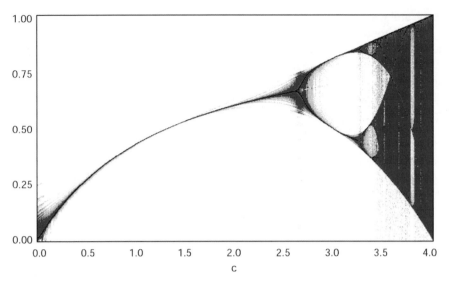

Figure 4. Bifurcation of the logistic map. Values for c are plotted on the x-axis range from 0.0 to 4.0 and are mapped onto the distribution of values of $f(n)$ after 1000 iterations starting from 2000 equally distributed initial seed values of f_n.

Mapping the logistic map
We now sonify the logistic map by using `rescale` to map function values onto sound parameters.

Example 1. The Logistic Map as key numbers

```
- - - - - - - - - - - - - - - - - - - - - - - - - - - - - - - - - - - - - - - - - - ·
(define (logmap chaos len rate dur key1 key2 amp)
   (let ((y (random 1.0))
         (k 0))
     (process repeat len
              set y = (* y chaos (- 1 y))
              set k = (rescale y 0 1 key1 key2)
              output (new midi time (now)
                          :keynum k
                          :duration dur
                          :amplitude amp)
              wait rate)))
- - - - - - - - - - - - - - - - - - - - - - - - - - - - - - - - - - - - - - - - - - ·
```

The `logmap` process maps values from the Logistic Map onto key numbers between *key1* and *key2*. The initial conditions f_0 are represented by the specified *chaos* parameter, which may range between 0 less than 4.0, and the initial random value for y.

Interaction 1. Listening to the Logistic Map

```
cm> (events (logmap 3.7 200 .125 .25 60 96 .6)
"logmap.mid")
"logmap-1.mid"
cm> (events (logmap 3.99 200 .125 .25 60 96 .6)
"logmap.mid")
"logmap-2.mid"
cm>
```

→ nm/17/snd/logmap-1.mid
→ nm/17/snd/logmap-2.mid

The second example increases the *chaos* factor close to the maximum. In the next example we explore chaotic rhythms.

Example 2. Chaotic rhythms

```
(define (groove chaos len pulse)
  (let ((y (random 1.0)))
    (process repeat len
             set y = (* y chaos (- 1 y))
             output (new midi :time (now)
                         :keynum 60
                         :duration .01)
             wait (* pulse y))))
```

Interaction 2. Listening to the Logistic Map

```
cm> (events (groove 3.99 50 .5) "logmap.mid")
"logmap-3.mid"
cm>
```

→ nm/17/snd/logmap-3.mid

This last example links rhythms and pitches together to form more distinctive gestures. The rhythms are quantized to increments of .1 using Common Music's quantize function.

Example 3. Two dimensional Logistic Map

```
(define (logmap-2d chaos len pulse key1 key2 dur)
  (let ((y (random 1.0)))
    (process repeat len
             set y = (* y chaos (- 1 y))
             output (new midi :time (now)
                         :keynum
                         (rescale y 0 1 key1 key2)
```

```
                              :duration dur)
            wait (quantize (rescale y 0 1 0 pulse)
                            .1)))))
```

Interaction 3. Listening to logmap-2d

```
cm> (events (logmap-2d 3.99 200 .125 60 96 1)
"logmap.mid")
"logmap-4.mid"
cm>
```

→ nm/17/snd/logmap-4.mid

Op. 6 No. 2, The Henon Map

The *Henon Map* is given by the two-dimensional function:

$$H(x,y) = ((y + 1) - ax^2, bx)$$

where *a* and *b* are constants, typically 1.4 and 0.3, respectively. The Henon Map is the two-dimensional analog to the logistic function in that it has an oscillating catalytic term $y+1=bx+1$ and an inhibiting part $-ax^2$ (Figure 5).

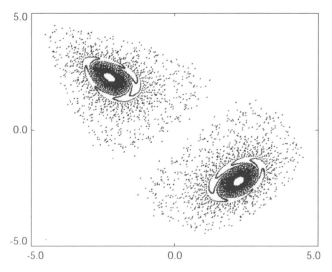

Figure 5. The Henon Map for standard values *a*=1.4 and *b*=.3 after 5000 iterations.

We can define two processes to map the Henon into musical space. The first maps Henon values onto frequency, the second does this in two voices.

Example 4. Henon Mapping

```
(define (henon1 len rate dur key1 key2)
  (let ((x 0)
        (y 0))
    (process repeat len
             for z =  (- (+ y 1) (* .2 x x))
             set y = (* .99 x)
             output (new midi :time (now)
                         :keynum
                         (rescale y -5 5 key1 key2)
                         :duration dur)
             wait (rescale z -5 5 0 rate)
             set x = z)))

(define (henon2 len rate key1 key2)
  (let ((x 0)
        (y 0)
        (k 0)
        (r 0))
    (process repeat len
             for z = (- (+ y 1) (* .2 x x))
             set y = (* .99 x)
             set k = (rescale y -5 5 key1 key2)
             set r = (rescale z -5 5 0 .4)
             output (new midi :time (now)
                         :keynum k
                         :duration r)
             sprout (new midi :time (+ (now) rate)
                         :keynum k
                         :duration .05)
             wait (+ rate r)
             set x = z)))
```

Interaction 4. Listening to Henon Mapping

```
cm> (events (henon1 250 .24 1 48 84) "henon.mid")
"henon-1.mid"
cm> (events (henon2 250 .25 48 84) "henon.mid")
"henon-2.mid"
cm>
```

→nm/17/snd/henon-1.mid

→nm/17/snd/henon-2.mid

Chapter Source Code

The source code to all of the examples and interactions in this chapter can be found in the file chaos.cm located in the same directory as the HTML file for this chapter. The source file can be edited in a text editor or evaluated inside the Common Music application.

References

Kramer, G. (1997). *Sonification Report: Status of the Field and Research Agenda* [On-line]. Available http://www.icad.org/websiteV2.0/References/nsf.html.

18

Randomness and Chance Composition

There is divinity in odd numbers, either in nativity, chance, or death.

— William Shakespeare

Music composition, and artistic expression in general, often reflects a tension between rational and irrational processes that underlie and motivate creative work. Perhaps more than at any other time in history, the 20th century witnessed the rational and irrational taking explicit shape in the techniques that composers used to create music. It should not be surprising that the same century that gave birth to Quantum Mechanics and Heisenberg's Uncertainty Principle also found artists consciously incorporating *non-deterministic*, or random processes into their artistic pallettes. One of the most important expressions of this influence was in the *chance procedures* adopted by some artists. Whether it is motion added to a dance by Merce Cunningham, an abstract painting by Jackson Pollock or the I Ching music of John Cage, randomness and chance are consciously embraced as generative techniques for making art. An interest in chance procedures also served as an important motivation in the development of the experimental music tradition in the 1950's, from which computer composition stems. The earliest examples of computer composition by Lejaren Hiller are largely based on some chance procedures that will be discussed in the next two chapters. These techniques can have a profound effect on the compositional process yet are very simple to perform with a computer. The computer also enables composers to experiment with more interesting types of randomness than the simple "coin tossing" model every composer is familiar with. It perhaps somewhat ironic then, that the computer programs that composers usually use to create chance compositions are not really generating randomness at all!

Random Number Generators

Computers are designed to function in a totally consistent and reproducible manner. This is a wonderful feature when your plane is landing or your tax returns are prepared but it means that randomness is inherently difficult to achieve with such a deterministic machine. Although some applications use specialized hardware to generate truly random signals, most computer programs only simulate randomness using a special type of algorithm called a *pseudo-random* number generator. Pseudo-random number generators are algorithms that calculate a series of numbers with statistically random properties. But, as the name suggests, these numbers are not really random at all. A pseudo-random generator is a completely deterministic algorithm that generates one series of numbers. Many random number generators, including Lisp's random function, allow the user to specify an initial random state seed that positions the algorithm at a certain location in its sequence of numbers. This means that each time the generator starts from the same seed the exact same sequence of numbers in the series will ensue. Composers who want to express randomness "philosophically" in a composition will therefore want to use different initial seeds each time a chance program runs to insure the program generates a different outcome each time. On the other hand, composers often want just the opposite: to save seeds in order to "back up" in the event that a random process has produced particularly satisfying results! This latter method is one way to implement the common *generate and test* compositional style in computer composition. By building random choice into the algorithms that generate music the composer can compute many possible "drafts" of a piece, each with its own random variations. These versions can then compared to determine which one(s) best satisfy the composer's goals. Sometimes a whole piece is generated in this manner, other times the composer collects the best features from different drafts and combines them into a final version. Since the initial seed for each draft was saved the composer can regenerate the best versions at any time, as long as the program code remains exactly the same.

Since the material in this book assumes that the reader is interactively experimenting with examples, we are virtually assured that the book's path through Lisp's random number series will not be repeated by the reader. For this reason none of the examples in this book make use of random number seeds. But by establishing different seeds each time you begin to work, or by saving the current seed before you run a chance program, you can minimize (or maximize) the likelihood that your program will generate the same results. To learn more about the process of seeding in Lisp consult the documentation on the random function in the Language specification.

Probability

A random process is a process in which outcomes have only a certain likelihood of happening. *Probability* is a measurement of the likelihood of these events actually occurring. Probability in our daily lives is often described in terms of a "percentage chance". For example, the weatherman might say: "There is a 25% chance that it will rain today". The percentage indicates that probability is *distributed* over all the events in a random process, where each event, or range of events, has a certain proportion of the total probability. So, although we do not know for certain if it will rain or not, probability allows us to infer several facts from the forecaster's statement:

1. there is a 25% chance that it will rain today
2. there is a 75% chance that it will not rain today
3. there is a 100% chance that it will either rain or not rain today
4. there is a 0% chance that neither will happen

Weather forecasts notwithstanding, probability factors are typically expressed as values between zero and one rather than as percentages between 0 and 100. The probabilities of all the events in a random process add up to 1.0 (100%) because there must be absolute certainty (1.0) that at least one of the outcomes will happen.

Some random processes are characterized by an equal distribution of probability over all of the events in the process. This is called a *uniform probability distribution*. For example, when a fair die is rolled there is an equal likelihood that any one of the six sides will land face up. Since the total probability must add up to 1 and there is an equal chance for any side to land on top, each of the six sides has a probability factor of 1/6. For a given event x, its probability, $P(x)$, is the ratio of the number of ways the outcome can happen to the total number of possible outcomes. For example, if x is a randomly chosen key number on a piano then $P(x)= 1/88$. If x is a randomly chosen black key on the piano, then there are 36 possible ways to do this and so $P(x)=36/88=9/22$. Similarly, the complementary probability of an event (all the events that are not x) is $1-P(x)$. So the probability of selecting a white key x on the piano can be calculated by complementing the probability of black keys, or $P(x)= 1-9/22=13/22$. In a continuous distribution, probability is defined over an area under a distribution curve. This means that the probability of any single event, or "point" is zero since it has no area. This sounds odd but since probability is the ratio of the number of ways an event can happen to the total number of events then if there are an infinite number of events the probability of any single event is zero.

Lisp's `random` function generates numbers in both discrete and continuous distributions. By specifying an integer range to `random` only integers will be returned. If the range is expressed as a real, or floating point value, then continuous values within the limits of floating point precision are returned. The `random` function always returns a value between zero less than the bounds specified to the function. To generate any other range of values, or to randomly generate non-numeric values, requires that the output from `random` be scaled and offset, or used as indices into lists of non-numeric data. These kinds of manipulations are such a common occurrence in composition that Common Music provides a number of different functions to facilitate chance operations in musical contexts. These functions are listed together here and then discussed at appropriate places later in this chapter.

(between *low high* [*skip*])	[Function]
(odds *prob* [*then*] [*else*])	[Function]
(pick ...)	[Function]
(pickl *list* [:start *i*] [:end *i*] [:skip *x*])	[Function]
(ran [:type *k*] [:a *n*] [:b *n*])	[Function]
(shuffle *list* [:start *i*] [:end *i*])	[Function]
(tendency *n env1 env2* [:offset *n*] [:scale *n*])	[Function]
(vary *n pct* [*where*])	[Function]

Probability Distributions

The probability of events in a random process is determined by a *probability distribution* — a mathematical function that describes the likelihood of all possible outcomes. Distributions can be characterized by a *mean,* or average, value that they produce and by a characteristic "shape" that the probability expresses over the events in the random process. One of the great advantages to using a computer to work with random processes is that it is possible for a composer to employ complex distributions without needing to understand the underlying mathematics of their implementation which can be quite complex for some types of randomness. Composers who are interested in a formal presentation of random number generation should read Knuth's Seminumerical Algorithms, volume 2 of The Art of Computer Programming (Knuth) , which contains the definitions of many random number generators with different probability characteristics. Computer Music (Dodge) by Charles Dodge and Thomas Jerse also contains an excellent discussion of probability theory and random number distributions.

In the next few sections we define the characteristics of some common distributions. Each example includes a graphical plot of sampled events together with a *histogram* that depicts a characteristic density of events that each probability distribution generates. The histograms were generated by analyzing the output from a musical process that maps random values onto a range of integer MIDI key numbers. The musical processes that generated the results are shown in each example. Such a process can be listened to in "discrete" mode — quantized to the closest MIDI key number — or in "continuous" mode, by using the channel tuning methods discussed in Chapter 14 to output microtonal frequency values. Example 1 contains the basic process definition we will use to sonify the distributions. The sound example provided for each distribution plays the distribution in continuous mode.

Example 1. Mapping distributions onto frequency space.

- -

```
(define (play-ran type len rate key1 key2)
  (process repeat len
           for r = (ran :type type)
           for k = (rescale r 0.0 1.0 key1 key2)
           output (new midi :time (now)
                             :keynum k
                             :duration (* rate 1.5)
                             :amplitude .5 )
           wait rate))

;;; channel tuning on first 9 channels

(define ct9 (list true 0 8))

(define (mean-ran type n a b)
  (/ (loop repeat n
           sum (ran :type type :a a :b b))
     n))
```

- -

The `play-ran` function in Example 1 maps values from Common Music's `ran` function onto a range of key numbers specified to the process. The `ran` function generates random numbers in a distribution specified using its `:type` keyword argument. The following distribution types are supported:

    `:uniform`   `:low`   `:high`   `:triangular`   `:beta`
    `:exponential`   `:cauchy`   `:poisson`   `:gamma`
    `:gaussian`

If the `:type` argument is not specified then the uniform distribution is generated. See the documentation on `ran` in the Common Music Dictionary for more information about this function.

The `mean-ran` function calculates the *mean*, or average, value of n outcomes of `ran`. This gives us some measure of how well the pseudo-random number generator approximates the theoretical mean value of each distribution type.

Uniform distribution

In a *uniform distribution* all events have an equal likelihood of being selected. This means that in a discrete selection over n events, each event has $1/n$ probability of being selected. In a continuous distribution the events under two equal portions of the total probability range will have an equal likelihood of selection with a mean value of .5. Lisp's `random` function return numbers in a uniform distribution. These values can then be filtered or processed in different ways to produce non-uniform behavior.

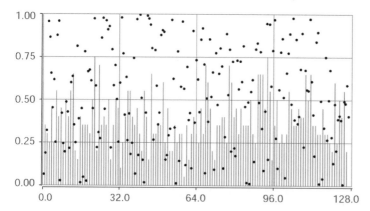

Figure 1. Two plots depicting values (points) and histogram (bars) of uniform distribution. The Y axis plots continuous random values normalized 0-1. The x axis plots the histogram range defined over 127 key numbers.

Interaction 1. Playing continuous uniform distribution.

```
cm> (events (play-ran :uniform 100 .1 20 100)
            "uniform.mid"
            :channel-tuning ct9)
"uniform-1.mid"
cm>
```

→ nm/18/snd/uniform-1.mid

Linear "low-pass" distribution

In a linear "low-pass" distribution the probability of larger numbers decreases linearly over the range of values returned by the process. The low-pass behavior is implemented by filtering a uniform process such that the minimum of two uniformly chosen numbers is returned:

```
(min (random 1.0) (random 1.0))
```

The expected mean value of the low-pass distribution is .2929.

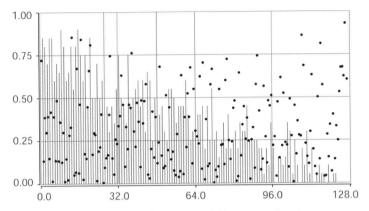

Figure 2. Low pass values (points) and histogram (bars).

Interaction 2. Playing the low pass distribution.

```
cm> (events (play-ran :low 50 .1 20 100) "low.mid"
            :channel-tuning ct9)
"low-1.mid"
cm>
```

⇢ nm/18/snd/low-1.mid

Linear "high-pass" distribution

In a linear "high-pass" distribution the probability of larger numbers increases linearly over the range of values. The distribution can be implemented by returning the maximum of two uniform random numbers:

```
(max (random 1.0) (random 1.0))
```

The expected mean value of the high distribution is .2929.

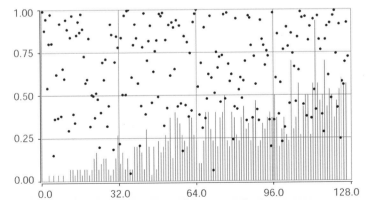

Figure 3. High pass values (points) and histogram (bars).

Interaction 3. Playing the high pass distribution.

```
cm> (events (play-ran :high 50 .1 20 100) "high.mid"
            :channel-tuning ct9)
"high-1.mid"
cm>
```

→ nm/18/snd/high-1.mid

Mean distribution

In a mean distribution the probability of numbers in the middle of the distribution increases linearly. A mean distribution can be implemented by averaging two uniform random numbers:

```
(/ (+ (random 1.0) (random 1.0)) 2))
```

The expected mean value of the distribution is .5.

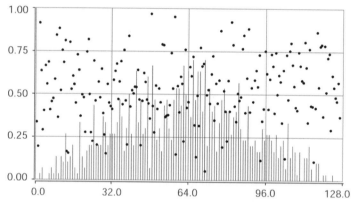

Figure 4. Mean distribution values (points) and histogram (bars).

Interaction 4. Playing the mean distribution.

```
cm> (events (play-ran :triangular 50 .1 20 100)
            "tri.mid" :channel-tuning ct9)
"tri-1.mid"
cm>
```

→ nm/18/snd/tri-1.mid

Exponential distribution

The exponential distribution returns the natural logarithm of a uniformly chosen number.

```
(/ (- (log (- 1 (random 1.0))))) a))
```

The *a* parameter provides a "stretching factor" that scales values closer to or further away from 0; the larger the value of *a* the more the values are pushed toward zero. If random returns 0 then $\log_e 1$ is 0, the minimum value in the distribution. As random values exceed *1/e* (0.367) the values returned in the distribution exceed 1.0. There is no upper limit to values produced in the exponential distribution but 99% of the time its value is less than 6.908. The expected mean value of the exponential distribution for *a=1* is .693.

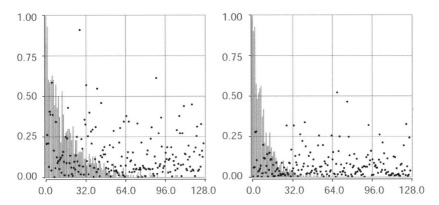

Figure 5. Exponential distribution (points) and histogram (bars) for *a=1* and *a=2*.

Example 2. An exponential distribution.

```
(define (play-exp len rate key1 key2 a)
  (process repeat len
           for r = (ran :type :exponential :a a)
           for k = (rescale r 0.0 6.908 key1 key2)
           when (< k 128)
           output (new midi :time (now)
                        :keynum k
                        :duration (* rate 1.5)
                        :amplitude .5 )
           and wait rate))
```

The play-exp process passes the *a* stretching factor to the ran function. Since the distribution is unbounded the conditional clause insures that only valid MIDI key numbers will be output.

Interaction 5. Playing the exponential distribution for a=1.

```
cm> (events (play-exp 50 .1 20 100 1) "exp.mid"
            :channel-tuning ct9)
"exp-1.mid"
cm>
```

→ nm/18/snd/exp-1.mid

Gaussian distribution

The Gaussian, or normal, distribution returns values that fall under the normal curve. The spread, or *standard deviation* is 1.0 centered at 0, so 68.26% of the results are between -1 and 1, and 99.74% of the results are between -3 and 3.

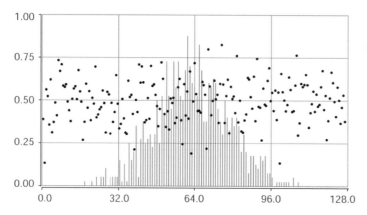

Figure 6. Gaussian distribution values (points) and histogram (bars).

Example 3. A Gaussian distribution.

```
(define (play-gauss len rate key1 key2)
  (process repeat len
           for r = (ran :type :gaussian)
           for k = (rescale r 0.0 3 key1 key2)
           when (<= 0 k 127)
           output (new midi :time (now)
                         :keynum k
                         :duration (* rate 1.5)
                         :amplitude .5 )
           and wait rate))
```

Interaction 6. Playing a Gaussian distribution.

```
cm> (events (play-gauss 50 .1 20 100) "gauss.mid"
            :channel-tuning ct9)
"gauss-1.mid"
cm>
```

→ nm/18/snd/gauss-1.mid

Beta distribution

The Beta distribution is one of the most musically interesting distributions to work with because it really describes a whole family of distribution shapes. The beta distribution is controlled by two parameters *a* and *b*. When *a=b=1* then a uniform distribution results. When *a=b*, the distribution is symmetric around .5. When *a<1* and *b<1* the density of large and small numbers increases. When *a>1* and *b>1* density is similar to the Gaussian distribution.

Example 4. The beta distribution.

```
(define (play-beta len rate a b key1 key2)
  (process repeat len
          for r = (ran :type :beta :a a :b b)
          for k = (rescale r 0.0 1.0 key1 key2)
          output (new midi :time (now)
                       :keynum k
                       :duration (* rate 1.5)
                       :amplitude .5 )
          wait rate))
```

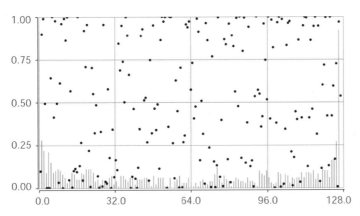

Figure 7. Beta distribution values (points) and histogram (bars).

Interaction 7. Playing the beta distribution for a=b=.4.

```
cm> (events (play-beta 50 .1 .4 .4 20 90) "beta.mid"
            :channel-tuning ct9)
"beta-1.mid"
cm>
```

➡nm/18/snd/beta-1.mid

Random Processes in Music Composition

Both continuous and discrete random processes are used in computer composition to control the evolution of parameterized data. But — as may be noticed in the preceding examples — simply mapping random distributions directly onto sound parameters does not really translate into interesting musical results. The lack of correlation between events in a random process causes our interest to diminish rapidly as we listen. There are really only two ways to deal with this issue. One method is to reserve the use of randomness for aspects in a composition that do not affect its structural integrity. The other method is to control randomness in some manner such that the listener either perceives an underlying structure unfolding or at least has some expectation of regularity, or *correlation* in the pattern. The remaining sections of the chapter present different approaches to controlling random processes such that they generate more interesting musical results than the basic distributions on which they are based.

Sampling Without Replacement

Generating discrete random values using an expression like (random 88) is called *sampling*. Sampling can be performed two different ways. *Sampling with replacement* means that once a value has been sampled it is still available to be sampled again. For example, if key number 60 is generated by (random 88) then 60 can be still be selected as a possible next value. *Sampling without replacement* describes a process in which generated values are not returned to the population once they have been selected. This is similar to how cards are dealt from a shuffled deck. By using sampling without replacement, a composer randomly *reorders* a set of specific values whose relationships are otherwise fixed. This reordering can be perceived as a kind of "freshness" in the data. The function shuffle can be used to implement sampling without replacement. Shuffle randomly permutes a list of values, which can then be sampled one at a time to produce a random ordering without repetition.

Example 5. Sampling without replacement.

```
- - - - - - - - - - - - - - - - - - - - - - - - - - - - - - - - - - - - - - - - - - - - - - - - - - - - .
(define (sampling reps rate notes )
  (let ((len (length notes)))
    (process for i below reps
             for j = (mod i len)
             when (= j 0)  ; need to reshuffle?
             set notes = (shuffle notes)
             output (new midi :time (now)
                         :keynum (list-ref notes j)
                         :duration (* rate 1.5)
                         :amplitude
                         (interp j 0 .4 (- len 1) .8))
             wait rate)))
- - - - - - - - - - - - - - - - - - - - - - - - - - - - - - - - - - - - - - - - - - - - - - - - - - - - .
```

Our `sampling` process also produces a crescendo that starts over again each time the values are shuffled so that each "period" in the population can be easily heard. Note that while shuffling avoids direct repetition within the period, there may still be a direct repetition between the last note of a period and the first note of the next.

Interaction 8. Calling shuffle.

```
cm> (events (sampling 80 .1 '(c d ef f g a bf c5))
            "shuffle.mid")
"shuffle-1.mid"
cm>
```

→ nm/18/snd/shuffle-1.mid

Direct Reselection

Direct reselection can be an issue anytime discrete random selection is used. When the range of random values is sufficiently large direct repetition may be so infrequent that it does not have a noticeable effect on the results. But as the number of events in a discrete random process diminishes the likelihood of direct reselection increases. At some point this may cause an unwanted regularity in musical results. One way to deal with this issue is to pass an optional *omit* value to the `between` function to avoid direct reselection. The following process can be used experiment with the effects of allowing or inhibiting direct reselection.

Example 6. Avoiding direct repetition in discrete distributions.

- -
```
(define (reps len lb ub skip?)
  (process repeat len
           for l = (if skip? k false)
           for k = (between lb ub l)
           output (new midi time (now)
                       :keynum k :duration .2)
           wait .125))
```
- -

If *skip?* is true then the variable *l* is the omit value so direct repetition of *l* cannot occur. If *skip?* is false then direct selection is possible.

Interaction 9. Random selection with and without direct repetition.

```
cm> (events (reps 30 60 63 false) "reps.mid")
"reps-1.mid"
cm> (events (reps 30 60 63 true) "reps.mid")
"reps-2.mid"
cm>
```

→ nm/18/snd/reps-1.mid
→ nm/18/snd/reps-2.mid

Variance

Continuous random selection is commonly used to provide variance for otherwise static parameter values. For example, by scaling a regular tempo or pulse value by a small random percentage the actual rate of events will fluctuate over time and produce a more natural effect than a fixed rate would. If the variance is small enough these fluctuations will not affect the perception of an underlying structural pulse. The process definition in Example 7 can be used to experiment with random variance applied to the pulse, amplitude and duration of events.

Example 7. The tapping process.

```
(define (tapping reps pct rate key amp)
  (let ((half (/ reps 2)))
    (process for i below reps
             for v = (if (< i half) 0 pct)
             output (new midi :time (now)
                         :duration (vary .1 v )
                         :keynum key
                         :amplitude (vary amp v :below))
             wait (vary rate v))))
```

The `tapping` process plays a single *key* number *reps* times at a specified *rate* and amplitude. The events in the first half of the process are played with fixed values and in the second half the values vary by up to *pct* amount of their values. By default the function `vary` distributes variance equally on either side of the fixed value. To produce variance that is always less than the value use `:below` as the third argument to `vary`. Similarly, the keyword `:above` will offset the variance above the value.

Interaction 10. Comparing 10% variance with 50% variance.

```
cm> (events (tapping 50 .1 .2 72 .6) "tap.mid")
"tap-1.mid"
cm> (events (tapping 50 .5 .2 72 .6) "tap.mid")
"tap-2.mid"
cm>
```

→nm/18/snd/tap-1.mid
→nm/18/snd/tap-2.mid

Even something as simple as random variation of a beat can be made musically interesting if it is controlled in some manner. In the next example the amount of variation applied to the beat is controlled by an envelope. When the envelope is at 0 then no variation occurs, when the envelope is at 1 then full variance is expressed. By using an envelope to control random variance the process can interpolate over the full continuum between completely random time increments and a strictly measured pulse. The same envelope that controls the beat will also be used to provide a value for the *a* and *b* beta distribution parameters that generates amplitude values for the process. When the control envelope is at zero (no random variance) then the beta distribution will be *a=b=.4* and will produce a large percentage of loud and soft values (Figure 7). When the envelope is at 1 then the beta distribution will be *a=b=1* and will produce values in the uniform distribution. When the control envelope is at zero (no random variance) then the beta distribution will be at (beta *a=b=1*) and produce values in the uniform distribution. When the envelope is at 1 (full random variance) then *a=b=.4*) and a large percentage of loud and soft values are produced. The shape of the envelope defined in Example 8 causes the process to begin and end with random time values and to express the strict pulse in the middle.

Example 8. The rain process.

```
(define (rain len rate env key1 key2 amp)
  (process for i below len
           for e = (interpl (/ i len) env)
           for v = (vary rate e :above)
           ;; rescale e to control shape of
           ;; beta distribution
           ;; when e=0 z=.4, and when e=1 z=1.
           for z = (rescale e 0 1 1 .4)
           for b = (ran :type :beta :a z :b z)
           output (new midi :time (+ (now) v)
                            :duration v
                            :keynum (between key1 key2)
                            :amplitude
                            (rescale b 0 1 .1 amp))
           wait rate))
(define rain-env '(0 1 .4 0 .6 0 1 1))
```

We listen to three simultaneous versions of the `rain` process, each with different length beats.

Interaction 11. Listening to rain.

```
cm> (events (list (rain 80 .5 rain-env 70 90 .8)
                  (rain 40 1 rain-env 40 60 .8)
                  (rain 20 2 rain-env 20 40 .9))
            "rain.mid")
"rain-1.mid"
cm>
```

➟ nm/18/snd/rain-1.mid

Shape-based composition

By applying a random variance to envelope values we can generate random variations on the basic shape of the envelope:

Example 9. Adding a random variance to envelope values.
- .
```
(define (shaper len rate env key1 key2)
  (process for i below len
           for e = (interpl (/ i len) env )
           for k = (rescale e 0 1 key1 key2)
           for r = (between -5 5)
           output (new midi :time (now)
                          :keynum (+ k r)
                          :duration rate)
           wait (* rate (pick .5 .25 1)))))

(define shape-env
  '(0 0 .2 1 .4 .25 .6 .5 .8 0 1 .5))
```
- .

The process in Example 9 scales and offsets values from an envelope to generate a range of key numbers specified to the process. A random amount is then added to the the key number to shift it upwards or downwards.

Interaction 12. Listening to two variations of the same envelope.

```
cm> (events (list (shaper 40 1 shape-env 70 90)
                  (shaper 40 1 shape-env 60 80)
                  (shaper 20 2 shape-env 60 48))
            "shape.mid")
"shape-1.mid"
cm> (events (list (shaper 40 1 shape-env 70 90)
                  (shaper 40 1 shape-env 60 80)
                  (shaper 20 2 shape-env 60 48))
            "shape.mid")
"shape-2.mid"
cm>
```

➙ nm/18/snd/shape-1.mid
➙ nm/18/snd/shape-2.mid

Tendency masks

Tendency masking, first described by the composer Gottfried Michael Koenig, is a technique related to the shape-based approach. A tendency mask uses two envelopes to specify the lower and upper boundaries for random selection. By describing each boundary as an envelope the range of the random variable can vary as a function of time, or of some other dynamic process. Common Music's `tendency` function returns a random value given an *x* lookup value, and a lower and upper envelope that define the boundaries.

Example 10. Tendency masking.

```
(define low-mask '(0 .4 .75 .4 1 0))
(define top-mask '(0  1 .25 .6 1 .6))

(define (masker len rate lower upper key1 key2)
  (let ((last (- len 1)))
    (process for i to last
             for e = (tendency (/ i last) lower upper)
             for k = (rescale e 0 1 key1 key2)
             output (new midi :time (now)
                         :duration rate
                         :keynum k)
             wait rate)))
```

In this example two envelopes *lower* and *upper* control the range of random selection. The variable *e* is set to a random value between an interpolated lower and upper bounds in the two envelopes specified to `tendency`. This random value, which lies between zero and one, is then rescaled to lie between the key numbers *key1* and *key2* passed as arguments to the process.

Interaction 13. Listening to masker.

```
cm> (events (masker 80 .1 low-mask top-mask 20 110)
            "masker.mid")
"masker-1.mid"
cm>
```

→nm/18/snd/masker-1.mid

Weighted Random Selection

In *weighted random selection* individual probability weights are assigned to each event in a discrete random process. This affords more precise control over the total mix of outcomes than would otherwise be possible using one of the basic distributions discussed in this chapter. Common Music's `odds` function implements a simple binary form of weighted random selection that is identical to the `chance?` function from Chapter 7 except that values other than true and false can be returned by `odds`). More complex forms of weighted selection are presented in Chapter 19 and Chapter 20, but these discussions assume an understanding of probability tables, which we present here.

Probability tables

A probability table associates each outcome in a discrete random process with a specific portion, or segment, of the total probability range. The size of each segment reflects the proportional likelihood of that value being generated from the random process. To generate the next value from a table, a uniformly distributed random value is generated and the table is searched to find the probability segment that contains the random lookup value. The datum associated with that segment is then returned from the table as the random value. The implementation defined in Example 11 allows us to specify probabilities in terms of relative *weights* that are associated with each possible outcome in the random process. The function that creates the probability table will convert these relative weights into absolute portions of the total probability interval from 0 to 1. To see how this works, consider a weighted random process that generates four rhythmic symbols: S, E, Q and H where S should be three times as likely Q, E should be twice as likely as Q and H should 1/4 as likely as Q (Table 1).

Table 1. Example probability table for four rhythmic outcomes.

index	0	1	2	3
outcome	s	e	q	h
weight	3	2	1	1/4
segment	0.0-0.48	0.048-0.8	0.8-0.96	0.96-1.0

Our implementation of probability tables (ptables) in Example 11 requires two functions. The first function `make-ptable` creates a ptable from a list of outcomes and weights. The `pran` function then generates a random outcome given a ptable.

Example 11. Implementing probability tables.

```
(define (make-ptable data)
  (let ((total (loop for d in data sum (second d)))
        (sum 0))
    ;; total holds sum of weights in data
    (loop for d in data
          for v = (first d)        ; outcome to return
          for w = (second d)       ; relative weight
          do (set! sum (+ sum w))
          ;; collect outcome and normalized probability
          collect (list v (/ sum total)))))

(define (pran table)
  ;; return outcome in table according
  ;; to its weighted probability
  (let ((x (random 1.0)))
    ;; x is uniform number < 1.
```

```
(loop for d in table
      for p = (second d)
      when (< x p )    ; x in this segment.
      return (first d))))
```

A probability table is represented as a list of lists, the first element of each sublist is an outcome and the second element is its weight relative to the other outcomes defined in the list. For example, the probability table described in Table 1 would be specified as the list:

```
((s 3) (e 2) (q 1) (h 1/4))
```

The make-ptable function creates a probability table from *data*, a list of values and weights as shown above. The table returned by make-ptable is identical to *data* except that the relative probability weights are converted to equivalent absolute segments along the probability interval 0-1. The variable *total* is set to the sum of the relative weights in *data*. The loop then iterates over each sublist *d* in *data* and sets the variable *v* to the outcome and *w* to its relative weight. This weight is summed and converted to increasing values between 0 and 1 by calculating the current ratio of *sum* to the *total* weight. Thus the ptable returned by the function contains the same outcomes as *data* but with relative weights converted to absolute points along the probability range 0-1.

The function pran implements weighted random selection given a ptable. It first generates a uniform random number *x* between 0 and 1. The loop iterates over each element in the table and compares *x* to its probability value *p*. Since probability values are stored in increasing order, the first occurrence of *x* less than *p* is the probability segment that stores the random outcome to return.

Given our implementation of probability tables we can now define a process to generate values using weighted random selection:

Example 12. Weighted random selection of notes and rhythms.

```
(define note-tabl
  (make-ptable '((c 3) (d 1) (ef 2) (f 1) (g 3)
                 (af 1) (bf 1) (c5 3) )))

(define rhy-tabl
  (make-ptable '((s 3) (e 2) (q 1)  (h 1/4))))

(define (play-pran reps notes rhys tempo)
  (process repeat reps for k = (keynum (pran notes))
           for r = (rhythm (pran rhys) tempo)
           output (new
                      midi :time (now) :keynum k
                      :duration (* r 1.5))
           wait r))
```

The probability table defined in *notes* "prefers" notes of a C-minor triad in the C-minor scale. The table stored in *rhys* contains the example shown in Table 1.

Interaction 14. Listening to Pran

```
cm> (events (play-pran 50 note-tabl rhy-tabl 100)
"ptab.mid")
"ptab-1.mid"
cm>
```

➙ nm/18/snd/ptab-1.mid

Random walks

The term *random walk* describes a random process in which a value is *incremented* by a random amount. The motion produced by a random walk is reminiscent of how a drunk staggers around when walking: on each step the location of the drunk changes by the amount of the random step. This type of motion is also characteristic of how molecules and very small particles move (Brownian motion) and for that reason it is sometimes referred to as *brown noise*.

Because the next value in a random walk must lie within a certain interval from the current value, the current value has a very strong influence on the next outcome. The influence of past values on successive values is called *correlation*. The correlation in a random walk is characterized by a $1/f^2$ spectrum, which means that small rates of change are much more present than larger ones. This is a very different behavior than the uniform distribution, or *white noise*, which exhibits large changes just as frequently as small ones since there is no correlation between successive values at all.

A random walk is easy to implement in a musical algorithm. A walking value x is initialized to some appropriate starting value and then incremented by a random amount (positive or negative) on each iteration of the process. A moment's reflection will tell us that at some point an *unbounded* walk will likely exceed the limits of whatever sound parameter it is controlling. For this reason random walks that control parameterized data are typically *bounded*, or constrained, in some manner such that they will always lie within minimum and maximum parameter values. There are no hard and fast rules on how to adjust values that wander past boundaries: common adjustments include resetting value to the boundary value, reflecting the value back into bounds, randomly repositioning the value to somewhere within the range, or stopping the process altogether.

Common Music's `drunk` function implements bounded or unbounded random walks and its optional keyword arguments constrain values to lie within specified `:low` and `:high` boundaries. A value that exceeds its bounds is adjusted according to the `:mode` argument. Possible modes are:

> `:reflect :limit :reset :jump :stop`

The default mode is `:reflect`, which "wraps" a value back into bounds by its excess amount. Example 13 defines a process that uses `drunk` to generate a random melody.

Example 13. Random walks applied to keynum and amplitude.

```
(define (stagger len low high step)
  (let ((k (/ (- high low) 2))
        (a (between .1 .9)))
    (process repeat len
         for r = (pick 1/8 1/4)
         set k = (drunk k step :low low :high high :mode :jump)
         output (new midi :time (now)
                      :duration (* r 1.5)
                      :keynum k :amplitude a)
             wait r)))
```

K is a key number controlled by a random walk between *key1* and *key2*. On each iteration of the process the key number can deviate by up to *step* steps from its current position. The :mode keyword argument controls the boundary rule of the walk. Its value :jump forces an out-of-bounds value to be reset to a randomly chosen position within bounds.

Interaction 15. Listening to the stagger process.

```
cm> (events (stagger 50 40 80 3) "drunk.mid")
"drunk-1.mid"
cm> (events (stagger 50 20 90 7) "drunk.mid")
"drunk-2.mid"
cm>
```

→ nm/18/snd/drunk-1.mid
→ nm/18/snd/drunk-2.mid

Example

The final example in this chapter was provided by Michael Klingbeil from some studies he made for an orchestra piece. The example generates a series of exponential gestures, each of which consists of an upward "arc" of microtonal notes. This short example uses many of the functions presented in this chapter as well as the exponential scaling functions from Chapter 16 and the harmonic series from Chapter 15.

Example 14. Using randomness in scaling and tuning.

- -.

```
(define (arpeggiate-exprhy keynums time rate
                          midpoint-frac amplow amphi
                          legato bass-legato
                          bass-cutoff last-legato)
  (let* ((segs (length keynums))
         (last (1- segs))
         (midpoint (floor (* segs midpoint-frac)))
         ;; deltas below midpoint follow one curve,
         ;; above another.
         (deltas (append (explsegs
                           midpoint
                           (* midpoint-frac time)
                           rate)
                         (explsegs
                           (- segs midpoint)
                           (* (- 1 midpoint-frac) time)
                           (/ 1 rate)))))
    (process for i from 0
             for k in keynums
             for d in deltas
             for r = (if (< k bass-cutoff)
                         bass-legato
                         (if (= i last)
                             (* last-legato d)
                             (* legato d)))
             for a = (between 0.45 0.5)
             then (drunk a 0.1 :low amplow :high amphi)
             output (new midi :time (now)
                             :keynum k
                             :amplitude a
                             :duration r)
             wait d)))
```

- -.

The argeggiate-exprhy process creates both upward and downward "arcs" of
MIDI events from a specified set of key numbers. The rhythms of each arc are
determined by dividing a total time duration into two segments of exponentially
related rhythms. The *midpoint-frac* is a proportion that determines the duration of
each relative to the total *time* specified to the process. This duration is then
"chopped up" into exponentially related time values that sum to the duration of the
arc using explsegs. The amplitude *a* for the each event is determined by a
random walk. The *amplow* and *amphi* parameters control the overall range of the
random walk. *Bass-legato* sets the duration of notes with keynum less than *bass-cutoff*. This allows the bass notes to ring even when the synthesizer does voice
stealing for the middle notes of the arpeggio. *Last-legato* extends the duration of the
final note of an arpeggio for similar reasons.

We now define a calling process that schedules a series of overlapping arpeggiations whose key numbers are determined by distorting the harmonic series:

Example 15. Arpeggiated harmonic distortions.

```
(define (distort-harmonics fund distort)
  (loop for h from 1 below (floor (/ 25.0 distort))
        if (odds (* 0.9 distort))
        collect (keynum (* fund (expt h distort))
                        :hertz)))

(define (arpa-harmonic note dur gap)
  (process with fund = (hertz note)
           for distort from 0.7 below 1.05 by 0.05
           for notes = (distort-harmonics fund distort)
           sprout
           (arpeggiate-exprhy notes
                              (* (vary dur 0.1) distort)
                              (between 4.0 0.25)
                              (between 0.3 0.6)
                              0.3   ; amplow
                              0.8   ; amphi
                              (* dur distort 0.7)
                              2.0    ; legato
                              59     ; bass cutoff
                              1.0)   ; last-legato
           wait (vary gap 0.4))))
```

Arpa-harmonic spawns overlapping arpeggios with maximum mean duration *dur* and rhythm of *gap* seconds. Each arpeggio is a distorted harmonic series. The distortion factor varies from 0.7 (compressed spectrum) to 1.0 (harmonic spectrum) by increments of 0.05. The greater the compression, the lesser the odds of selecting an element of the spectrum. When the distortion reaches 1.0 the spectrum is harmonic and on average 90% of the elements will be selected.

Interaction 16. Arpeggiated harmonic distortions.

```
cm> (events (arpa-harmonic 'g1 7.0 5.0) "arp.mid"
            :channel-tuning ct9)
"arp-1.mid"
cm> (events (arpa-harmonic 'g1 6.0 5.0) "arp.mid"
            :channel-tuning ct9)
"arp-2.mid"
cm>
```

→ nm/18/snd/arp-1.mid
→ nm/18/snd/arp-2.mid

Chapter Source Code

The source code to all of the examples and interactions in this chapter can be found in the file chance.cm located in the same directory as the HTML file for this chapter. The source file can be edited in a text editor or evaluated inside the Common Music application.

References

Knuth, D.E. (1981). *The Art of Computer Programming*. Reading: Addison-Wesley.
Dodge, C. & Jerse, T. (1985). *Computer Music*. New York: Schirmer Books.

19

Markov Processes

The previous chapter introduced random number generation and presented some simple strategies for producing musical results that are more interesting than directly mapping distributions onto sound parameters. Without these controls probability distributions sound incoherent due to a lack of correlation between the generated samples. But in a random walk there is a great deal of correlation between successive events and the results can sound almost too coherent! A *Markov process*, or *Markov chain*, is a type of random process closely related to the random walk that is capable of producing different degrees of correlation between its random outcomes. In a Markov process past events represent a *state*, or context, for determining the probabilities of subsequent events. The number of past events considered by the process is called its *order*. In a first order process the probabilities for choosing the next event depend only on the immediately preceding event. In a second order Markov process the probabilities for the next choice depend on the last two events. A Markov process can reflect any number of past choices, including the degenerate case of no past choices. A zero order Markov Process is equivalent to weighted random selection.

Because past choices influence subsequent choices, a Markov process can model, or mimic, different degrees of variation in patterns of data. The higher the order, the closer the process comes to matching the pattern it models. The pattern on which a Markov process is based can be invented by the composer or determined by a statistical analysis of data. We will examine both methods for creating Markov processes later in this chapter.

Conditional Probability and Transition Tables

A Markov process exhibits *conditional probability*, in which the probability of the next outcome depends on one or more past outcomes. This means that the probability distribution of the random process changes dynamically as a function of the outcomes that the process has already produced. For two independent events x and y, the conditional probability $P(x|y)$ is equal to the product of the probability of x and y alone. For example, the probability of "heads" appearing in a coin toss is $P(h)=.5$. The conditional probability of consecutive heads $P(h|h)$ is equal to the products $.5*.5=.25$. The probability of tossing three heads is $.5*.5*.5=.125$ and so on. Higher order processes can be described by multiplying the probabilities stored in a first order table or by explicitly storing past outcomes in a table and then matching these against a *history* of outcomes to determine the probability of future outcomes. A table that establishes this linkage is called a *transition table*. A transition table is really a table of probability tables. Each transition represents a probability distribution for a specific set of past outcomes. In a first order Markov process there is only one past outcome for each transition. In a second order process each transition would refer to a pair of past outcomes.

We demonstrate the relationship between probability tables and transition tables by transforming the probability table shown in Table 1 into a transition table and then implementing new behavior not possible using a probability table alone. Table 1 is a model of a fair coin toss. There are only two possible outcomes, h (heads) and t (tails), each of which has an equal probability of being selected. The outcomes appear as columns in the table and the cells hold each outcome's probability.

Table 1. Probability table for a fair coin toss. Heads is labeled h and tails t.

h	t
0.50	0.50

Table 1 can be turned into a first order transition table by adding a *transition row* for each possible outcome. In our example there are only two possible outcomes (h and t) so our table will have two transition rows. The converted table acts as a kind of "feed back" loop: random outcomes are generated from the "top" of the table (labeled next in Table 2) and then return to the table as past outcomes (marked past). The transition row that matches the current past outcome will then generate the next outcome according to its particular probability distribution.

Table 2. Transition table for a fair coin toss.

		next	
		h	t
past	h	0.50	0.50
	t	0.50	0.50

The random outcomes generated by Table 2 will have the same probability distribution as Table 1. The following sequence depicts 20 representative outcomes:

t h t t h h h t t t h h t h h h t h t t

But using the transition table shown in Table 2 we can now implement two different patterns of outcomes that are impossible to produce using the probability table in Table 1. These new patterns can be created simply by changing the weights in the cells, without altering the structure of the table at all. For example, the next table (Table 3) produces a "biased" coin toss that always favors heads, particularly if the last value chosen was tails:

Table 3. Transition table for a biased coin toss.

		next	
		h	t
past	h	0.75	0.25
	t	1.00	0.00

Representative outcomes from Table 3:

t h t h h h h h t h h t h h h h h t h h

The weights in Table 3 cause tails to always produce heads, and heads to usually produce heads.

In Table 4 we implement a "persistent" coin toss in which the next outcome (heads or tails) tends to be the same as the past outcome.

Table 4. Transition table for a persistent coin toss.

		next	
		h	t
past	h	0.60	0.40
	t	0.20	0.80

Representative outcomes from Table 4:

t t h t h t h h h t t t t t t t t h t t

Implementing transition tables

As we have seen in the previous section, transition tables can be represented by adapting our design for probability tables described in Chapter 18. Recall that the constructor function make-ptable created a probability table from a list of data that associated random events with their relative weights in the table. We start by observing what these probability lists would look like for each transition row in Table 4:

Table 5. Probability lists for Table 4.

	h	t
transition 1	((h .6)	(t .4))
transition 2	((h .2)	(t .8))

To turn these probability lists into transition lists only requires that we explicitly associate the past outcome with each set of probabilities. We can do this by adding the past outcome to the front of each probability list:

Table 6. Transition lists for Table 4.

	h	t
(h	(h .6)	(t .4))
(t	(h .2)	(t .8))

Each transition list is now a structure linking a past outcome with a probability distribution for generating the next outcome. The first element in each transition is the past outcome and the rest of the elements in the list are the probability pairs. Note that to implement a second order table each past value would be a list of past values. For example, a second order representation might look like:

Table 7. Second order transition lists.

	h	t
((h h)	(h .9)	(t .1))
((h t)	(h .9)	(t .1))
((t t)	(h .9)	(t .1))
((t h)	(h .9)	(t .1))

Notice that as the order of the Markov process increases so does the length of the transition table since each possible combination of past outcomes must be explicitly represented in the table.

In our implementation of transition tables, each ttable will consist of a list of transition rows. Each transition row will itself be a list that associates one or more past outcomes with a ptable (probability table) for generating the next outcome (Table 6.) To implement ttables will require only three new functions.

1. `make-ttable` creates a ttable from an external specification of its data.
2. `find-ptable` finds the ptable of a specified past outcome in a ttable.
3. `mran` returns the next random outcome given a ttable and past outcome.

Our implementation assumes that we have already defined the required ptable definitions presented in Example 11 of the previous chapter. These definitions are shown again here for the reader's convenience (Example 1).

Example 1. Ptable functions discussed in Chapter 18.

```
(define (make-ptable data)
  (let ((total (loop for d in data sum (second d)))
        (sum 0))
    ;; total holds sum of weights in data
    (loop for d in data
          for v = (first d)        ; outcome to return
          for w = (second d)       ; relative weight
          do (set! sum (+ sum w))
          ;; collect outcome and normalized probability
          collect (list v (/ sum total)))))

(define (pran table)
  ;; return outcome in table according
  ;; to its weighted probability
  (let ((x (random 1.0)))
    ;; x is uniform number < 1.
    (loop for d in table
          for p = (second d)
          when (< x p )    ; x in this segment.
          return (first d))))
```

We start by defining the function `make-ttable` that creates a transition table for generating Markov chains (Example 2).

Example 2. Defining a transition table constructor.

```
(define (make-ttable data)
  ;; create a transition table from data.
  (loop for trans in data
        for past = (first trans)
        for probs = (rest trans)
        ;; each row transition is a past value
        ;; and a ptable
        collect (list past (make-ptable probs))))
```

The function `make-ttable` creates a ttable (transition table) from a list of *data*. Each element in *data* is a transition list *trans*. The first element of each *trans* is a past outcome and the rest of the data are the probability pairs *probs* of its distribution. The `make-ttable` returns a ttable list as its value. Each element in the table is transition row that associates a past outcome with a probability table created by `make-ptable`.

Interaction 1. Creating a transition table from Table 4.

```
cm> (define coin
        (make-ttable '((h (h .6) (t .4))
                       (t (h .2) (t .8)))))

cm> (pprint coin)
((h ((h 0.6) (t 1.0)))
 (t ((h 0.2) (t 1.0))))
cm>
```

The next step is to define the function `find-ptable` which returns a `ptable` for a specified past outcome. This function will accept two arguments, the transition table *ttable* and the past outcome *past*, and will return the probability table associated with *past* in the transition table. The function will find the ptable by iterating over transition rows and matching each row's past outcome with *past*. If they are the equal then the probability table for that transition is returned. But what does "equal" actually mean? The past outcomes we search for might be numbers, symbols (as is the case in our example table) or even lists of data. How can we test for the equivalence of symbols and lists? The Lisp function `equal?` is a predicate for testing general equivalence between two Lisp objects:

Interaction 2. The equal? general equivalence predicate.

```
cm> (equal? 1 1)
#t
cm> (equal? 1 1.0)
#f
cm> (equal? 'a 'a)
#t
cm> (equal? '(t t) '(t t))
#t
cm> (equal? '(h t) '(t h))
#f
cm>
```

As a general rule of thumb, two objects are considered `equal?` if they look the same, otherwise they are not equal. Given the `equal?` general equivalence predicate we can define the probability table lookup function:

Example 3. A lookup function to find the ptable for a specified past outcome.

```
(define (find-ptable ttable past)
  ;; find the row matching past and return its ptable
  (loop for trans in ttable
        for this = (first trans)
        if (equal? this past)
        return (second trans)))
```

The function `find-ptable` searches a ttable and returns the ptable whose past outcome is equal to *past*. A loop iterates over each transition row *trans* in the table and compares *past* with the row's past outcome *this*. If these outcomes are `equal?` then the loop immediately returns the probability table stored as the second element of *trans*. Note that the case of not finding a match for a past outcome should not happen. If it does (through mistaken input by the caller) the function will return false.

Interaction 3. Looking up ptables for past outcomes.

```
cm> (find-ptable coin 't)
((h 0.2) (t 1.0))
cm> (find-ptable coin 'h)
((h 0.6) (t 1.0))
cm> (find-ptable coin 'xyz)
#f
cm>
```

The final step in the implementation is to define the function `mran` that implements Markov selection. The function is passed two inputs, a *ttable* and a *past* outcome and returns the next outcome. The outcome is generated by calling the `pran` function on the probability table returned by `find-ptable`. The `pran` function was discussed in the previous chapter and its definition is included here as well.

Example 4. Defining the Markov selection function.

```
(define (pran table)
  ;; return outcome in table according
  ;; to its weighted probability
  (let ((x (random 1.0)))
    ;; x is uniform number < 1.
    (loop for d in table
          for p = (second d)
          when (< x p )     ; x in this segment.
          return (first d))))
```

```
(define (mran ttable past)
  ;; find row matching past and return its ptable
  (let ((ptab (find-ptable ttable past)))
    (if ptab
        (pran ptab)
        #f)))
```

We can now use Markov selection to return values from our "coin":

Interaction 4. Two methods for Markov selection.

```
cm> (loop with past = 'h
          repeat 20
          for y = (mran coin past)
          collect y
          do (set! past y))
(h h t t t h h h h t t t t t h h t t t t)
cm> (loop repeat 20
          for next = 'h then (mran coin next)
          collect next)
(h h t t t t t h h t t h h t t t h h h t)
cm>
```

Interaction 4 demonstrates two different strategies for controlling Markov selection. The first method initializes a *past* to one of the possible outcomes in the table. Each iteration of the process then generates a value from the transition table and updates *past* with that value for the next iteration through the loop. The second method starts with a particular *next* outcome and then updates that value on each subsequent iteration. The second method is not only simpler than the first, it also allows the composer to start the random process with a specific initial value. Other strategies for controlling the starting and ending points of Markov processes will be presented in the next few examples.

Musical Examples

We will now use our implementation of transition tables in a several musical contexts. For examples of higher order Markov processes please see the discussion of the Markov pattern in Chapter 20.

Markov rhythmic patterns

Imagine generating a melody for a soloist in which rhythmic values are determined by random selection. Even if only very simple rhythms are used, a moments reflection should tell us that the patterns produced by the process will not reflect any underlying pattern of beat. For example, assume that the process is restricted to quarters, dotted-eights, eighths, and sixteenths (which we notate q, e., e, and s respectively). Since the random process can place sixteenths and dotted eighths anywhere within a beat, the sequence of rhythmic values that result will only occasionally line up with the start of a metric pulse:

→ nm/19/snd/uni-1.mid Uniform rhythmic distribution with tempo curve and random walk melody.

In this first Markov example we generate random rhythms that nevertheless express an underlying beat and tempo curve.

Example 5. Comparison of uniform and Markov rhythmic patterns.

```
(define rhy-table
  '((q   (q .5) (e  2) (e. .75) )
    (e   (e 3) (q 1) )
    (e.  (s 1))
    (s   (e 2) (q 1))))

(define tcurve '(0 1 .7 .75 1 1))   ; tempo envelope

(define (markov-rhythms len)
  ;; rhythms generated from first order Markov
  (let ((tbl (make-ttable rhy-table)))
    (process for i below len
             for k = 60 then (drunk k 6 :low 40 :high 80
                                          :mode :jump)
             for r = 'q then (mran tbl r)
             for d = (* (rhythm r 120)
                        (interpl (/ i len) tcurve))
             output (new midi :time (now) :keynum k
                         :duration d)
             wait d)))
```

The Markov table *rhy-table* assigns highest weight to eighth notes and the least weight to dotted eighths. If a dotted-eighth is played then the next value must be a sixteenth, which forces the pattern to return back to the beginning of the beat again. A random walk generates the melody.

Interaction 5. Listening to Markov rhythm patterns.

```
cm> (events (markov-rhythms 80) "rhy.mid")
"rhy-1.mid"
cm>
```

→ nm/19/snd/rhy-1.mid

The next version of the rhythmic example demonstrates an alternate method for controlling the Markov process. The table in Example 6 encodes two extra transitions that represent unique states in the process. A starting state for the table is represented by start transition row. The output from this transition is either a dotted-eighth or a quarter. A stopping state for the table is represented by the stop outcome of the whole note (w) transition row. If a whole note is selected then the table will be forced to return the unique outcome stop as its next value. A calling process can check for this symbol and terminate iteration as soon as it occurs.

Example 6. Markov rhythm with start and stop transitions.

```
(define rhy-table2
  '((start (e. 2) (q 1))
    (q  (q .5) (e  2) (e. .75) (w .2))
    (e  (e 3) (q 1) )
    (e. (s 1))
    (s  (e 2) (q 1))
    (w  (stop 1))))

(define (markov-rhythms2 )
  ;; rhythms generated from first order Markov with
  ;; explicit start and stop transitions.
  (let ((tabl (make-ttable rhy-table2))
        (past 'start))
    (process for k = 60 then (drunk k 6 :low 40 :high 80
                                                :mode :jump)
             for r = (mran tabl past)
             until (equal? r 'stop)
             for d = (rhythm r 120)
             output (new midi :time (now) :keynum k
                         :duration d)
             wait d
             set past = r)))
```

The process markov-rhythms2 checks to see if *r* is equal to stop, in which case the process immediately terminates. The disadvantage with this method is that there is no way to determine ahead of time how long the process will actually run!

Interaction 6. Listening to Markov rhythm patterns.

```
cm> (events (markov-rhythms2 ) "rhy.mid")
"rhy-2.mid"
cm>
```

→ nm/19/snd/rhy-2.mid

Markov melody

In our next example we use a Markov process to generate a pseudo Gregorian Chant. The intention is not to generate a stylistically correct chant, but rather to see how melodic motion can be constrained using a Markov chain and how the processes can mimic composition styles. For a much larger example of style generation see the Markov process example in Chapter 20 that implements the second order Stephen Foster table discussed in Computer Music (Dodge)

In the crudest of terms, a Gregorian Chant is characterized by mostly step wise motion within a range of modal degrees. From any given tone there is more likelihood that a chant will move a step up or down than leap to a tone further away. The larger the skip, the more unlikely it is to occur. In addition, certain tones, such as the final and tenor, have more influence over the melody than other tones. In the For example, in the Dorian mode the tenor A is occasionally decorated by the B-flat directly above it. This B-flat almost always returns back to the tenor tone. In an authentic mode, the final of the mode also acts as a kind of "reflecting boundary" that redirects the melody in the opposite direction. We can mimic these stylistic tendencies using a first order Markov process:

Example 7. Dorian Gregorian Chant

```
(define dchant
  '((d4   (d4 .1) (e4 .35) (f4 .25) (g4 .1) (a4 .15))
    (e4   (d4 .35) (f4 .35) (e4 .1) (g4 .1) (a4 .1))
    (f4   (d4 .2) (e4 .2) (f4 .1) (g4 .2) (a4 .12))
    (g4   (d4 .2) (e4 .1) (f4 .3) (g4 .1) (a4 .3)
          (bf4 .2))
    (a4   (d4 .1) (e4 .2) (f4 .25) (g4 .3) (a4 .1)
          (bf4 .3))
    (bf4  (a4 1))))

(define (monks1 len chant rhy)
  (let ((tbl (make-ttable chant)))
    (process repeat len
             for k = 'd4 then (mran tbl k)
             output (new midi :time (now)
                         :keynum k duration rhy)
             wait rhy)))
```

In Example 7 the Gregorian Chant is represented by a transition table that "prefers" step wise motion. Certain leaps, for example to the B-flat, are not allowed at all. B-flat can only be approached and left from the tenor note A. D4 is the final of the mode and reflects the melody upward, usually by step, but occasionally to the mediant or tenor tones as well.

Interaction 7. Listening to Markov monks.

```
cm> (events (monks1 30 dchant .8) "monks.mid")
"monks-1.mid"
cm>
```

➜ nm/19/snd/monks-1.mid

In this next example we look at several strategies for shaping a Markov process such that its results are more musically satisfying. We know, for example, that in Gregorian Chant the tenor and final notes are more likely to be agogically stressed than the other tones. Moreover, the chant should begin and end on the final of the mode.

Example 8. Markov with external conditional checks.

```
(define (chant-dur tone dur)
  ;; adjust dur if tone is D, F or A.
  (let ((doub (* dur 2)))
    (if (scale= tone 'd4)
        (odds .7 doub dur)
      (if (scale= tone 'a4)
          (odds .5 doub dur)
        (if (scale= tone 'f4)
            (odds .25 doub dur)
          dur)))))

(define (monks2 end chant rhy oct)
  (let ((tabl (make-ttable chant)))
    (process for k = 'd4 then (mran tabl k)
             for dur = (chant-dur k rhy)
             output (new midi :time (now)
                             :keynum (transpose k oct)
                             :amplitude .8
                             :duration dur)
             wait dur
             until (and (> (now) end)
                        (scale= k 'd4)))))
```

The monks2 process generates a note *k* from a first order Markov chant and then calls chant-dur to determine the rhythmic value for that tone. chant-dur tests *k* to see if it is the final (d), tenor (a) or mediant (f) tone. If *k* is the final then there is a 70% chance that its duration will be doubled. If *k* is the tenor then there is a 50% chance the tone will be doubled and if it is the mediant there is a 25% chance it will be doubled. The until clause stops the process if the current note is the mode's final and enough notes have been sung. The *oct* parameter allows us to transpose the monk process up and down without having to alter the process definition. We can now listen to monks in octaves and other interval relations.

Interaction 8. Listening to Monks2.

```
cm> (events (list (monks2 24 dchant .8 12)
                  (monks2 24 dchant .8 0)
                  (monks2 24 dchant .8 -12))
            "monks.mid")
```

```
"monks-2.mid"
cm> (events (list (monks2 24 dchant .8 -6)
                  (monks2 24 dchant .8 0)
                  (monks2 24 dchant .8 11))
          "monks.mid")
"monks-3.mid"
cm>
```

→nm/19/snd/monks-2.mid
→nm/19/snd/monks-3.mid

Markov harmonic rules

In this next example we use a Markov process to generate the interval relations for a series of chords. The same rules will be used to generate an underlying melody on which the chords will be transposed.

Example 9. Markov interval patterns.

```
(define int-mix
  '((1 (3 .4) (4 .4) (6 .1))
    (2 (2 .2 ) (3 .4) (4 .4) (6 .1))
    (3 (1 .2 )(2 .6 )  (4 .4) )
    (4 (2 .2 ) (3 .4) (4 .4) )
    (6 (2 .4) (3 .2) (4 .2))))

(define (markov-chorder len int-mix note size ud
                        rhy dur)
  (let ((tabl (make-ttable int-mix))
        (int 1)
        (key (keynum note))
        (chord #f))
    (process repeat len
             set int = (mran tabl int)
             set key = (fit (transpose key
                                 (odds ud int (- int)))
                           50 90)
             set chord = (loop with n = key
                               repeat size
                               collect n
                               do
                               (set! int
                                     (mran tabl int))
                               (set! n (transpose
                                          n (- int))))
             each c in chord
             output (new midi :time (now)
                         :keynum c duration dur)
             wait rhy)))
```

The `markov-chorder` process uses the interval content defined in *int-mix* to generate *len* number of chords. Each chord has *size* number of notes. The starting point for the series of chords is specified by *note* and *ud* is a ratio controlling the odds of the melody wandering upward or downward where a *ud* value greater than .5 prefers ascending melodic motion. The *int* variable will hold the current value from the Markov table and is initialized to 1. This value is then updated to a new interval from the Markov table at the beginning of each process iteration. The *key* variable serves as the key number on which each chord is based. Its value is calculated by transposing the current *key* value up or down *int* intervals according to the *ud* probability factor. The `fit` function insures that this value lies between key numbers 50 and 90. The next clause sets the value *chord* to a list of key numbers based on the current value of *key*. These key numbers are computed from the current key and the Markov interval table. The chord loop initializes the variable *n* to the current value of *key* and then iterates *size* number of times. On each iteration the value of n is first collected and then transposed downward by each interval read from the Markov table. (The transposition is downward simply to allow us to hear the melodic tone on which the chord is based.) The `each` process clause then applies an `output` action to each element in the chord.

Interaction 9. Listening to Markov generated harmony.

```
cm> (events (markov-chorder 25 int-mix 'g4 6 .6
                            1.2 1.2 )
            "chord.mid")
"chord-1.mid"
cm>
```

→ nm/19/snd/chord-1.mid

Markov texture
In this last example we use a Markov process to generate a melodic texture reminiscent of both the persistent coin toss model in Table 4 and the Gregorian Chant process discussed earlier in this section. In this example "heads" is represented by black keys and "tails" by white keys. Each black or white key is weighted to prefer moving to nearer tones of the same color. The basic weighting strategy for moving from key to key is shown in Table 8

Table 8. Transition categories and weight spread.

Repeat current key:	0.5
Near-to-far spread same color	2.0-0.5
Near-to-far spread other color	0.2-0.1

Example 10. Persistent black and white keys.

```
(define bw-intervals
  ;; first line of each transition hold weights
  ;; for keys of same color. second lines contains
  ;; weights for moving to other color
  '((0   (0 .5) (2 2) (4 1.5) (5 1) (7 .5) (9 .5)
         (11 .5)(1 .2) (3 .1) (6 .1)  (8 .1) (10 .1))
    (1   (1 .5) (3 2) (6 1.5) (8 1) (10 1) (0 .2) (2 .2)
         (4 .1)  (5 .1) (7 .1) (9 .1) (11 .1))
    (2   (0 2)  (2 .5) (4 2)   (5 1.5) (7 1) (9 .5)
         (1 .2) (3 .2) (6 .1) (8 .1) (10 .1) (11 .1) )
    (3   (1 2)  (3 .5) (6 1.5) (8 1) (10 .5)
         (0 .1) (2 .2) (4 .2) (5 .1) (7 .1) (9 .1)
         (11 .1))
    (4   (0 1.5)(2 2) (4 .5) (5 2) (7 1.5) (9 1) (11 .5)
         (1 .1) (3 .2) (6 .2) (8 .1) (10 .1))
    (5   (0 1)  (2 1.5)(4 2) (5 .5) (7 2) (9 1.5) (11 1)
         (1 .1) (3 .2) (6 .2) (8 .1) (10 .1))
    (6   (1 1.5)(3 2)  (6 .5) (8 2) (10 1.5)
         (0 .1) (2 .1) (4 .1) (5 .2) (7 .2) (9 .1)
         (11 .1))
    (7   (0 .5) (2 1)  (4 1.5) (5 2) (7 .5) (9 2)
         (11 1.5)
         (1 .1) (3 .1) (6 .2) (8 .2) (10 .1))
    (8   (1 1)  (3 1.5)(6 2) (8 .5) (10 2)
         (0 .1) (2 .1) (4 .1) (5 .1) (7 .2) (9 .2)
         (11 .1))
    (9   (0 .5) (2 .4) (4 1) (5 1.5) (7 2) (9 .5) (11 2)
         (1 .1) (3 .1) (6 .1) (8 .2) (10 .2))
    (10  (1 .5) (3 1) (6 1.5) (8 2) (10 .5)
         (0 .1) (2 .1) (4 .1) (5 .1) (7 .1) (9 .2)
         (11 .2))
    (11  (0 .5) (2 .5) (4 .5) (5 1) (7 1.5) (9 2)
         (11 0.5) (1 0.1) (3 .1) (6 .1) (8 .1) (10 .2))))

(define bw-octaves
  '((c3 (c3 2)    (c4 1)   (c5 .5) (c6 .25))
    (c4 (c3 1)    (c4 2)   (c5 1)  (c6 .5))
    (c5 (c3 .5)   (c4 1)   (c5 2)  (c6 1))
    (c6 (c3 .25)  (c4 .5)  (c5 1)  (c6 2))))

(define (bw len oct rate)
  (let ((ints (make-ttable bw-intervals))
        (octs (make-ttable bw-octaves))
        (reps 0)
        (int 0))
    (process repeat len
```

```
--------------------------------------------------------------------
          if (= reps 0)
          set reps = (pick 4 8 12 16)
          and set oct = (mran octs oct)
          set int = (mran ints int)
          output (new midi :time (now)
                       :keynum (transpose oct int)
                       :duration (* rate 1.5))
          wait rate
          set reps = (- reps 1))))
--------------------------------------------------------------------
```

The bw process uses two Markov tables to project an interval pattern of black and white key motion onto a pattern of octave transpositions. The Markov table *octs* controls the octave register and "prefers" motion to near octaves than to octaves further away. This causes the octave register of the pattern to usually shift in a smooth manner. The *reps* variable holds the number of notes remaining to play in the current octave. If *reps* is zero then a new octave is selected from *octs* and *reps* is reset to a random length of 4, 8, 12, or 16 events. The key number for each event is determined by transposing the current octave offset *oct* by an interval *int* generated from the Markov interval table *ints*. The last statement in the process decrements the value of *reps* by 1.

Interaction 10. Listening to Black and White.

```
cm> (events (bw 120 'c4 .125) "bw.mid")
"bw-1.mid"
cm> (events (list (bw 120 'c4 .125)
                  (bw 120 'c3 .125))
            "bw.mid"          '(0 4))
"bw-2.mid"
cm> (events (list (bw 120 'c4 .125)
                  (bw (* 120 21/13)
                      'c4
                      (* .125 13/21)))
            "bw.mid")
"bw-3.mid"
cm>
```

→ nm/19/snd/bw-1.mid
→ nm/19/snd/bw-2.mid
→ nm/19/snd/bw-3.mid

The third call in Example 10 creates two rhythmic strata related by the Golden Mean ratio 21/13.

Markov Analysis

The weights for all of the preceding Markov processes were determined only by the preference of the author. But by analyzing data and extracting a set of outcomes and weights, one can create Markov processes that generate chains with statistically similar characteristics. In a "Markov analysis", data is analyzed using a "window" that moves over successive positions in the sequence. The width of this window is determined by the order of the analysis. An analysis for a first order table uses a window width of 2: the first element in the window represents a past outcome and the second represents its successor. In a second order analysis the window is 3 elements wide, the first two elements are the past outcomes and the third element is that past's successor. The analysis proceeds by moving the window over successive elements in the data and counting the number of times each unique outcome follows each unique past. We can perform an example analysis on the following short data sequence:

a a b c b a

Recall that first order window examines pairs: the first element in the pair represents a past value and the second element is its outcome. Windowing over the example sequence therefore produces the following pairs:

aa, ab, bc, cb, ba, aa

The very last window in the analysis (aa) is produced by "wrapping" the final window around to the front of the sequence again so that the last element in the sequence also has a successor. An analysis that wraps around creates a "seamless" chain without any terminating condition. An alternate method of analysis encodes a unique terminal value, call it z, as the consequent of the last a. When z appears from the chain the caller will knows that the Markov process cannot generate any more events.

The next step in the analysis is to count each unique outcome for each unique past, giving us the raw counts shown in Table 9 and their normalized probabilities in Table 10. Past events are represented as row labels and successor events are labeled as columns.

Table 9. Raw count tally.

	a	b	c
a	2	1	—
b	1	—	1
c	—	1	—

Table 10. Counts normalized to probabilities.

	a	b	c
a	0.667	0.333	—
b	0.500	—	0.500
c	—	1.000	—

It should be obvious from even this very short example that doing a Markov analysis "by hand" is both tedious and error prone. Luckily for us, its iterative nature makes it a chore that computers can easily do!

Analysis by computer

Common Music provides the function markov-analyze to generate *nth* order Markov analysis of a sequence of data.

(markov-analyze   *seq*   [:order   *i*]   [:print?   *b*]   [Function]
[:pattern?   *b*]   [:key   *p*])

The type of results returned by the function vary according to its :print? and :pattern? keyword arguments. One or more of the following are possible:
1. A printed table of results from the statistical analysis.
2. A pattern definition that implements the pattern.
3. A pattern object that generates the pattern.

Only the first and third possibilities will be demonstrated in this chapter, see the discussion of the Markov pattern in Chapter 20 for information about the second option.

The following analyses generate different orders of Markov from the melody Happy Birthday. The examples were first demonstrated to me by the composer Paul Berg, who works at the Institute of Sonology. Because higher orders of analysis generate tables too large to fit on a book page our analyses include tables for only the first two orders. However, the reader can generate tables of higher orders interactively in Lisp. Happy Birthday is fully expressed by a fifth-order Markov process.

We first define the note sequence for Happy Birthday and a process to play the Markov renditions:

Example 11. Happy Birthday, data and player.

```
(define bday
  (note '(c4 c d c f e c c d c g f
          c c c5 a4 f e d bf bf a f g f)))

(define (play-bday order reps rate)
  ;; process to play happy birthday in various orders.
  (let ((pat (markov-analyze bday :order order
                                  :print? false)))
    (process repeat reps
             output (new midi :time (now)
                             :keynum (next pat)
                             :duration (* rate 1.5))
             wait rate)))
```

Happy birthday, zero order Markov (weighted random selection)
```
(markov-analyze bday :order 0 :print? :table
                :pattern? false)
```

Table 11. Zeroth order transition weights.

c4	d4	e4	f4	g4	a4	bf4	c5
0.32	0.12	0.08	0.20	0.08	0.08	0.08	0.04

Interaction 11. Listening to zero order Happy Birthday.

```
cm> (events (play-bday 0 40 .15) "bday.mid")
"bday-1.mid"
cm>
```

• → nm/19/snd/bday-1.mid

Happy birthday, first order Markov
```
(markov-analyze bday :order 1 :print? :table
                :pattern? false)
```

Table 12. First order transition weights.

	c4	d4	e4	f4	g4	a4	bf4	c5
c4	0.38	0.25	—	0.13	0.13	—	—	0.13
d4	0.67	—	—	—	—	—	0.33	—
e4	0.50	0.50	—	—	—	—	—	—
f4	0.40	—	0.40	—	0.20	—	—	—
g4	—	—	—	1.00	—	—	—	—
a4	—	—	—	1.00	—	—	—	—
bf4	—	—	—	—	—	0.50	0.50	—
c5	—	—	—	—	—	1.00	—	—

Interaction 12. Listening to first order Happy Birthday.

```
cm> (events (play-bday 1 40 .15) "bday.mid")
"bday-2.mid"
cm>
```

→ nm/19/snd/bday-2.mid

Happy birthday, second order Markov
```
(markov-analyze bday :order 2 :print? :table
                :pattern? false)
```

Table 13. Second order transition weights.

	c4	d4	e4	f4	g4	a4	bf4	c5
c4 c4	—	0.67	—	—	—	—	—	0.33
c4 d4	1.00	—	—	—	—	—	—	—
c4 f4	—	—	1.00	—	—	—	—	—
c4 g4	—	—	—	1.00	—	—	—	—
c4 c5	—	—	—	—	—	1.00	—	—
d4 c4	—	—	—	0.50	0.50	—	—	—
d4 bf4	—	—	—	—	—	—	1.00	—
e4 c4	1.00	—	—	—	—	—	—	—
e4 d4	—	—	—	—	—	—	1.00	—
f4 c4	1.00	—	—	—	—	—	—	—
f4 e4	0.50	0.50	—	—	—	—	—	—
f4 g4	—	—	—	1.00	—	—	—	—
g4 f4	1.00	—	—	—	—	—	—	—
a4 f4	—	—	0.50	—	0.50	—	—	—
bf4 a4	—	—	—	1.00	—	—	—	—
bf4 bf4	—	—	—	—	—	1.00	—	—
c5 a4	—	—	—	1.00	—	—	—	—

Interaction 13. Listening to second order Happy Birthday.

```
cm> (events (play-bday 2 40 .15) "bday.mid")
"bday-3.mid"
cm>
```

➙ nm/19/snd/bday-3.mid

Happy Birthday, orders 3-5
```
(markov-analyze bday :order 3 :print? :table
                :pattern? false)
(markov-analyze bday :order 4 :print? :table
                :pattern? false)
(markov-analyze bday :order 5 :print? :table
                :pattern? false)
```

Interaction 14. Listening to Happy Birthday, orders 3, 4 and 5.

```
cm> (events (play-bday 3 40 .15) "bday.mid")
"bday-3.mid"
cm> (events (play-bday 4 40 .15) "bday.mid")
"bday-4.mid"
cm> (events (play-bday 5 40 .15) "bday.mid")
"bday-5.mid"
cm>
```

→ nm/19/snd/bday-3.mid

→ nm/19/snd/bday-4.mid

→ nm/19/snd/bday-5.mid

Amazing Grace

As a final example of Markov processes I offer a piece I composed from a Markov analysis of the spiritual Amazing Grace. The piece also employs weighted random selection and envelopes, which have been covered in Chapters 15 and 17. The only real difference between the Markov processes you will hear in the composition and the process described in this chapter is in the manner in which probability weights were controlled in the table. Rather than develop multiple tables to represent different orders of the folk song, I implemented a single large table whose probability weights were expressed as envelopes. The probability envelopes in this large Markov table were then controlled as a function of time.

Amazing Grace is an algorithmic fantasy for the Yamaha Disklavier (a MIDI controlled piano) based on the American folk song of the same name. The fantasy involves a processes of "becoming", in which melodic and rhythmic contours of the folk song serve as gravitational centers for the musical texture to coalesce around, like dust spiraling inward to form a star. Amazing Grace begins in a mode and texture very distant from the folk melody. As the composition unfolds the original tune gradually exerts more and more influence over the stochastic texture. Short melodic motives and rhythmic figures first appear and are followed by progressively longer gestures and melodic figures from the original tune coming to the fore. This process continues until the point of maximum influence, at which time the fantasy has congealed into a block texture with a single rhythmic motive and melodic content completely determined by the folk song. Amazing Grace was commissioned for the opening ceremony of the Multimedial III Festival in Karlsruhe Germany, where it received its world premiere in 1995.

→ nm/19/snd/Amazing-Grace-KA.mp3 stereo MP3, 8 Mbytes, 7 minutes.

Chapter Source Code

The source code to all of the examples and interactions in this chapter can be found in the file markov.cm located in the same directory as the HTML file for this chapter. The source file can be edited in a text editor or evaluated inside the Common Music application.

References

Dodge, C. & Jerse, T. (1985). *Computer Music*. New York: Schirmer Books.

20

Patterns and Composition

Art is the imposing of a pattern on experience, and our aesthetic enjoyment is recognition of the pattern.

— Alfred North Whitehead

It is hard to conceive of a musical work that does not express patterns somehow. Patterns can operate at all levels of a composition, from the transitory surface flow of notes and rhythms to its deep structural organization. A pattern might involve a single sound parameter such as frequency, or it may involve multiple sound attributes evolving in parallel over time. Because patterns permeate musical expression, inventing and manipulating them is fundamental to the work that a composer does. In this chapter we explore an object oriented language for musical pattern description based on a class of object called `pattern`. The pattern language provides a number of different patterns to work with. Every type of pattern organizes and generates data according to class specific ordering rules. These patterns can be used individually or combined together to form *composite patterns* that simultaneously exhibit the characteristics of several different pattern types. Table 1 contains a summary of the basic pattern classes that will be discussed in this chapter. Be sure to consult the Common Music Dictionary for full details about each type of pattern.

Table 1. Table of pattern classes.

class	description
cycle	sequences elements in a continual loop.
line	sequences elements and sticks on last.
palindrome	sequences elements forwards and backwards.
heap	permutes elements randomly.
random	selects elements in weighted distribution.
rotation	permutes elements by rotation rules.
markov	generates elements by markov process.
graph	generates elements by state transition rules.
funcall	computes elements by calling a function.
rewrite	rewrites elements using grammar rules.

The pattern language also provides some pattern classes that implement specialized functionality. These specialized patterns (Table 2) are almost always used in conjunction with the general patterns listed in Table 1. Their use will be discussed at appropriate places over the course of this chapter.

Table 2. Table of specialized pattern classes.

class	description
join	forms a single pattern out of multiple patterns.
copier	repeats periods of a pattern.
chord	produces lists of elements.
transposer	transposes patterns and lists.
range	generates numerical ranges.
pval	evaluates a Lisp expression inside a pattern.

Before examining the pattern classes in more detail we first describe some characteristics that all patterns share and demonstrate how patterns are created and used.

Pattern Properties

The manner in which a pattern generates data is influenced not only by what specific pattern type it is but also by a set of common properties that control the way in which all patterns behave. The *period length* is one of the most important properties that all patterns possess. Patterns group their data into "chunks" called periods and the period length of a pattern determines the number of elements that constitute a chunk's worth of data. All patterns also possess a *repeat* property that places an optional ceiling on the number of periods, or chunks, that the pattern will be allowed to produce. If a pattern reaches its repeat factor it will only generate an *end of data* marker from that point onward. This marker allows a caller to determine when a pattern is done producing elements without knowing in advance how many elements the pattern will actually produce.

Working with Patterns

Patterns are created using the new macro.

All patterns support the following property initializations:
: of *data*

> Sets the pattern's elements to *data*. This initialization can also be specified using the : notes or : keynums aliases, in which case *data* is parsed as a list of note names or key numbers, respectively.

: name {*string* | *symbol*}

> Sets the name of the pattern to *string* or to the print name of *symbol*.

: for {*number* | *pattern*}

> Sets the period length of the pattern to *number* or *pattern* of numbers.

: repeat {*number* | *pattern*}

> Sets the repetition factor of the pattern to *number* or *pattern* of numbers.

: counting {:periods | :values}

> Determines how the pattern counts subpatterns. The default value is : periods, which means each period of a subpattern is counted as a single choice in the pattern.

Example 1 demonstrates three simple pattern definitions.

Example 1. Pattern creation using the new macro.

```
(new cycle :of '(a b c))

(new heap :keynums '(c4 b d5 ef3) :for 20
     :name 'gesture1)

(new heap
     :of (list (new cycle :of 'q :for 3)
               (new palindrome :of '(e. s e))
               (new random :of '(h w h.) :for 1)))
```

The first expression in Example 1 creates a cyclic pattern of three symbols: a, b and c. The second expression defines a random permutation of key numbers with twenty key numbers per period. The third expression creates a composite rhythmic pattern built from three different subpatterns.

Reading pattern values

Once a pattern has been created its elements are accessed, or *read*, using the next function:

(next *pattern* [*amount*]) [Function]

The next function returns the next value, or list of values, from *pattern*. The optional *amount* parameter determines how many values are read from the pattern. If *amount* is not specified then just the next element in the pattern is returned. If *amount* is an integer then that many values are read and returned in a list. Otherwise, if *amount* is not false, then a period's worth of elements is read from the pattern and returned in a list.

Interaction 1. Creating and reading patterns.

```
cm> (define p (new cycle :of '(a b c)))

cm> (next p)
a
cm> (next p)
b
cm> (next p)
c
cm> (next p #t)
(a b c)
cm> (next p 7)
(a b c a b c a)
cm> (next p #t)
(b c)
cm>
```

Example 1 creates a cyclic pattern and reads elements from it using the next function. A cycle pattern generates its elements in sequential order and then loops back to its first element after the last value has been produced. Since no :for initialization was specified in the cycle's period length was automatically set to three, the number of elements in the pattern's data. The fourth call to next specifies true for the *amount* parameter, which returns one full period of the pattern's elements in a list. Note that the last expression only returns two value in the period because only two values were left in the current period due to the previous call reading seven values.

Subpatterns

Patterns can contain any type of Lisp data, including other patterns. A *subpattern* defines a local ordering of elements within the scope of the surrounding pattern. As a general rule, any value specified to a pattern can be replaced by a subpattern of values. This rule applies not only to pattern data, but to many of the pattern's properties as well. In this way the behavioral characteristics of a pattern can change and evolve along with the data that the pattern generates.

Subpatterns typically produce an entire period of their elements before any other element in the surrounding pattern's data can be chosen and normally all of these elements count as only one choice in the containing pattern's period count. In contrast, a subpattern specified as a pattern property produces just the next element each time the surrounding pattern starts a new period. We will use a simple first example to demonstrate some of the basic features of subpatterns.

Figures and motives
Every composer is familiar with the *Alberti Bass*, a "broken chord" figure that appears in many works from the Common Practice period. Example 2 shows the definition of two Alberti figures using the cycle pattern.

Example 2. Alberti figures implemented as patterns.

```
(new cycle :notes '(c3 e g e) :name 'm1)

(new cycle :notes '(d3 f g f) :name 'm2)
```

The figures were given the names m1 and m2 so that they can be referenced repeatedly as motivic units inside a larger pattern. Naming is a convenience that allows a pattern to be "fetched" using the #& feature without having to define global variables to store them. In Example 3 the m1 and m2 patterns are treated as building blocks to form a little bass line in which each subpattern appears several times. Since a cycle continually loops its data from back to front, the Alberti figures in Example 2 begin with their first note each time they are repeated in the surrounding pattern.

Example 3. Alberti figures used in a short Alberti bass line.

```
(new cycle :name 'bass-line
     :of (list #&m1 #&m1 #&m2 #&m2
              #&m1 #&m2 'c3))
```

→ nm/20/snd/pat-1.mid

Multidimensional patterns
The short bass line pattern defined in Example 3 generates values for a single sound parameter. But musical motives and gestures are often defined across more than one dimension of sound. For example, the opening motive of Beethoven's Fifth symphony is as much a rhythmic contour as it is a pitch contour. In simple cases multiple sound parameters can be managed using separate, independent patterns that control the parameters in parallel. However, this parallelism ignores the underlying unity of the motive and will become confusing as the size and complexity of the

motivic patterns increases. Worse yet, if the motivic patterns are not completely deterministic then the two independent, parallel patterns will not generate values in the required synchronized order.

Common Music's pattern language provides a special type of pattern called join which can be used to link more than one pattern together to form an aggregate unit of structure that will always produce synchronized values regardless of how the joined patterns are organized inside a larger pattern. Example 4 rewrites the bass line from the preceding example using joins to form two-dimensional musical motives with both pitch and rhythm linked together.

Example 4. Frequency and rhythm joined together.

```
(new cycle
  :of (list (new join :name 'j1
                  :of (list #&m1
                              (new cycle
                                  :of '(te ts te ts))))
            #&j1
            (new join :name 'j2 :of (list #&m2 's))
            #&j2 #&j1 #&j2 '(c3 h)))
```

→ nm/20/snd/pat-2.mid

In the first join every note from m1 combines with a corresponding triplet rhythm from a cyclic rhythm pattern. The second join links each note in m2 with a sixteenth note value. The very last element in the pattern (c3 h) defines a half-note C3 value.

Joined motives with random characteristics will still maintain their conceptual integrity as single units of structure. Example 5 demonstrates a pattern that joins frequency, rhythm and amplitude values to form gestures involving three dimensions of sound. The overall pattern is a cycle of three local gestures, the second and third gesture produce random variations each time they are generated from the larger pattern.

Example 5. Three dimensional motives with random variation.

```
(new cycle
  :of (list (new join
                  :of (list (new cycle :of '(ef5 e4 r))
                            (new cycle :of '(s s q) )
                            'ff))
            (new join
                  :of (list (new heap :of '(g4 fs4 fn5 b5))
                            (new cycle
                                :of (list (new heap
                                                :of '(e q e))
                                          'h))
                            'p))
```

```
                    (new join
                      :of (list (new cycle
                                      :of '(af5 f5 a4 cs4 c5))
                                 (new heap :of '(e s q) :for 5)
                                 (new cycle
                                      :of '(pp p mp mf f))))))
```

→ nm/20/snd/pat-3.mid

Composite patterns

Composite patterns are patterns that exhibit the characteristics of more than one type
of pattern at the same time. Example 6 presents a simple example of combining
cyclic and random behaviors together. The outer `cycle` pattern sequences three
`heap` subpatterns. The heaps in Example 6 collectively partition a single octave into
three groups of chromatic notes, where each group lies a major third above the
previous group. A `heap` pattern behaves like a deck of cards: it shuffles its elements
each time it starts over. Since the heaps in Example 6 randomly permuted their
elements the series of values that results from the composite pattern will exhibit
localized random orderings within a larger periodic ascent.

Example 6. Cycles of random permutation.

```
(new cycle
  :of (list (new heap :notes '(c3 cs d ef))
            (new heap :notes '(e3 f fs g))
            (new heap :notes '(gs3 a as b))))
```

→ nm/20/snd/pat-4.mid

If the pattern in Example 6 is turned "inside out" then randomly ordered cycles will
result:

Example 7. Randomly permuted cycles.

```
(new heap
  :of (list (new cycle :notes '(c3 cs d ef))
            (new cycle :notes '(e3 f fs g))
            (new cycle :notes '(gs3 a as b))))
```

→ nm/20/snd/pat-5.mid

Pattern Periods

The period length of a subpattern has a large impact on how the overall pattern
evolves. If, as in the preceding examples, the period length is the same as the
number of elements then all the elements of a subpattern will be generated before
any other data in the surrounding pattern will be considered. This sort of traversal is

called *depth first ordering*. By setting the period length of a subpattern to less than the number of its elements, the subpattern will yield to other patterns in the surrounding data and produce *breadth first* ordering.

We can observe the effect of a breadth-first traversal by setting the period lengths of the of inner heaps in Example 6 to 1. A period length of 1 will cause each heap to produce only 1 note per period of the outer cycle. This will generate a different four notes from the three heaps each period of the outer cycle, thus turning the pattern into a "random generator" of Alberti-like figures.

Example 8. Randomized Alberti figures.

```
(new cycle
   :of (list (new heap :notes '(c3 cs d ef) :for 1)
             (new heap :notes '(e3 f fs g) :for 1
                  :name 'm)
             (new heap :notes '(gs3 a as b) :for 1)
             #&m) )
```

→ nm/20/snd/pat-6.mid

Note that the fourth element #&m in the pattern does not produce a repeated value in the melodic output because #&m is a repeated pattern, not a repeated value. To make our generator repeat the exact same value for the second and fourth element will require that the fourth element literally reference whatever value the middle pattern (named m) produced. The function `pattern-value` can be used to return the last value that a pattern generated:

Interaction 2. Referencing the last value a pattern produced.

```
cm> (define p (new cycle :of '(a b c)))

cm> (pattern-value p)
:not-a-datum
cm> (next p)
a
cm> (pattern-value p)
a
cm>
```

The first call to `pattern-value` returned the special keyword token `:not-a-datum` because the pattern had no value at that point. Once `next` reads a value then `pattern-value` can fetch that value again from the pattern that produced it. Note that in the case of our random Alberti generator the `pattern-value` expression will have to be evaluated *inside* the pattern, every time the fourth element is to be read. This means that the expression (`pattern-value #&m`) must appear in the list of data specified to the pattern when it is created. But this presents a problem: the list of data is evaluated when the pattern is *created*, not when the pattern is read. This means our call to `pattern-value` must somehow be delayed until the call is actually read using `next`. A special pattern macro called `pval` (pattern value) can be used to delay the evaluation of a Lisp expression until it is encountered by the `next` function in a pattern.

(pval *expr*)   [Macro]

Pval delays the evaluation of a Lisp expression *expr* until it is encountered in a pattern by `next`. Pval allows any Lisp expression to be evaluated inside a pattern. A pval expression will be re-evaluated every time it is encountered by `next`.

Example 9. Using pval to delay the evaluation of an expression.

```
(new cycle
  :of (list (new heap :notes '(c3 cs d ef) :for 1)
            (new heap :notes '(e3 f fs g) :for 1 :name
'm)
            (new heap :notes '(gs3 a as b) :for 1)
            (pval (pattern-value #&m))))
```

→nm/20/snd/pat-7.mid

The pval in Example 9 delays the evaluation of the call to `pattern-value` until the pattern is read using the `next` function. When the fourth element is accessed the pval returns the value of its expression in its place. This expression will be re-evaluated each time the fourth element is accessed, effectively repeating whatever value was previously produced by the subpattern named m.

As a final variation on the Alberti bass idea we will place our randomized Alberti generator inside a `copier` pattern (Example 10).

Example 10. Using a copier to repeat pattern periods.

```
(new copier
  :of
  (new cycle
    :of (list (new heap :notes '(c3 cs d ef) :for 1)
              (new heap :notes '(e3 f fs g) :for 1
                  :name 'm)
              (new heap :notes '(gs3 a as b) :for 1)
              (pval (pattern-value #&m))))
  :for (new heap :of '(2 3 5))))
```

→nm/20/snd/pat-8.mid

A `copier` is a specialized pattern that generates a period from a source pattern and then repeats, or copies, that period some number of times before generating the next new period of data from the source. The period length of our copier is set to a heap that produces either two, three or five iterations of each period of the random figure.

Zero-length periods

A subpattern that sets its period length to zero "disappears" from the surrounding pattern until it is reselected with a period length greater than zero. In the following example, the note B4 will periodically appear three, two and then zero times in the surrounding pattern.

Example 11. Subpatterns with zero period length are skipped over.

```
(new cycle :of `(c4
                  ,(new cycle :of 'ef4
                       :for (new cycle :of '(1 2)))
                  ,(new cycle :of 'b4
                       :for (new cycle :of '(3 2 0)))
                  d4))
```

→ nm/20/snd/pat-9.mid

Example 11 also demonstrates a very useful Lisp feature called the *backquoted list*. The pattern's data list contains two note names (C4 and D4) that are tokens for the pattern to generate and two expressions that, when evaluated, create subpatterns. Recall from Chapter 5 that a backquoted list acts just like a quoted list except that expressions preceded by a comma "," are explicitly evaluated. In the case of pattern data, the backquote is useful for notating data lists in which some elements are pattern tokens while others elements are *expressions* that create subpatterns.

Patterns and Processes

Patterns can greatly simply the overall design and implementation of a musical process. For example, most of the code in the first processes definition in Chapter 14 (Piano Phase) was specifically related to treating lists in a cyclic manner. Recasting the process to use a cycle pattern to hold the phasing trope eliminates the need for several local variables and makes the code more compact and easier to understand.

Example 12 demonstrates the basic manner in which patterns are incorporated into a process definition. Data for the pattern is usually passed to the process as a list and the process creates a local pattern object to hold the data. Each iteration of the process then sets a stepping variable to successive values read from the pattern. In Example 12 the stepping variable *k* becomes the keynum value of each MIDI object output to the score.

Example 12. Process from Chapter 14 converted to use a pattern.

```
(define (piano1 trope amp chan)
  (let* ((cycl (new cycle :keynums trope
                    :repeat (length trope)))
         (rate (rhythm->seconds pp-pulse pp-tempo)))
    (process for k = (next cycl)
             until (eod? k)
             output (new midi :time (now)
                         :keynum k
                         :duration (* rate 1.5)
                         :amplitude amp
                         :channel chan)
             wait rate)))
```

Creating patterns inside a process is almost always better than defining patterns globally in the Lisp environment. There are several reasons for this. First, a pattern created inside a process is guaranteed to start from its initial conditions each time the process function is called. In contrast, a pattern that is defined globally will resume from the point it last stopped unless the composer remembers to redefine it before it is used again. Second, if the composer uses a local process variable to hold the pattern then no other process can share that exact same pattern object. If a single pattern is read by multiple processes then each process reads alternate values from the pattern rather than successive values. Sharing a pattern between processes can be useful but in most cases it is probably not what the composer intends.

Pattern state

The current *state* of a pattern can be just as important to a process as the data that the pattern produces. To illustrate, the :repeat initialization in Example 12 established a limit on the number of periods the cyclic trope produced. A process can use this information to determine when to stop generating events instead of keeping count of its iterations. The pattern facility provides several functions that allow pattern states to be "inspected" and tested for certain conditions.

(eop? *pattern*)	[Function]
(eod? *pattern*)	[Function]
(pattern-value *pattern*)	[Function]
(pattern-period-length *pattern*)	[Function]

The eop? (end of period) function returns true if *pattern* is currently at the end of a period, and the eod? (end of data) predicate returns true if a pattern has reached an established :repeat limit. The pattern-value function returns the previous value read from a pattern (if any) and pattern-period-length returns the current period length of the pattern if one has been established. Example 13 demonstrates how these functions might be used to control the actions of a process.

Example 13. Using pattern states to control a process.

```
(define (play-pat reps rate dur amp )
  (let ((pat (new heap
                 :notes '(c4 d ef f g af bf c5)
                 :for (new random :of '(8 12 16))
                 :repeat reps))
        (x 0)
        (r #t ))
    (process for k = (next pat)
             until (eod? k)
             for p = (pattern-period-length pat)
             if r set x = 0
             output
             (new midi :time (now)
                  :keynum k
                  :amplitude (interp x 0 .4 (- p 1) amp)
                  :duration dur)
             wait rate
             set r = (eop? pat)
             set x = (+ x 1))))
```

The play-pat process creates a heap pattern to generate *reps* periods of notes. Since the heap was given a random period length the process cannot know in advance how many events it will generate. A test using the eod? function allows the process to determine that the pattern's end-of-data marker has appeared after all of the events in *reps* periods have been produced. The until clause kills the process as soon as that point has been reached.

The process in Example 13 produces a crescendo over every period in the heap pattern without knowing in advance how long each period actually is. The amplitudes of events within a single period are calculated using linear interpolation (Chapter 16) and range from .4 to the maximum *amp* value specified to the process. The variable *x* provides the interpolation lookup value, and ranges from 0 to one less than *p*, the heap's current period length as determined by the pattern-period-length function. The variable *r* is a flag that marks the beginning of each new period. When *r* is true then the *x* lookup variable is reset to 0 to begin a new crescendo. The variable *r* is updated at the end of each iteration by the eop? function, which returns true only if the pattern is at the end of its current period. Note that eod? testing will typically occur at the beginning of a process definition, before dependent operations actually reference pattern values, and eop? testing will usually occur at the end of the process definition, after a value has been read and processed.

Interaction 3. Listening to a pattern.

```
cm> (events (play-pat 10 .1 .3 .8) "pat-10.mid")
"pat-10.mid"
cm>
```

→ nm/20/snd/pat-10.mid

Sharing patterns between processes

If multiple processes share pattern data then each process can output its own stream of musical events in which some sound properties depend on a common shared "idea" while others remain local to each process definition. One simple way to implement a shared idea is to treat one of the processes as a "master" that creates and manages the shared pattern and to then treat the other processes as "slaves" that only reference the pattern. Care must be taken to insure that the master process executes ahead of the slave processes so that the shared data is ready before the slaves start using it. This can be done either by scheduling the master process slightly ahead of the slaves, or by insuring that the master process is the first process in the list of processes passed to the events function.

Example 14 defines two processes that harmonize a random bass line using a shared pattern value *the-note*. The first process is the "master" process, it reads a value from its random bass line pattern, outputs a midi event to play the note, and sets the shared variable *the-note* to that pattern value. The second process is a "slave" process that generates a chord on whatever bass note the master process has last produced. The slave process sets *c* to a randomly selected chord from a pattern of chord templates and then transposes each chord two octaves above the current value of *the-note*. The slave's each clause iterates over each value in the current chord list and outputs a midi event.

Example 14. Sharing pattern values between processes.

```
(define (two-hands end tempo)
  (let ((the-note #f))  ; shared pattern value
    (list
     ;; master process sets the shared variable.
     (let ((bass (new random
                       :keynums '(e1 f g a b c2 d)))
           (rhys (new random :of '( h.. h e))))
       (process while (< (now) end)
                for k = (next bass)
                for r = (rhythm (next rhys) tempo)
                set the-note = k
                output (new midi :time (now)
                            :keynum k :duration r
                            :amplitude .8)
                wait r))
     ;; slave procees adds random harmony
```

```
-------------------------------------------------------------------
     (let ((rhys (new random :of '((q :max 3) (e :max 2)
                                   (s :max 1)
                                   (t :weight .5
                                      :max 1))))
           (harm (new heap :of '((0 3 7 8) (1 5 8 10)
                                 (0 3 7 10) (1 5 8 12)
                                 (1 3 7 10) (3 5 8 12)
                                 (1 5 7 10)))))
       (process while (< (now) end)
               for c = (transpose (next harm)
                                  (+ the-note 24))
               for r = (rhythm (next rhys) tempo)
               each k in c
               output (new midi :time (now)
                           :keynum k :duration (* r 2)
                           :amplitude .4)
               wait r)))))
-------------------------------------------------------------------
```

→ nm/20/snd/pat-11.mid

Pattern Classes

In this section we examine some pattern classes that, like the random pattern used in the preceding slave process, involve more complex formats for their data specification or control properties.

Palindrome

A palindrome pattern enumerates its data forwards and backwards. Subpatterns are visited in palindromic order but will continue to yield their own internal orderings within the palindrome. The palindrome's :elide initialization controls how the beginning and ending elements in the pattern data are treated when the palindrome reverses direction. Table 1 demonstrates the effect of the all the possible :elide values given example data of four letters: a b c d.

Table 3. Effects of :elide on palindrome data.

elide value	result
false	a b c d d c b a	a b ...
true	a b c d c b	a b ...
:first	a b c d d c b	a b ...
:last	a b c d c b a	a b ...

The palindrome in Example 15 contains 5 elements, the first of which is a heap subpattern with a period length of 1. The `:elide` value of the palindrome is set to choose between `:first`, which causes the heap pattern to not repeat as the last element in the palindrome, and false, which causes it to repeat.

Example 15. A palindrome with subpattern.

```
(new palindrome
  :notes `(, (new heap :notes '(c4 b3 bf a af g) :for 1)
            d4 ef f gf)
  :elide (new random :of '(:first #f)))
```

→ nm/20/snd/pat-12.mid

Rotation

A `rotation` pattern permutes its elements according to rules specified in the `:rotations` initialization. The value of `:rotations` should be a *rotation list* or a pattern that generates rotation lists. A rotation list contains (up to) four numbers that describe which elements in the pattern will be "swapped", or exchanged, to produce the next rotation. This swapping is applied iteratively over all the data to produce the rotation for the next period. The format of a rotations list is:

(*start step width end*)

where *start* is the initial index (zero based) in the data to begin swapping, *step* is the distance to move in the data after each swap, *width* is the distance between swapped elements, and *end* marks the index in data to stop element swapping. If the `:rotations` initialization is not provided it defaults to (0 1 1 *end*), which causes the front element to shift to the back on each new period. For example, if a b c d represents the initial order for a rotation, then the default rule (0 1 1) iterates over all elements and swaps adjacent pairs, thus moving the first element a to its next position at the end of the list:

Table 4. Rotation of front element A to back.

initial	**a** b c d
swap first pair	b **a** c d
swap second pair	b c **a** d
swap last pair	b c d **a**

The rotation in Example 16 consists of five elements, the first of which is a subpattern.

Example 16. The rotation pattern.

```
-------------------------------------------------------------------------
(new rotation
   :notes `(, (new range :by -2 :initially (keynum 'c6))
             b3 f4 g5 ef6)
   :rotations (new cycle :of '((0 1 1) (0 1 2)))))
-------------------------------------------------------------------------
```

→ nm/20/snd/pat-13.mid

The first element in the rotation is a specialized pattern called a range that can generate either bounded or unbounded number ranges. The range used in Example 16 returns a series of descending key numbers a whole step apart starting from key number 84 (C6). The :rotations for the pattern is expressed as a cycle of of two rules so that the pattern alternates rules on each period of the pattern. The first rule is the default rotation (0 1 1) and the second swaps elements two steps apart, i.e. elements separated by one element between them.

The example file nm/20/cring.cm contains some examples of rotations that implement *change ringing* patterns, complex rotational schemes developed by English church bell ringers for generating long sequences of peals without direct repetition.

Random

The random pattern generates elements in a discrete weighted distribution. By default, each element in a random pattern has an equal probability of selection and may be repeated in direct succession any number of times. This default behavior can be modified by specifying the element as a *node*, a list containing the element followed by a set of optional keyword constraints to place on the element:

$$(x \ [\texttt{:weight} \ n] \ [\texttt{:min} \ i] \ [\texttt{:max} \ i])$$

X is the pattern element, :weight sets the probability of the node relative to other elements in the pattern, :min sets a lower bound on how many direct repetitions of the node element must be made before a new element might be selected, and :max sets a ceiling on how many direct repetitions of the node element may be made before a new element must be selected. An element's :weight value may be specified as a *pattern* of weights, in which case a new weight will be selected for each period of the random pattern. Note that the :min and :max node values will affect the statistical accuracy of the node's probability weight. The process in Example 17 uses the random pattern to generate transposition offsets, rhythmic patterns, and amplitude values.

Example 17. Random 12-tone generator.

```
-------------------------------------------------------------------------
(define (ranrow end)
   (let ((rows (new transposer
                  :of (new cycle :of '(0 1 6 -5 10 11 5
                                         16 15 21 26 20))
                  :on (new random
                         :keynums '(c4 cs3 b3 fs4 fs3))))
-------------------------------------------------------------------------
```

```
(rhys (new random
            :of `((t :min 4) (s :min 2)
                  (q :weight 3)
                  (te :min 3) (tq :min 3)
                  ,(new cycle :of '(e. s))
                  (e :weight 2))))
    (amps (new random :of '((mf :weight 7)
                            (mp :weight 3)
                            p))))
  (process while (< (now #t) end)
          for k = (next rows)
          for r = (rhythm (next rhys) 70)
          for a = (amplitude (next amps))
          output (new midi :time (now)
                           :keynum k :amplitude a
                           :duration r)
          wait r )))
```

→ nm/20/snd/pat-14.mid

In this example the twelve-tone row is specified as a cycle pattern that is transposed to key numbers selected from a random pattern. (The intervals in the row are not notated within a single octave to provide a slight contour to the melodic line.) A transposer is a specialized pattern that transposes either patterns or lists of key numbers or notes. The rhythmic values are selected at random; the :min feature is used to insure that rhythmic values of less than an eighth note duration are reselected enough times so as to place the next different rhythm at the beginning of an eighth note pulse.

Markov

The markov pattern implements nth order Markov chains. The data specified to the pattern is a list of *transition rules* where each rule is a list of the form:

(*past...* -> *next...*)

where *past* is zero or more identifiers that define the transition trigger of the rule and values to the right of the marker -> define the transition's outcomes. The number of ids in the left-hand side determines the Markov order of the pattern. These ids are ordered left to right from most past to most recent past. The special id * can appear in the left-hand side to match any past id at that position. This allows higher order tables to "collapse" transitions with identical outcomes and near-identical left-hand sides into a single transition rule.

By default each transition outcome has the same probability of being selected. To alter the weight of an particular outcome relative to the other outcomes, specify its id in a list together with its weight. For example the transition rule:

(c -> a (b 2) c)

defines a 1st order Markov transition whose outcome b has twice the selection probability than either the a or c outcomes. The transition rule:

(q * a -> e r (d 3) g)

describes a third-order transition triggered whenever a is the most recent past outcome and q is the third past outcome. Example 18 shows a second order markov pattern that generates rhythms with an underlying pulse. Using the wildcard token * reduces the number of transition rules that would otherwise have to be entered.

Example 18. A second order Markov rhythm pattern.

```
(new markov
  :of '((e s -> s)
        (q s -> e.)
        (q. s -> s)
        (h s -> e.)
        (e e -> s e e. q q. q.. h)
        (* e -> e)
        (* s -> e e. q q. q.. h)
        (* h -> e e. q q. q.. h)
        (* q.. -> s)
        (* q. -> e s)
        (* q -> e e. q q. q.. h)
        (* e. -> s))
  :for 20
  :past '(q q))
```

The optional :past initialization for Markov patterns presets the pattern's memory buffer with an explicit past outcome. The value (q q) in Example 18 will cause the second to last transition rule in the pattern to be triggered the first time the pattern is read.

→nm/20/snd/pat-15.mid Drum Track (Ride Cymbal)

The example files nm/20/foster.cm and nm/20/snd/foster-1.mid contain a large example of a second order Markov process that generates melodic material based on the analysis of Stephen Foster's folk songs described in chapter eight of Computer Music (Dodge).

Graph

A graph pattern generates elements from *transition rules* associated with the elements in the pattern. Elements and their transitions are represented as *graph nodes*. A graph node is a list in the form:

         (x [:id n] [:to ids])

where x is the element in the graph node, :id sets the node's *identifier*, or name, and :to is its transition rule. The transition rule determines the next node to select if the current node is selected. The value of :to can be a node identifier or pattern of identifiers. If the :to value of each node is a random pattern then the graph will implement a first order Markov process. The graph in Example 19 generates a melodic line using both random and cyclic transition rules. The graph contains 5 elements. Each element is a graph node with an identifier that uniquely "names" that element in the graph and a transition rule that produces the name of the next node.

In Example 19 the transitions are subpatterns that produce the identifiers of the successor nodes. The first four nodes in the graph select their successor nodes by randomly choosing between two possible successors (first order Markov). The fifth node selects its successor by cycling through the first four nodes. Note that the pattern element of the fifth node is itself a subpattern (heap) that produces a four note melodic fragment each time it is selected. The entire graph is embedded in a cyclic pattern that generates one period of the graph followed by a rest.

Example 19. A quasi-markov graph

```
(new cycle
  :of `(, (new graph
            :of `((c4 :id 1 :to , (new random :of '(2 5)))
                  (d4 :id 2 :to , (new random :of '(1 3)))
                  (ef4 :id 3 :to , (new random
                                        :of '(2 4)))
                  (f4 :id 4 :to , (new random :of '(3 5)))
                  (, (new heap :of '(g4 fs4 b4 c5))
                   :id 5
                   :to , (new cycle :of '(1 2 3 4)))))
       r))
```

→ nm/20/snd/pat-16.mid

Funcall

The funcall pattern implements patterns by function call. Each time a funcall pattern requires a new period of elements it calls a user specified function to return a list of value that becomes the next period of values in the pattern. The best way to work with the funcall pattern is to define functions that create and return them. That way the function can be called with different arguments to create different versions of the funcall pattern, as shown in Example 20.

Example 20. Implementing a pattern with the funcall pattern.

```
(define (noreps low hi n)
  (define (thunk )
    (loop repeat n
          for x = (between low hi x)
          collect x))
  (new funcall :of #'thunk))
```

The noreps function creates a funcall pattern to return *n* random values per period between a *low* and *high* bounds without any direct repetition. noreps defines a helper function, called thunk, to do most of its work. (The term thunk is used by Lisp programmers to describe a function without any arguments.) The thunk for noreps collects a list of random values without any direct repetitions. Our funcall pattern is then passed the thunk to call whenever it needs a new period of values. Interaction 4 demonstrates some sample output from a `noreps` pattern.

Interaction 4. Defining a noreps pattern.

```
cm> (define p (noreps 60 72 5))

cm> (next p t)
(63 61 64 62 70)
cm> (next p t)
(66 61 67 69 61)
cm>
```

We can use `noreps` in conjunction with the `copier` pattern to create a wandering melody in which locally random figures are repeated to produce larger scale periodicity.

Example 21. Repetition and randomness.

```
(define (wander tmpo)
  (let ((bass (new copier :of (noreps 41 60 5)
                    :for (new random :of '(1 3 5))
                    :repeat 10))
        (amps (new heap :of '(.6 .4 .4 .4 .4))))
    (process for k = (next bass)
             for a = (next amps)
             until (eod? k)
             output
             (new midi :time (now)
                  :keynum k
                  :duration (if (> a .5) 5 3)
                  :amplitude a)
             wait (rhythm 1/20 tmpo))))
```

The `wander` melody selects random fragments from a range and then plays each fragments one, three or five time before selecting a new one. The amplitude pattern accents exactly one note during each fragment so that an irregularly spaced melodic line is "brought out" from the steady background of notes.

Interaction 5. Listening to wander.

```
cm> (events (wander 48) "pat-17.mid")
"pat-17.mid"
cm>
```

➙ nm/20/snd/pat-17.mid One channel, monotimbral.

In this next example we use funcall to implement three new patterns. The revpat function creates a funcall that reverses (retrogrades) a source pattern. The invpat pattern will invert a pattern and mirror will produce a strict palindrome of a pattern.

Example 22. Retrograding and inverting patterns.

```
(define (revpat pat)
  ;; return the reverse of pat
  (define (thunk )
    (let ((vals (next pat true)))
      (reverse vals)))
  (new funcall :of #'thunk))

(define (invpat pat)
  ;; return the inversion of pat,
  ;; which must contain keynums or notes.
  (define (thunk )
    (let ((vals (next pat true)))
      (invert vals)))
  (new funcall :of #'thunk))

(define (mirror pat)
  ;; return a period of pat followed
  ;; by its strict retrograde
  (define (thunk )
    (let ((vals (next pat true)))
      (append vals (reverse vals))))
  (new funcall :of #'thunk))
```

Note that the funcall patterns in Example 22 can be applied to any pattern, regardless of how that pattern generates values.

Interaction 6. Palindrome of random values.

```
cm> (define p (mirror (noreps 0 12 6)))

cm> (next p t)
(0 2 7 0 2 7 7 2 0 7 2 0)
cm> (next p t)
(4 3 5 10 0 4 4 0 10 5 3 4)
cm>
```

The thunks for revpat, invpat and mirror all operate in a similar manner. Each thunk sets a local variable *vals* to the next period of values from the source pattern *pat* and then performs the appropriate operation on that list of data: revpat reverses the list, invpat inverts the list (which must therefore contain either key

numbers or note names), and mirror appends the list of values to the reverse of
that list. The process in Example 23 uses funcall patterns to generate randomly
shuffled prime, inversion, retrograde and retrograde-inversion forms of a randomly
generated 12-tone row.

Example 23. Random rows with retrograde and inversion.

```
(define (ranrow2 end offset tmpo chan)
  ;; get a row, any row.
  (let* ((arow (shuffle
                 (loop for i below 12
                       collect i)) )
         (main (new cycle :of arow)) ; prime form
         (rows (new transposer
                 ;;  heap of p, i, r and ri forms.
                 :of (new heap
                       :of (list main
                                  (invpat main)
                                  (revpat main)
                                  (revpat
                                    (invpat main))))
                 :on (new cycle
                       :keynums
                       (transpose arow offset)))))
         (rhys (mirror
                 (new random
                   :of (list
                          (new cycle :of 't :for 4)
                          (new cycle :of 's :for 2)
                          '(q :weight 3)
                          (new cycle :of 'te :for 3)
                          (new cycle of 'tq :for 3)
                          (new cycle :of '(e. s))
                          '(e :weight 2)))))
         (amps (new random :of '((mf :weight 7)
                                 (mp :weight 3)
                                 p))))
    (process while (< (now #t) end)
             for k = (next rows)
             for r = (rhythm (next rhys) tmpo)
             for a = (amplitude (next amps))
             output (new midi :time (now)
                         :keynum k
                         :amplitude a
                         :duration r
                         :channel chan)
             wait r )))
```

Each time the `ranrow` process is called it will create a new 12-tone row. `invpat` and `revpat` produce the inversion, retrograde and retrograde inversion forms. The *rows* variable contains a heap pattern that randomly permutes the different row forms. Each new permutation determines transposition levels from the key number *offset* specified to the process. *Rhys* produces rhythmic palindromes in which the first half of each period contains randomly generated rhythms and the second half contains its reverse. In Interaction 7 we listen to four versions of the process, each on a separate channels and offset by 8 seconds.

Interaction 7. Random 12-tone music.

```
cm> (events (loop for i below 4
                  collect
                  (ranrow2 32
                             (transpose 'c3 (* i 12))
                             40
                             i))
            "pat-18.mid"
            (loop for i from 0 by 8 to 16
                  collect i))
"pat-18.mid"
cm>
```

➝ nm/20/snd/pat-18.mid Four channels.

Rewrite

The `rewrite` pattern produces successive *generations* of elements, where each generation is created by rewriting the previous generation using a *grammar* defined by the user. A grammar is a set of *rewrite rules*, instructions for "respelling" elements to produce successive generations. Consider a rewrite pattern whose first generation consists of A and B and whose grammar is the following two rules:

     rule 1: a -> b a
     rule 2: b -> a a b

The first rule says that every A in the current generation is replaced by the sequence B A in the next. The second rule replaces every B in the current generation with A A B. If the initial generation is A B then the rules will produce the following generations:

Table 5. Rewriting generations with grammar rules.

Generation	Pattern elements
1	a b
2	b a a a b
3	a a b b a b a b a a a b
4	b a b a a a b a a b b a a a b b a a a b b a b a b a a a b

Generation 2 was created by applying the grammar rules to generation 1. Rule 1 replaced every A in generation 1 with B A and rule 2 replaced every B with B A A. This transformed the initial generation A B into the second generation's sequence B A A A B. Successive generations are produced in a similar manner. The rewrite rules defined above are additive, which means that successive generations become longer and longer. Rewrite sequences can become very long. The rewrite pattern's :generations initialization can be used to control the maximum number of generations that the pattern will produce. If a rewrite pattern reaches this optional limit it will simply cycle over the last generation from that point onward.

The rewrite pattern supports two different styles of rule specification. *Context free* rules are rules that are associated with specific elements in the pattern. Context sensitive rules are rules that are applied to a set of elements at the same time.

Context free grammars

In a context free rewrite pattern each element of data is represented by a node in the pattern. The node associates a single element with a rule to replace that element in the next generation. This type of rule is termed "context free" because the rule depends only on the node itself and not its context, or position, in the surrounding nodes in the pattern. The form of a context free node is almost identical to the graph pattern:

$$(\{element\} \quad [:id \quad x] \quad [:to \quad \{id \quad | \quad (id \quad ...) \quad |$$
$$pattern \quad | \quad false\})$$

The only difference is that the value of :to can be an id, a list of ids, a pattern that produces ids, or false. Interaction 8 shows the rules discussed in the preceding section implemented as a context-free rewrite pattern:

Interaction 8. Three generations from a context-free pattern.

```
cm> (define p
      (new rewrite :of '((a :to (b a))
                         (b :to (a a b)))
           :initially '(a b)))

cm> (next p 19)
(a b b a a a b a a b b a b a b a a a b)
cm>
```

Example 24 shows a rewrite pattern similar to Example 23 that generates a melodic line. The pattern contains two tokens +2 and -2 that are treated as *increments* between the notes of a melodic line. This is same grammar that the composer Tom Johnson used in his piece *Formulas for String Quartet*. Given an alphabet of +2 and -2 the pattern rewrites each +2 with the sequence +2 -2 +2 and -2 with -2 -2 +2. In our example we interpret +2 or -2 as whole step up or down. The range pattern in the example describes a "walk" that starts from a key number *from* and proceeds according to the steps returned by the rewrite pattern. The range pattern presets the position of the walk using its :initially argument, and the :stepping initialization forces the range's increment to be read in parallel with the offset.

Example 24. Rewrite melody.

```
(define (stepper end rate from)
   (let ((pat (new range :initially (keynum from)
                  :stepping
                     (new rewrite
                        :of '((+2 :to (+2 -2 +2))
                              (-2 :to (-2 -2 +2)))))))
      (process while (< (now) end)
              output (new midi :time (now)
                               :keynum (next pat)
                               :duration rate)
              wait rate)))
```

We listen to four simultaneous versions of the stepper process, each with a different rhythm and pitch offset.

Interaction 9. Listening to four voice stepper.

```
cm> (events (list (stepper 20 (rhythm 's 100) 'c5)
                  (stepper 20 (rhythm 'te 100) 'f4)
                  (stepper 20 (rhythm 'e 100) 'bf3)
                  (stepper 20 (rhythm 'tq 100) 'ef3))
            "pat-19.mid")
"pat-19.mid"
cm>
```

→ nm/20/snd/pat-19.mid Four channels.

Context sensitive rules

In a context sensitive rewrite pattern, nodes in the current generation are matched against a separate rule set to find successor rules to apply to the node. The first rule in the set that matches is "triggered" and the ids in the right-hand side of the rule provide the names of the successor nodes in the next generation.

Node specification for the context sensitive patterns is similar to the context free method except that:

- the -> option is not part of the node declaration.
- if the node's id value is the same as the element itself then the element itself can be specified in place of the node.

Each rule in a context sensitive rule set is a list of the form:

(id... -> id ...)

The -> rule operator divides each rule into two sides. The left-hand side of the rule defines a "matching target" and the right-hand side defines the rewrite succession. Either or both sides of the rule may contain more than one id. If the left-hand side of the rule is a single id then the rule matches any node with the same id. If the left-hand side has more than one id (a context-sensitive rule) then the rule matches if the *strict predecessor* in the left-hand side matches the current node and adjacent nodes in the generation match the ids adjacent to the strict predecessor. The strict predecessor id is notated as a list. Every context sensitive rule must contain exactly one strict predecessor in its left-hand side. Note that the right-hand side may be empty and that the left-hand side may contain the wild card * which matches any single element in the current generation.

```
(1 (1) 2 -> 3)
(1 * (2) -> 1 2)
(5 (3) 3 4 -> )
```

The first rules specifies that node 1 rewrites to node 3 wherever 1 is preceded by itself and followed by 2 in the current generation. The second rule says that node 2 rewrites to 1 and 2 whenever 1 occurs two positions earlier in the current generation. The third rule means node 3 rewrites to nothing if preceded by 5 and followed by itself and 4 in the current generation.

Example 25. Harmonies from a context sensitive rewrite.

```
(define (lsystem-harmonies len rhy dur)
  (let ((lsys (new rewrite :of '(((0 4 7) :id f)
                                 ((0 3 7) :id g)
                                 (+1 :id +) (-1 :id -))
                     :initially '(f + f - g - f)
                     :rules '((f -> f f - g - - g - f)
                              (g -> g f + f)))))
        (term false)
        (knum 60))
    (process repeat len
             do
             (set! term false)
             (loop until term
                   for x = (next lsys)
                   do
                   (if (list? x)
                       (set! term x)
                       (set! knum (fit (+ knum x)
                                       48 72))))
             each c in (transpose term knum)
             output (new midi :time (now)
                         :keynum c
                         :duration dur
                         :amplitude .7)
             wait rhy)))
```

The lsystem-harmonies process uses a context sensitive rewrite pattern to generate a harmonic grammar of chords and offsets that are then transposed to specific pitches. The variable *lsys* holds the pattern and *knum* holds the current transposition level for the process. There are four nodes in the rewrite pattern, the first two define major and minor chords (0 4 7) and (0 3 7) named F and G in the pattern, respectively. The other two nodes define transposition increments of +1 and -1 and are named + and -. The list of terms specified to :initially sets the first generation of the pattern to a specific list of node ids. Two rules are specified to the pattern, the first rule rewrites F terms and the second G terms. The process uses a loop to read successive terms from the pattern until a major or minor chord list has been produced. If -1 or 1 is encountered during this process the loop adjusts the current offset level *knum* by that amount. The fit function is used to ensure that this value remains within a two octave range from key number 48 to 72. Once the loop has produced the next chord list from the pattern the each clauses iterates every value in the chord and outputs a midi object to play it.

Interaction 10. Listening to context-sensitive rewrite.

```
cm> (events (lsystem-harmonies 200 .2 .35)
            "pat-20.mid")
"pat-20.mid"
cm>
```

→ nm/20/snd/pat-20.mid Four channels.

Gloriette for John Cage

Gloriette for John Cage (1994) is a completely pattern based algorithmic composition. It was written in 1994 as a memorial tribute to John Cage and was commissioned for the Busy Drone mechanical organ at the Stedelijk Museum in Amsterdam. The Busy Drone organ reads a large cardboard score that functions just like a piano roll except that the size and weight of the cardboard score restricts the mechanical organ to pieces that last only a few minutes in duration. Keep in mind as you listen to the piece that every note you hear was punched into heavy cardboard sheets by hand!

In keeping with Cage's interest in aleatoric music, the main algorithm in the piece uses a random pattern in which the likelihood of the musical notes C, A, G, and E gradually increases as a function of time, causing the composer's name to slowly emerge out of a background of G Dorian. The rhythmic scheme and number of voices are similarly inspired by the composer's name. Gloriette for John Cage was composed at the Zentrum fuer Kunst und Medientechnologie in Karlsruhe, Germany and has been included on several CDs.

→ nm/20/snd/gloriette.mp3 Gloriette for John Cage, performed by the Busy Drone mechanical organ at the Multimediale II Festival in Karlsruhe Germany, 1994.

The code for a simplified version of this composition is show in Example 26.

Example 26. Probability as a function of time.

```
(define (cage offset)
  (let* ((w 0)                        ; weight of CAGE
         (d (pval w))                 ; delay eval of w
         (p (new random
            :of `((g3 :weight ,d)     ; delay weight of G
                  (a3 :weight ,d)     ; delay weight of A
                  bf3
                  (c4 :weight ,d)     ; delay weight of C
                  d4
                  (e4 :weight ,d)     ; delay weight of E
                  f4
                  (g4 :weight ,d)     ; delay weight of G
                  (r :max 1 :weight .25)) ; add rests
            :for 1))
         (q (new random
            :of (list 1/16 1/8
                    (new cycle :of 1/32 :for 2 )))))
    (process repeat 100
             for n = (next p)
             for r = (rhythm (next q) 65)
             for i from 0
             ;; interpolate new weight value
             ;; for CAGE notes.
             set w = (interp i 0 .5 90 4)
             output (new midi :time (now)
                         :duration r
                         :keynum (transpose n offset))
             wait r)))
```

The cage process demonstrates how the probability of a random pattern can be controlled as a function of time. Over the course of 100 iterations the notes C, A, G and E gradually gain more probability than the other notes in a G Dorian collection. The variable *w* controls the probability of the CAGE notes being selected relative to others. The variable *d* holds a pval object to delay the evaluation of *w* until is it read by next. The set clause sets the interpolation at the start of the process to .5, so the CAGE notes are only half as likely to be selected as the other notes in G Dorian. But since *w* is set to a new weight value on each iteration of the process, the likelyhood of the CAGE notes will increased slightly over the course of the work. By the 90th iteration the CAGE notes will be four times as likely as the others to be selected. Interaction 11 generates four cage processes in several different octaves, each offset by a half note a tempo 65.

Interaction 11. Listening to the Cage algorithm.

```
cm> (events (loop for o in '(-12 0 12 24)
```

```
                    collect (cage o))
            "pat-21.mid"
            (loop for r in '(0 h w w.)
                    collect (rhythm r 65)))
"pat-21.mid"
cm>
```

→ nm/20/snd/pat-21.mid

Chapter Source Code

The source code to all of the examples and interactions in this chapter can be found
in the file patterns.cm located in the same directory as the HTML file for this
chapter. The source file can be edited in a text editor or evaluated inside the
Common Music application.

References

Dodge, C. & Jerse, T. (1985). *Computer Music*. New York: Schirmer Books.

21

Etudes, Op. 7: Automatic Jazz

In this Etude we examine a program that performs pattern-based jazz improvisation. The code is derived from a program originally written by Erik Flister at CCRMA, Stanford University, as a project for his undergraduate computer music class. (His original code has been simplified and adapted to work with General MIDI instruments.) Flister's improviser generates music for a MIDI jazz combo consisting of piano, acoustic bass and percussion parts. Our first step will be to learn how to specify the appropriate MIDI *program changes* to establish the Jazz Combo instruments on three channels of the synthesizer.

MIDI Messages

Until this point we have worked exclusively with midi events — object-oriented representations of MIDI note information. It may surprise you to learn that these objects are not actually defined in the MIDI protocol, they are high-level abstractions that represent a pair of low-level MIDI *messages*. A MIDI message is a packet of numbers sent to the synthesizer to control its operation. These messages consists of a series of *bytes*, where each byte holds up to 7 *bits* of information, enough to represent 2^7 different states, or the series of integers ranging from 0 to 127. The two messages that a midi event represents are called *Note On* and *Note Off* messages. These messages are what MIDI keyboards send when keys are depressed and released.

Common Music represents low-level MIDI messages as specially formatted integers containing up to 3 MIDI bytes of information. All of the different message types defined in the MIDI protocol are supported. Each of these messages is implemented by a constructor function, a predicate, and one or more byte accessors, if appropriate. Interaction 1 demonstrates the creation and display of low-level MIDI Note On and Note off messages.

Interaction 1. Creating and displaying MIDI messages.

```
cm> (make-note-on 0 60 90)
155226
cm> (midi-print-message 155226)
#<Note-On 0 60 90>
155226
cm> (make-note-off 9 48 127)
2496639
cm> (midi-print-message 2496639)
#<Note-Off P "Hi-Mid-Tom" 127>
2498175
cm>
```

The Note On message was created with a channel value of 0, key number 60 and key velocity 90. The utility function midi-print-message "decodes" low-level midi messages into a readable text format. The Note Off message was created with a channel value of 9, the channel (in zero based counting) that General MIDI reserves for the percussion map. When a Note On or Note Off message references the drum map the midi-print-message function prints P for the channel number and also displays the sound associated with the key number

Program changes

A MIDI *program change* message assigns a MIDI instrument (sometimes referred to as a program, patch or tone) to a specific channel of the synthesizer. Program change values between 0-127 can be sent to any non-percussion channel of a General MIDI synthesizer. The program change values needed for our Jazz Combo are 0, the Acoustic Grand Piano, and program 32, the Acoustic Bass. A program change is not necessary to select percussion parts since General MIDI already reserves channel 9 for the drum map. Interaction 2 shows the creation of our MIDI program changes using the make-program-change constructor, which takes a channel number and a program change value and returns a MIDI program change message. When program messages are displayed, midi-print-message includes the name of the instrument in the message information it prints.

Interaction 2. Program changes for Jazz Instruments

```
cm> (make-program-change 0 0)
196608
cm> (midi-print-message 196608)
#<Program-Change 0 "Acoustic-Grand-Piano">
196608
cm> (make-program-change 1 32)
462848
cm> (midi-print-message 462848)
#<Program-Change 1 "Acoustic-Bass">
462848
cm>
```

The midimsg Object

The MIDI specification defines many different types of messages that collectively implement all of the ways that a MIDI synthesizer can be controlled. The midimsg object can represent any MIDI message defined in the MIDI 1.0 specification in high-level score generation.

midimsg   [Class]

A midimsg is an object-oriented representation of a low-level MIDI message.

midimsg supports the following initializations:
:time *number*
   The score time of the midimsg.
:msg *integer*
   The 28 bit integer MIDI message.
:data *list*
   A list of any additional data bytes required by *message*.

We are now ready to define program changes for setting up the synthesizer to play the Jazz Combo. We use two midimsg objects, the first sends a program change 0 on channel 0 to select Acoustic Grand Piano and the second sends program change 32 on channel 1 to select an Acoustic Bass.

Example 1. A seq of program changes for the Jazz Combo
```
--------------------------------------------------------------------
(new seq :name 'combo-setup
     :subobjects
     (list (new midimsg :time 0
                :msg (make-program-change 0 0))
           (new midimsg :time 0
                :msg (make-program-change 1 32))))
--------------------------------------------------------------------
```

Example 1 uses a `seq` object to hold the program changes so that it is easy to mix them into the output when it comes time to generate the score. We can test our setup by writing a score containing program changes and two test tones:

Interaction 3. Testing the program changes.

```
cm> (events (list #&combo-setup
                  (new midi :time 1 :channel 0
                       :keynum 60)
                  (new midi :time 3 :channel 1
                       :keynum 48))
            "pctest.mid")
"pctest-1.mid"
cm>
```

→ nm/21/snd/pctest-1.mid (two channels, program changes)

Playing the file should cause the Acoustic Grand Piano to play on channel 0 and the Acoustic Bass on channel 1.

The Automatic Jazz Program

The automatic jazz program executes a "conductor" process. The conductor runs for a specified number of measures and sprouts piano, percussion and bass processes to improvise each measure. Each instrument process uses data passed to it from the main process. This data includes the jazz scale to improvise with, a transposition level for the jazz scale, a tempo factor and an overall amplitude level. The amplitude level is adjusted on a per measure basis by the main conductor process. The other data are defined as global variables that can be adjusted and redefined by the composer.

Example 2. Global control data for the jazz improviser.

```
---------------------------------------------------------------------------------
(define jazz-scale ; dorian with decorated octave
  '(0 2 3 5 7 9 10 12 14))

(define jazz-changes ; key changes
  '(bf3 ef4 bf3 bf ef4 ef bf3 bf f4 ef bf3 bf))

(define jazz-tempo 120)
---------------------------------------------------------------------------------
```

We will examine each instrument process in detail before looking at the main conductor algorithm.

The percussion parts

The percussion parts for the Jazz Combo consist of two ride cymbals, a high hat, snare and bass drums. We will introduce these parts in their order of complexity,

from simplest to most difficult. As mentioned in the previous section, each
percussion sound is addressed by a specific key number in the General MIDI Drum
Map. Example 3 contains the definition of the percussion sounds we will use:

Example 3. Percussion key numbers in the GM drum map.

```
(define hihat 42)  ; Closed Hi Hat
(define snare 40)  ; Electric Snare
(define bdrum 35)  ; Acoustic Bass Drum
(define ride1 51)  ; Ride Cymbal 1
(define ride2 59)  ; Ride Cymbal 2
```

The high hat

The High Hat percussion process is very simple, it just plays the High Hat on the
second and fourth beats of every measure. Each hit sounds for the duration one
triplet eighth note:

Example 4. The High Hat process.

```
(define (jazz-high-hat tmpo ampl)
  ;; generate a 4/4 measure of high-hat
  (let ((rhy (rhythm 'q tmpo))
        (dur (rhythm 't8 tmpo))
        (amp (amplitude 'mp))
        (pat (new cycle
                  :of `(r ,hihat r ,hihat ))))
    (process repeat 4
             output
             (new midi :time (now)
                  :keynum (next pat)
                  :channel 9 :duration dur
                  :amplitude (* amp ampl))
             wait rhy)))
```

The variable *pat* holds a cyclic pattern that rests (r) on the first and third beats, and
plays the key number of *hihat* on the other second and fourth beat.

We now listen to eight measures of the High Hat. Since the process computes
only one measure, we sprout eight versions of the process and offset each copy by
two seconds, exactly the duration of the combo's 4/4 measure at tempo 120.

Interaction 4. Playing eight measures of the high hat.

```
cm> (events (loop repeat 8
                  collect (jazz-high-hat 120 1))
            "perc.mid" '(0 2 4 6 8 10 12 14))
"perc-1.mid"
cm>
```

→ nm/21/snd/perc-1.mid

The jazz drums

The jazz-drums process (Example 5) randomly selects playing the snare, the bass drum or resting one quarter of the time. One tenth of the time the process produces a very loud tone.

Example 5. Jazz drums

```
(define (jazz-drums tmpo ampl)
  (let ((knums (new random
                 :of `((r :weight .25) ,snare ,bdrum)))
        (rhys (new cycle :of '(t4 t8)))
        (amps (new random :of '(f (ffff :weight .1)))))
    (process repeat 8
             for k = (next knums)
             for a = (amplitude (next amps))
             for r = (rhythm (next rhys) tmpo)
             output
             (new midi :time (now)
                  :keynum k :channel 9
                  :duration r
                  :amplitude (* a ampl))
             wait r)))
```

We now listen to eight measures of the drum process (Interaction 5).

Interaction 5. Playing eight measures of the drums.

```
cm> (events (loop repeat 8
              collect
              (list (jazz-high-hat 120 .99)
                    (jazz-drums 120 .99)))
            "perc.mid"
            '(0 2 4 6 8 10 12 14))
"perc-2.mid"
cm>
```

→ nm/21/snd/perc-2.mid

The jazz cymbals

The jazz-cymbals process is slightly more complex than either the high hat or the drums. The cymbals process performs a constant stream of triplet eighths in which the *ride1* cymbal is played on the beginning or every quarter note. The second and third triplets of each beat are either rests or a random choice between *ride1*, *ride2* or a rest. Table 1 shows the beat map for a measure of the process, where 1 means the *ride1* cymbal is played, r means a rest and x means a random choice between *ride1*, *ride2* or a rest:

Table 1. Beat map for one measure of the ride cymbals.

triplet	1	2	3	4	5	6	7	8	9	10	11	12
cymbals	1	r	x	1	r	1	1	x	x	1	x	1

The random elements marked x in Table 1 are created by a helper function called `or12r`:

Example 6. Random cymbal element.

```
(define (or12r wt)
  ;; wt is weight of resting relative to playing
  ;; r1 pattern plays ride1 or rests
  ;; r2 pattern plays ride2 or rests
  (let ((r1 (new random
               :of `(,ride1 (r :weight ,wt) )
               :for 1))
        (r2 (new random
               :of `(,ride2 (r :weight ,wt) )
               :for 1)))
    ;; return random pattern that slightly
    ;; prefers r1 pattern over r2 pattern
    (new random
      :of `((,r1 :weight 1.5)
            ,r2)
      :for 1)))
```

The `or12r` function returns a pattern that randomly selects between two sub-patterns, *r1* or *r2*. Each sub-pattern, in turn, randomly selects between playing a cymbal (ride1 in the case of *r1* and ride2 in the case of *r2*) or a rest. The probability weight *wt* is the probability of playing a rest relative to playing either one of the ride cymbals. The pattern returned by `or12r` assigns the overall weight of 1.5 to the *r1* sub-pattern, which means that probability of *r1* relative to *r2* is 3:2.

Given this helper function, the `jazz-cymbals` process creates the pattern described in Table 1 to improvise one measure of music:

Example 7. Jazz cymbals.

```
(define (jazz-cymbals tmpo ampl)
  (let* ((rhy (rhythm 't8 tmpo))
         (amps (new cycle
                  :of '(mf mp fff f mp ffff mf
                        mp fff f mp ffff)))
         (knums (new cycle
                  :of (list ride1 'r (or12r 5)
                            ride1 'r ride1
                            ride1 (or12r 7) (or12r 7)
                            ride1 (or12r 3) ride1))))
```

```
(process repeat 12
        for k = (next knums)
        for a = (amplitude (next amps))
        output
        (new midi :time (now)
              :keynum k
              :channel 9
              :duration rhy
              :amplitude (* a ampl ))
        wait rhy)))
```

The *knums* variable holds the random pattern that produces ride1, ride2 or the random choices created by the helper function. We can now listen eight bars of all the percussion together:

Interaction 6. Listening to the percussion sounds.

```
cm> (events (loop repeat 8
              collect
              (list (jazz-high-hat 120 1)
                    (jazz-drums 120 1)
                    (jazz-cymbals 120 1)))
            "perc.mid"
            '(0 2 4 6 8 10 12 14))
"perc-3.mid"
cm>
```

→ nm/21/snd/perc-3.mid

The jazz piano part
The jazz piano plays "improvised" jazz chords based on a pattern of root changes and a scale pattern that is transposed to each root. The piano randomly choose between playing triplet eighths or straight eights for a given measure.

Example 8. The jazz piano process.

```
(define (jazz-piano scale on tmpo ampl)
  ;; generate a measure of jazz harmony.
  ;; measure contains either 8 or 12 notes.
  (let* ((reps (odds .65 8 12))
         (rhys (if (= reps 8)
                   (new cycle :of '(t4 t8))
                   (new cycle :of 't8)))
         (amps (if (= reps 8)
                   (new random
                        :of (list (new cycle :of '(mp f))
                                  (new cycle :of '(mf ff))))
```

```
                        (new random
                          :of (list (new cycle :of '(mp p f))
                                    (new cycle
                                         :of '(mf mp ff)))))))
              (knms (new random
                      :of `((,(new heap :of scale
                                        :for (new random
                                                :of '(1 2 3 4)))
                              :weight ,(new random
                                              :of '(1.15 1.65)))
                            r))))
      (process repeat reps
              for r = (rhythm (next rhys) tmpo)
              for a = (amplitude (next amps))
              for l = (transpose (next knms true) on)
              each k in l
              output (new midi :time (now)
                             :channel 0 :keynum k
                             :duration r
                             :amplitude (* a ampl))
              wait r)))
```

The `jazz-piano` process creates a measure of jazz harmonies given a *scale*, a transposition level *on*, a tempo factor *tmpo* and an amplitude level *ampl* that scales the local amplitude value produced in the process. Each measure of the `jazz-piano` part will contain *reps* number of notes as determined by the `odds` function, which in this process chooses 8 notes per measure approximately 65% of the time, otherwise 12 notes. The *rhys* variable is set to a pattern of rhythms that depends on the value of *reps*. If the piano plays 8 notes in the measure then the rhythmic pattern for the process will consists of triplet quarter (tq) followed by a triplet 8ths (te), otherwise the piano will play twelve triplet 8ths. The harmonies are generated by a random pattern that selects between a rest and a heap of notes created from the *scale* that was passed into process. Probability of choosing a note is either 1.16 or 1.65 relative to the rest and each time the heap is selected it will generate one to four notes.

The process iterates *reps* times. On each iteration it selects a new rhythm, amplitude and list of key numbers to play. The key numbers are always returned in a list because the `next` function is called with its optional second argument set to true, which means that an entire period of key numbers is returned each time. This list will therefore hold between one and four key numbers on each iteration and the each clause iterates every key number *k* in the list and outputs a midi event to play it. Since the key numbers are all output at the same current time the piano produces up to four simultaneous notes on every rhythm in the measure. We now listen to the piano part in isolation. We will create four measures using the jazz-scale we defined transposed to B-flat at tempo 120.

Interaction 7. Playing four measures of the piano part.

```
cm> (events (loop repeat 4
                collect (jazz-piano jazz-scale
                                    'bf3 120 1))
            "piano.mid"
            '(0 2 4 6))
"piano-1.mid"
cm>
```

→ nm/21/snd/piano-1.mid

The acoustic bass part

The acoustic bass part is perhaps the most complex in terms of its implementation. The bass part plays a melodic line built out of tones from the jazz scale's tonic seventh chord alternating with color tones outside the tonic chord. The process first divides the jazz-scale (0 2 3 5 7 9 10 11 12 14) into two sets. The tonic set, designated "t" in the code below, contains the tonic seventh pitches 0 2, 4, 6 and 7, and the color set, designated c, contains the decoration pitches 1, 3, 5, 7 and 9. The bass plays a series of 12 triplets per measure, on each triplet only one of the two sets is possible. On all but the first triplet a rest is also possible. A tonic note always sounds on the 1st triplet eighth of the measure, but in the next three groups of three triplets there are five alternate patterns possible, of which only one is selected at random to be played. The top line in Table 2 shows the triplet 8th sub-groupings within the measure, and the five possible choices for each group appear on the lines below it. Each of these lines, labeled A through E, designates the probability of selection from most to least likely. Within each triplet grouping, the letter r stands for rest, t stands for a tonic note and c stands for a color note. The 11th and 12th triplets in the measure are simply random choices between either a tonic note and a rest (t|r) or a color note and a rest (c|r)

Table 2. Possible sub-patterns a-e within one measure's triplet beat map.

	1	2-4	5-7	8-10	11	12
a	t	r r c	r r t	r r c	t|r	c|r
b	t	r r r	r r r	r t c	t|r	c|r
c	t	r t c	r c t	r r r	t|r	c|r
d	t	c t c	t c t	c t c	t|r	c|r
e	t	c t r	t c r	c t r	t|r	c|r

The `acoustic-bass` process defines two helper functions to assist in pattern creation:

Example 9. Helper functions for the acoustic bass process.

```
(define (getset scale ints)
    ;; return the notes in scale
```

```
;; at the positions in ints.
(loop for i in ints
      collect (list-ref scale i)))

(define (rancyc data prob)
  ;; create cyclic pattern to be used
  ;; as element in random pattern with weight prob
  (list (new cycle :of data) :weight prob))
```

The getset function returns the list of notes in *scale* whose indices are specified in the list *ints*. The rancyc function creates the sub-pattern groups shown in Table 2. It returns a pattern node whose element is a cyclic pattern with an associated probability weight *prob* in the surrounding random pattern.

The jazz-bass process uses the helper functions to create the pattern data. It first uses getset to partition the jazz-scale into two random patterns, *tonics* and *colors*. The *bmap* variable holds the "beat map" for the measure. The pattern will returns twelve values, each value is either the symbol t c or r. The t value means the process should read a note from the *tonic* pattern, c means to read from the color pattern and r means to rest. The beatmap divides the twelve triplets of the measure into pattern subgroups containing 4+3+3+1+1 values. Each of first three subgroups chooses one of five possible patterns created by the rancyc helper function.

Example 10. The acoustic bass process.

```
(define (jazz-bass scale on tmpo ampl)
  (let ((rhy (rhythm 'te tmpo))
        (tonics (new random
                   :of (getset scale '(0 2 4 6 7))))
        (colors (new random
                   :of (getset scale '(1 3 5 6 8))))
        (amps (new cycle
                 :of '(mp p ffff fff p fff
                       mp p ffff fff mp fff)))
        (durs (new cycle :of '(tq t8 t8)))
        ;; beat map
        (bmap
         (new cycle
           :of
           (list
            ;; 5 possible patterns for 1-4
            (new random :for 1
                 :of (list (rancyc '(t r r c) 1.0)
                           (rancyc '(t r r r) .25)
                           (rancyc '(t r t c) .22)
                           (rancyc '(t c t c) .065)
                           (rancyc '(t c t r) .014)))
            ;; 5 possible patterns for 5-7
```

```
                    (new random :for 1
                         :of (list (rancyc '(r r t) 1.0)
                                   (rancyc '(r r r) .25)
                                   (rancyc '(r c t) .22)
                                   (rancyc '(t c t) .038)
                                   (rancyc '(t c r) .007)))
                    ;; 5 possible patterns for 8-10
                    (new random :for 1
                         :of (list (rancyc '(r r c) 1.0)
                                   (rancyc '(r t c) .415)
                                   (rancyc '(r r r) .25)
                                   (rancyc '(c t c) .11)
                                   (rancyc '(c t r) .018)))
                    ;; two possible values for 11
                    (new random :for 1
                         :of '((r :weight 1)
                               (t :weight .25)))
                    ;; two possible values for 12
                    (new random :for 1
                         :of '((r :weight 1)
                               (c :weight .25))))))))
           (process repeat 12
                    for x = (next bmap)
                    for k = (if (equal? x 't)
                                (next tonics)    .
                                (if (equal? x 'c)
                                  (next colors)
                                  x))
                    for d = (rhythm (next durs) tmpo)
                    for a = (amplitude (next amps))
                    output
                    (new midi :time (now)
                         :keynum (transpose k on)
                         :channel 1
                         :duration d
                         :amplitude (* a ampl))
                    wait rhy)))
```

The process plays twelve notes per measure, on each note a value *x* is read from the beat map. If *x* is either t or c then *k* is set to a value from the *tonic* or *color* pattern, otherwise *x* is a rest (r). The key number of each midi event is determined by transposing the scale degree *k* to the transposition level *on* specified to the process. We now listen to eight measures of jazz-bass in isolation:

Interaction 8. Listening to eight bars of the acoustic bass.

```
cm> (events (loop repeat 8
                  collect (jazz-bass jazz-scale
                                     'bf2 120 1))
            "bass.mid"
            '(0 2 4 6 8 10 12 14))
"bass-1.mid"
cm>
```

→ nm/21/snd/bass-1.mid

The main process

The main process of the automatic jazz program is quite simple: jazz-combo iterates *measures* number of times and sprouts the combo's instrument at the start of each measure. Every 12 measures the process adjusts its overall amplitude level so that the combo's amplitude changes dynamically during the performance. Similar adjustments could be made to the tempo, scale and root movements of the jazz improvisation. These improvements are left to the reader to implement.

Example 11. The main process.

```
(define (jazz-combo measures changes tempo scale)
  (let ((roots (new cycle :of changes))
        (ampl 1))
    (process for meas below measures
             for root = (next roots)
             if (= 0 (mod meas 12))
             set ampl = (between .5 1)
             sprout (jazz-piano scale root tempo ampl)
             sprout (jazz-cymbals tempo ampl)
             sprout (jazz-high-hat tempo ampl)
             sprout (jazz-drums tempo ampl)
             sprout (jazz-bass scale
                               (transpose root -12)
                               tempo ampl)
             wait (rhythm 'w tempo))))
```

We now generate a 24 bar improvisation from the jazz combo. Sound examples from two different runs are provided.

Interaction 9. Two different versions of the Jazz Combo.

```
cm> (events (list #&combo-setup
                  (jazz-combo 48 jazz-changes
                              jazz-tempo jazz-scale))
            "jazz.mid")
```

```
"jazz-1.mid"
cm> (events (list #&combo-setup
                  (jazz-combo 48 jazz-changes
                              jazz-tempo jazz-scale))
            "jazz.mid")
"jazz-2.mid"
cm>
```

→ nm/21/snd/jazz-1.mid
→ nm/21/snd/jazz-2.mid

Chapter Source Code

The source code to all of the examples and interactions in this chapter can be found in the file jazz.cm located in the same directory as the HTML file for this chapter. The source file can be edited in a text editor or evaluated inside the Common Music application.

22

Etudes, Op. 8: An Algorithmic Model of György Ligeti's *Désordre*

In this Etude we look at a pattern-based description of György Ligeti's first Piano Etude, *Désordre*. The program examples and most of the commentary were written by Tobias Kunze at CCRMA, Stanford University. *Désordre* has been analyzed in great depth by Kinzler in György Ligeti: decision and automatism in `Désordre', 1er Étude, Premier Livre (Kinzler). Jane Piper Clendinning's The Pattern Meccanico Compositions of György Ligeti (Clendinning) discusses Ligeti's use of patterns in a number of different compositions.

The intent of this Etude is to consider Ligeti's composition from the perspective of algorithmic control — to arrive at some idea of what specific "algorithmic knobs" could be implemented that might offer a possible analog to the composer's actual decisions. We first present a general analysis of the Etude's essential features, and then model the composition in software using process descriptions. The model makes an honest attempt to be realistic but trades off accuracy against flexibility. After all, there is no point in implementing an algorithm that cannot be manipulated or adjusted so that it can explore different paths through a composition's theoretical parameter space.

A note regarding references to the score: since the left and right hands are essentially independent, each point of interest in the score will be indicated by page, system and measure numbers. Page numbers are prefixed by *p*, systems by *s* and measures by *m*. For example "p3s2m1" stands for page 3, system 2, measure 1. Where necessary, an indication of the part will also be provided. In systems starting with a partial measure, the first complete measure is counted as measure 1. All numbers follow the facsimile edition of Études pour piano: premier livre. published by B. Schott's Söhne, Mainz, 1985.

Structure

The textural make-up of the Etude is rather straightforward. Each hand is assigned its own part and both parts share a common, layered substructure and a continuously pulsating eighth-note motion. Each hand is restricted to a particular set of notes: the right-hand plays only the white keys and the left-hand plays only black keys. In addition to establishing the essential dramatic opposition in the piece, the partitioning also allows the relatively difficult parts to occupy the same register at certain points in the composition. In keeping with the harmonic partitioning, each part follows its own internal logic and is essentially independent from the other "horizontally" as well. That is, both hands are largely unsynchronized on the metrical level although stretches with semi-synchronized phrase structures do exist. This metrical independence is central to the composition of *Désordre* and most of the form-defining features of the work stem from this basic independence.

The internal structure of each part is a combination of constantly rising eighth notes in the background and a rhythmically pronounced, slower foreground, all within the constant running motion of the eighth notes. The foreground layer is played *forte* throughout the piece and heavily accented. The foreground layer in both hands features a phrase structure that is reminiscent of traditional A-A'-B forms, where two closely related shorter phrases are followed by a longer developmental third phrase. In spite of the distortion by the asymmetrical meter employed in each part, the phrasing hints at an underlying simple and song-like two-beat meter. The similarly asymmetric "meter" that is induced in the backgrounds by eighth-note groups of differing lengths is relatively negligible compared to the prominent metric structure in the foreground layers.

On a formal level, the piece is structured by both the temporal behavior and pitch behavior of its two parts. A first section, 404 eighth notes long, (from the beginning of the piece to p3s4m4) is quite static in tempo except for the slight accelerando towards the end. The next section, which extends until p4s4m7 (231 eighth notes in duration) accelerates the foreground parts until they are reduced to eighth notes, at which point a typical "ligetiesque" cut interrupts the lower part (which had by then hit the bottom of the piano range) and resumes in the descant as well as in the original foreground tempo. This third section (429 measures) extends to the end and is characterized by a static tempo in the upper part and a slowing down of the lower part.

The patterns
The foreground in both the upper and lower parts will consist of cyclic repetitions of a constant, stepwise pattern. Within each cycle the pattern is transposed diatonically

by a constant amount. The pattern for the upper part consists of 26 steps, 7 for each of the A phrases and 12 for phrase B:

Table 1. Step Pattern for white keys.

Phrase A	0 0 1 0 2 1 -1
Phrase A'	-1 -1 2 1 3 2 -2
Phrase B	2 2 4 3 5 4 -1 0 3 2 6 5

The pattern for the lower part has 33 steps, again 7 for each of the A phrases and 19 in the extended phrase B:

Table 2. Step Pattern for black keys

Phrase A	0 0 1 0 2 2 0
Phrase A'	1 1 2 1 -2 -2 -1
Phrase B	1 1 2 2 0 -1 -4 -3 0 -1 3 2 1 -1 0 -3 -2 -3 -5

There are a total of 14 cycles in the upper part, each of which is transposed *diatonically* one step upwards. Due to its greater length, there only 11 cycles in the lower part. The smaller number of cycles — which translates into fewer transpositions — is more than compensated for by (1) a two-step diatonic transposition downwards and (2) the lower part's pentatonic mode having fewer steps per octave than the heptatonic mode of the upper part. The cycles align with the score as shown in Table 2

Table 3. Cycles and transpositions for both parts.

Lower Part				Upper Part		
#	Transp.	Score		#	Transp.	Score
			Section I			
1:	ds3	p2s1m0		1:	b4	p2s1m0
2:	as2	p2s3m5		2:	c5	p2s2m7
3:	fs2	p3s2m2		3:	d5	p2s4m7
				4:	e5	p3s2m6
			Section II			
4:	cs2	p3s4m4		5:	f5	p3s4m4
5:	gs1	p4s1m3		6:	g5	p3s4m11
6:	ds1	p4s2m3		7:	a5	p4s1m7
7:	as0	p4s3m2		8:	b5	p4s2m5
8:	fs0	p4s4m1[1]		9:	c6	p4s3m3
				10:	d6	p4s3m10
			Section III			
		(p4s4m7)		11:	e6	p4s4m7
9:	cs5	p5s1m2		12:	f6	p5s2m4
10:	gs4	p5s3m7		13:	g6	p5s4m4
11:	ds4	p6s2m4[2]		14:	a6	p6s2m4 [3]

1. Cycle 8 in the lower part reaches the bottom of the piano range and discontinues after m. 4 in phrase B only to resume immediately in the treble clef (p4s4m7). The first note of this continuation should read fs but for obvious reasons is given as fs5 to the right-hand.
2. Cycle is cut off after m. 3 in Phrase B.
3. Cycle is cut off after m. 2 in Phrase A'.

The rhythmic picture is less clear due to acceleration and deceleration of the patterns. The sequence of rhythms in the upper and lower parts read as follows:

Table 4. Upper part, foreground rhythms.

Sect. I: Little Disorder (404 eighths)	
3 5 3 5 5 3 7	cycle 1
3 5 3 5 5 3 7	
3 5 3 5 5 3 3 4 5 3 3 5	
3 5 3 4 5 3 8	cycle 2
3 5 3 4 5 3 8	
3 5 3 4 5 3 3 5 5 3 3 4	
3 5 3 5 5 3 7	cycle 3
3 5 3 5 5 3 7	
3 5 3 5 5 3 3 4 5 3 3 5	
3 5 3 4 5 2 7	cycle 4 (accel.)
2 4 2 4 4 2 5	
2 3 2 3 3 1 1 3 3 1 1 3	
Sect. II: Rapid accelerando (231 eighths)	
1 2 1 2 2 1 3	cycle 5
1 2 1 2 2 1 3	
1 2 1 2 2 1 1 2 2 1 1 2	
1 2 1 2 2 1 3	cycle 6
1 2 1 2 2 1 3	
1 2 1 2 2 1 1 2 2 1 1 2	
1 2 1 2 2 1 3	cycle 7
1 2 1 2 2 1 2	
1 2 1 2 2 1 1 2 2 1 1 2	
1 2 1 2 2 1 2	cycle 8
1 2 1 2 2 1 2	
1 2 1 2 2 1 1 2 2 1 1 2	
1 2 1 2 2 1 2	cycle 9
1 2 1 2 1 1 2	
1 2 1 2 2 1 1 1 2 1 1 1	
1 2 1 1 1 1 2	cycle 10
1 1 1 1 1 1 2	
1 1 1 1 1 1 1 1 1 1 1	
Sect. III: Static (429 eighths)	
3 5 3 5 5 3 8	cycle 11
3 5 3 5 5 3 8	
3 5 3 5 5 3 3 5 5 3 3 5	
3 5 3 5 5 3 8	cycle 12 (same)
3 5 3 5 5 3 8	

3 5 3 5 5 3 3 5 5 5 3 3 5	
3 5 3 5 5 3 8	cycle 13 (same)
3 5 3 5 5 3 8	
3 5 3 5 5 3 3 5 5 3 3 5	
3 5 3 5 5 3 8	cycle 14
3 5 3 5 5 3 8	
3 5 3 5 5 8	(cuts off here)

Table 5. Lower part, foreground rhythms.

Sect. I: Static (404 eighths)	
3 5 3 5 5 3 8	cycle 1
3 5 3 5 5 3 8	
3 5 3 5 5 3 3 5 5 3 3 5 3 5 3 5 5 3 8	
3 5 3'5 5 3 8	cycle 2
3 5 3 5 5 3 8	
3 5 3 5 5 3 3 5 5 3 3 5 3 5 3 5 5 3 8	
3 5 3 5 5 3 8	cycle 3
3 5 3 5 5 2 7	(accel.)
3 4 3 4 4 2 2 4 4 2 2 3 2 3 1 3 3 1 4	
Sect. II: Rapid Accelerando (231 eighths)	
1 3 1 2 2 1 3	cycle 4
1 2 1 2 2 1 3	
1 2 1 2 2 1 1 2 2 1 1 2 1 2 1 2 2 1 3	
1 3 1 2 2 1 3	cycle 5
1 2 1 2 2 1 3	
1 2 1 2 2 1 1 2 2 1 1 2 1 2 1 2 2 1 2	
1 2 1 2 2 1 2	cycle 6
1 2 1 2 2 1 2	
1 2 1 2 2 1 1 2 2 1 1 2 1 2 1 2 2 1 2	
1 2 1 2 2 1 2	cycle 7
1 2 1 2 2 1 2	
1 2 1 2 2 1 1 2 1 1 1 2 1 1 1 1 1 1 2	
1 1 1 1 1 1 2	cycle 8
1 1 1 1 1 1 2	
1 1 1 1 1 1 1 1	
Sect. III: Allargando (429 eighths)	
5 3 3 5 3 5 3 5 5 3 8	
3 5 3 5 5 3 8	cycle 9
3 5 3 5 5 3 8	
3 5 3 5 5 3 3 5 6 3 3 5 3 5 3 6 5 3 8	
3 6 3 5 5 3 9	cycle 10
3 5 3 5 6 3 8	
3 5 3 6 5 3 3 5 6 3 3 5 3 5 3 6 5 3 9	
3 7 3 8 9 3 13	cycle 11
3 11 3 21	

The Model

The brief analysis presented in the previous section will allow us to translate the combined foreground structure of *Désordre* into pattern descriptions. We begin by defining an 8th note pulse for the piece according to the specification in the score. A helper function `eighth-time` will allow us to convert from duration values expressed as number of 8th notes into time in seconds:

Example 1. Global tempo and amplitude.

```
(define eighth-pulse (rhythm 'e 76.0 'w))

(define (eighth-time number-of-eighths)
  ;; Convert duration in eighth notes
  ;; to time in seconds
  (* eighth-pulse number-of-eighths))

(define fg-amp .7)   ; foreground amp

(define bg-amp .5)   ; background amp
```

The global variable *eighth-pulse* holds the duration in seconds of an 8th note pulse at tempo 76 with a whole note beat. This value works out to 15/152, or approximately 0.098 seconds per 8th note. The function `eighth-time` translates a specified *number-of-eighths* into time in seconds by multiplying that number by the speed of one eighth note. The variables *fg-amp* and *bg-amp* define global amplitude levels for the foreground and background processes, respectively. These can be adjusted as needed to increase or decrease the amplitude level of the foreground relative to the background.

Upper foreground materials

As suggested by our analysis in the preceding section, the algorithms to implement the upper and lower parts to *Désordre* will be driven by four sets of data: the part's mode, its step pattern, its transposition pattern, and its rhythmic pattern.

Upper foreground melody

We examine the melodic materials first. Example 2 contains the definitions of the white key mode and the step pattern for the upper part. A *step* is an interval that describes relative melodic motion between notes, i.e. the intervallic distances between successive notes in a sequence.

Example 2. Upper foreground mode and step patterns.

```
(define white-mode
  (new mode :steps '(c d e f g a b c)))

(define white-fg-steps
  '(0   0   1   0   2   1  -1            ; Phrase a
    -1  -1   2   1   3   2  -2            ; Phrase a'
     2   2   4   3   5   4  -1  0  3  2  6  5)') ; Phrase b

(define (make-white-fg-notes note)
  ;; convert note in MIDI scale to modal equivalent
  (let ((step (keynum note :to white-mode)))
    ;; pattern of steps is offset
    ;; from a constantly rising offset
    (new transposer
      :of (new cycle :of white-fg-steps)
      :by (new range :initially step :by 1))))
```

The *white-mode* global variable is set to a mode object that implements the white key mode for the upper part. Each octave has only eight tones, and adjacent key numbers in the mode will be either one or two semi-tones apart in the chromatic scale. The *white-fg-steps* variable contains the sequence of *step motion* that describes the upper part. Each step in *white-fg-steps* describes the *relative* distance from the previous step. For example, if the initial position for the step pattern were c4 then the steps (0 0 1 0 2) would produce the notes (c4 c4 cs cs ds) in the chromatic scale but (c4 c4 d4 d4 e4) in *white-mode*.

The `make-white-fg-note` function returns a pattern that implements the melodic foreground of the upper part. The starting point for the melody is the *note* specified to the function which is converted to its key number equivalent in *white-mode*. The `transposer` pattern transposes a cycle pattern of foreground steps (intervals) onto the diatonic degrees of the white mode.

Upper foreground rhythmic pattern
For reasons of clarity the rhythmic pattern for the upper part is presented here in its entirety even though is is fairly long. It would certainly be possible to define this pattern in terms of repeated subpatterns.

Example 3. The upper foreground rhythmic pattern.

```
-------------------------------------------------------------------------
(define (make-white-fg-rhythms)
  (new cycle
    :of `(3 5 3 5 5 3 7              ; cycle 1
          3 5 3 5 5 3 7
          3 5 3 5 5 3 3 4 5 3 3 5
          3 5 3 4 5 3 8             ; cycle 2
          3 5 3 4 5 3 8
          3 5 3 4 5 3 3 5 5 3 3 4
          3 5 3 5 5 3 7             ; cycle 3
          3 5 3 5 5 3 7
          3 5 3 5 5 3 3 4 5 3 3 5
          3 5 3 4 5 2 7             ; cycle 4
          2 4 2 4 4 2 5
          2 3 2 3 3 1 1 3 3 1 1 3
          1 2 1 2 2 1 3             ; cycle 5
          1 2 1 2 2 1 3
          1 2 1 2 2 1 1 2 2 1 1 2
          1 2 1 2 2 1 3             ; cycle 6
          1 2 1 2 2 1 3
          1 2 1 2 2 1 1 2 2 1 1 2
          1 2 1 2 2 1 3             ; cycle 7
          1 2 1 2 2 1 2
          1 2 1 2 2 1 1 2 2 1 1 2
          1 2 1 2 2 1 2             ; cycle 8
          1 2 1 2 2 1 2
          1 2 1 2 2 1 1 2 2 1 1 2
          1 2 1 2 2 1 2             ; cycle 9
          1 2 1 2 1 1 2
          1 2 1 2 2 1 1 1 2 1 1 1
          1 2 1 1 1 1 2             ; cycle 10
          1 1 1 1 1 1 2
          1 1 1 1 1 1 1 1 1 1 1 1
          ,(new cycle
             :of
             (new cycle
               :of
               '(3 5 3 5 5 3 8    ; cycle 11-14
                 3 5 3 5 5 3 8
                 3 5 3 5 5 3 3 5 5 3 3 5))
             :for 3)
          3 5 3 5 5 3 8             ; cycle 14
-------------------------------------------------------------------------
```

```
        3 5 3 5 5 3 8
        3 5 3 5 5 3)))                              ; cuts off here
```

Lower foreground materials

The algorithm for the lower foreground part is driven by the same types of data. However, since it is eventually shifted into the treble clef after it hits the bottom of the keyboard (p4s4m7), its transposition pattern adds a "warp" that transposes the whole pattern up five octaves, or 20 black mode steps (see the *warp-point* variable in Example 4).

Lower foreground melody

Our lower foreground melody is defined in a manner analogous to the upper foreground, except of course that the pattern and mode are quite different. The implementation is made slightly more complex because the lower pattern "warps", or shifts, when it reaches the bottom of the keyboard by jumping back up to the middle register of the keyboard.

Example 4. Lower foreground mode and step patterns.

```
(define black-mode
  (new mode :steps '(cs ds fs gs as cs)))

(define black-fg-steps
  '(0   0   1   0   2   2   0              ; Phrase a
    1   1   2   1  -2  -2  -1              ; Phrase a'
    1   1   2   2   0  -1  -4  -3   0      ; Phrase b
    0  -1   3   2   1  -1   0  -3  -2  -3  -5))

(define (make-black-fg-notes note)
  (let* ((cycle-length (length black-fg-steps))
         (warp-point (+ (* cycle-length 7)
                        7 7 8))
         (step (keynum note :to black-mode)))
    (new transposer
      :of
      (new transposer
        :of (new cycle
              :of black-fg-steps)
        :stepping (new line
                    :of
                    (list (new cycle :of 0
                            :for warp-point)
                          20)))
      :by (new range :initially step :by -2)))))
```

Warp-point specifies the point at which the lower process jumps from the bottom of the keyboard up to the middle register. The inner transposer replicates step intervals relative to an offset produced by a `line`. The line generates 0 (no offset) until *warp-point* but then transposes by 20 thereafter. The surrounding pattern applies the descending stepwise transposition (-2) to the warped pattern values.

Lower foreground rhythm

The definition of the lower foreground rhythmic pattern is derived directly from the data in Table 4. Although it is not shown here, there is enough inner repetition to make the definition of subpatterns worthwhile.

Example 5. The lower foreground rhythmic pattern.

```
(define (make-black-fg-rhythms)
  (new cycle
    :of '(3 5 3 5 5 5 3 8      ; cycle 1
          3 5 3 5 5 5 3 8
          3 5 3 5 5 3 3 5  5 3 3 5 3 5 3 5 5 3 8
          3 5 3 5 5 3 8      ; cycle 2
          3 5 3 5 5 3 8
          3 5 3 5 5 3 3 5  5 3 3 5 3 5 3 5 5 3 8
          3 5 3 5 5 3 8      ; cycle 3
          3 5 3 5 5 2 7
          3 4 3 4 4 2 2 4  4 2 2 3 2 3 1 3 3 1 4
          1 3 1 2 2 1 3      ; cycle 4
          1 2 1 2 2 1 3
          1 2 1 2 2 1 1 2  2 1 1 2 1 2 1 2 2 1 3
          1 3 1 2 2 1 3      ; cycle 5
          1 2 1 2 2 1 3
          1 2 1 2 2 1 1 2  2 1 1 2 1 2 1 2 2 1 2
          1 2 1 2 2 1 2      ; cycle 6
          1 2 1 2 2 1 2
          1 2 1 2 2 1 1 2  2 1 1 2 1 2 1 2 2 1 2
          1 2 1 2 2 1 2      ; cycle 7
          1 2 1 2 2 1 2
          1 2 1 2 2 1 1 2  1 1 1 2 1 1 1 1 1 1 2
          1 1 1 1 1 1 2      ; cycle 8
          1 1 1 1 1 1 2
          1 1 1 1 1 1 1 1  5 3 3 5 3 5 3 5 5 3 8
          3 5 3 5 5 3 8      ; cycle 9
          3 5 3 5 5 3 8
          3 5 3 5 5 3 3 5  6 3 3 5 3 5 3 6 5 3 8
          3 6 3 5 5 3 9      ; cycle 10
          3 5 3 5 6 3 8
          3 5 3 6 5 3 3 5  6 3 3 5 3 5 3 6 5 3 9
          3 7 3 8 9 3 13     ; cycle 11
          3 11 3 21)))       ; cuts off here
```

Foreground process description

We are now ready to define a process that will play our foreground material:

Example 6. Foreground process.

```
(define (fg-mono mode keynums rhythms)
   (process for key = (keynum (next keynums)
                                  :from mode)
            for rhy = (eighth-time (next rhythms))
            output (new midi :time (now)
                          :keynum key
                          :amplitude fg-amp
                          :duration rhy)
            wait rhy
            until (eop? rhythms)))
```

The `fg-mono` process takes a *mode*, a pattern of *keynums* and a pattern of *rhythms*. The process generates a melody with every keynum *key* and rhythm *rhy* in the patterns for one rhythmic period. Since the pattern *keynums* that is passed to the function describes relative intervallic motion within a particular mode, the :from keyword argument to keynum is used to convert scaler positions in *mode* into their equivalent positions in the standard chromatic scale used by MIDI. Since this mode is passed into the process, fg-mono is a completely generic description that can be used to generate both the upper and lower foreground parts. We now listen to each foreground part, first individually and then mixed together.

Interaction 1. Play upper foreground.

```
cm> (events (fg-mono white-mode
                     (make-white-fg-notes 'b4)
                     (make-white-fg-rhythms))
           "ligeti.mid")
"ligeti-1.mid"
cm>
```

→ nm/22/snd/ligeti-1.mid

Interaction 2. Play lower foreground.

```
cm> (events (fg-mono black-mode
                     (make-black-fg-notes 'ds4)
                     (make-black-fg-rhythms))
           "ligeti.mid")
"ligeti-2.mid"
cm>
```

→ nm/22/snd/ligeti-2.mid

Interaction 3. Play both foregrounds together.

```
cm> (events (list
              (fg-mono white-mode
                       (make-white-fg-notes 'b4)
                       (make-white-fg-rhythms))
              (fg-mono black-mode
                       (make-black-fg-notes 'ds4)
                       (make-black-fg-rhythms)))
           "ligeti.mid")
"ligeti-3.mid"
cm>
```

→ nm/22/snd/ligeti-3.mid

Enhancement 1

The first improvement to our model will add octaves to the foreground and simulate a background layer by filling in the 8th note pulse using randomly selected mode notes centered around each of the foreground notes.

Example 7. Add octaves and a fake background

```
(define (desordre-w/octaves mode ntes rhys)
  (let ((fg-time 0)
        (fg-eighths 0)
        (mode-deg 0))
    (list
     ;; foreground process
     (process with dur and key
              set fg-time = (now)
              set mode-deg = (next ntes)
              set key = (keynum mode-deg :from mode)
              set fg-eighths = (next rhys)
              set dur = (eighth-time fg-eighths)
              output (new midi
                          :time fg-time
                          :keynum key
                          :duration (- dur .01)
                          :amplitude fg-amp)
              output (new midi
                          :time fg-time
                          :keynum (+ key 12)
                          :duration (- dur .01)
                          :amplitude fg-amp)
              wait dur
              until (eop? rhys))
     ;; background process fills in 8th note pulses with
```

```
;; randomly selected mode notes based on current
;; foreground note.
(let ((pat (new range
               :from (pval mode-deg)
               :stepping (new random
                              :of
                              '((1 :weight 3)
                                2
                                (3 :weight .5
                                   :max 1)))
               :for (pval fg-eighths))))
   (process repeat 1064
            for k = (keynum (next pat)
                            :from mode)
            unless (or (= (now) fg-time)
                       (not (<= 0 k 127)))
            output (new midi
                        :time (now)
                        :keynum k
                        :duration (- eighth-pulse
                                     .01)
                        :amplitude bg-amp)
            wait eighth-pulse)))))
```

The Desordre-w/octaves process takes the same arguments as our original play-fg process but its definition is more involved. Notice that desordre-w/octaves returns a list of two processes, the first produces our foreground materials and the second generates the background. The first process is equivalent to our original play-fg definition except that it outputs *two* MIDI objects per interaction to create the octave passage work. Our first process description also sets two shared variables that the second process will use. The *mode-deg* variable holds the current mode degree of the foreground and the variable *fg-eighths* is set to the duration (in eighth notes) of the note the process is currently playing.

The second process description creates a harmonic background to support the foreground material. It creates a pattern *pat* that generates random steps from whatever *mode-deg* the first process is currently playing. The range pattern produces each step using a random pattern that generates three different step sizes: steps to adjacent degrees (1), steps that skip one degree (2) and steps that skip two degrees (3). The actual intervallic distances these steps produce will depend on the mode to which it is applied. For example a single step (1) can produce either half steps or whole steps in our white mode but whole steps or minor thirds in our pentatonic black mode. Since the range's initial position as well as its period length depend on whatever the first process is currently generating, the pattern uses pval to delay the evaluation of *fg-eighths* and *mode-deg* until the pattern is actually running. Otherwise, these variables would be evaluated when the pattern is *created*, rather than when the pattern was used.

The rest of the process description is relatively straightforward. Because the foreground material extends to the top and bottom of the keyboard, our random background process could potentially generate random key number above or below the legal range of key numbers specified by MIDI. The unless clause checks to see if the current key number of the background is within the legal limits and, if not, omits that event from the score. We now listen to the octaves and background material:

Interaction 4. Listening to enhancement 1.

```
cm> (events (append
              (desordre-w/octaves
                white-mode
                (make-white-fg-notes 'b3)
                (make-white-fg-rhythms))
              (desordre-w/octaves
                black-mode
                (make-black-fg-notes 'ds3)
                (make-black-fg-rhythms)))
           "ligeti.mid")
"ligeti-4.mid"
cm>
```

→ nm/22/snd/ligeti-4.mid

Enhancement 2

As our final enhancement we implement processes that add more realism by simulating the foreground chords that occur in section three:

Example 8. Process with foreground chords.

```
(define (desordre-voices mode ntes rhys chord
                         voimap fgchan bgchan)
  (let ((moct (scale-divisions mode))
        (fg-time 0)
        (fg-8ths 0)
        (mode-deg 0))
    (list
     ;; foreground process
     (process with rhy and voi and key
              and voices =
              (new transposer
                :of (new heap :of chord
                         :for (pval voi))
                :on (pval mode-deg))
              for count from 0
              set fg-time = (now)
```

```
           set mode-deg = (next ntes)
           set key = (keynum mode-deg
                           :from mode)
           set fg-8ths = (next rhys)
           set rhy = (eighth-time fg-8ths)
           set voi = (lookup count voimap)
           output
           (new midi :time (now)
                 :channel fgchan
                 :keynum key
                 :duration rhy
                 :amplitude fg-amp)
           wait rhy
           if (equal? voi true)
           ;; add lower octave ...
           output
           (new midi :time (now)
                 :channel fgchan
                 :keynum (- key 12)
                 :duration rhy
                 :amplitude fg-amp)
           else
           ;; ... else add cluster
           each k in (next voices true)
           output
           (new midi
              :channel fgchan
              :time (now)
              :keynum (keynum k :from mode)
              :duration (- rhy .01))
           until (eop? rhys))
   ;; background process.
   (let ((notes
          (new range
             :from
             (pval (- mode-deg
                     moct))
             :stepping
             (new random
                :of '((1 :weight 3)
                      2
                      (3 :weight .5 :max 1)))
             :for (pval fg-8ths))))
     (process for i below 1064
              for k = (keynum (next notes)
                              :from mode)
              unless (or (= (now) fg-time)
                         (not (<= 0 k 127)))
```

```
output (new midi
          :channel bgchan
          :time (now)
          :keynum k
          :duration (- eighth-pulse
                         .01)
          :amplitude bg-amp)
       wait eighth-pulse)))))
```

As in the first enhancement (desordre-w/octaves) our second enhancement creates a foreground and background process. The background process is essentially unchanged from the first enhancement and will not be discussed here. However, the foreground process is considerably more complex in our new definition because it now generates both octaves and random chords of notes. The intervallic content of these clusters is specified to the process by the *chord* parameter. The value of *chords* is a list of intervals that the *voices* random pattern will transpose to the foreground's current mode degree. The density, or number of notes, in each random cluster is controlled by a "voice map" specified in the *voimap* parameter. The voice map is a list that contains pairs of values. The first value in each pair specifies a beat number in the score (calculated in eighth notes) and the second value specifies the number notes that each cluster should contain from that beat forward until the next pair in the beat map. Since our foreground process will produce both octaves and chords, a boolean true value in the voice map will be interpreted as meaning that octaves instead of random clusters should be output. For example the beat map:

    (0 3 10 #t 15 6)

would specify 3-voice clusters starting at beat 0, octaves starting at beat 10 and 6-voice clusters staring at beat 15. The function lookup is used to look up the current voice number *voi* in *voimap*. lookup is similar to interpl in that it assumes lists of pairs whose *x* value is monotonically increasing. However lookup does not perform linear interpolation, it simply returns whatever *y* value is in the list. Since no interpolation is performed the *y* value does not even have to be numeric.

We now listen to our final version. Foreground and background processes for both parts are given their own MIDI channels so that each individual processes can heard in isolation or in combination with other specific voices.

Interaction 5. Listening to enhancement 2.

```
cm> (events (append
            (dsordre-voices white-mode
                            (make-white-fg-notes 'b4)
                            (make-white-fg-rhythms)
                            '(-1 -2 -3 -4 -5 -6)
                            '(0 #t 261 1 284 2 297 3)
                            0 1)
            (dsordre-voices black-mode
                            (make-black-fg-notes 'ds4)
                            (make-black-fg-rhythms)
                            '(-1 -2 -3 -4)
                            '(0 #t 254 1 286 2)
                             2 3))
            "ligeti.mid")
"ligeti-5.mid"
cm>
```

→ nm/22/snd/ligeti-5.mid (four channels)

Chapter Source Code

The source code to all of the examples and interactions in this chapter can be found in the file ligeti.cm located in the same directory as the HTML file for this chapter. The source file can be edited in a text editor or evaluated inside the Common Music application.

References

Kinzler, H.. (1991). Gyorgy Ligeti: decision and automatism in Desordre 1er Etude, Premier Livre. *Journal of New Music Research, 20(2),* 89.
Clendinning, J. (1992). The Pattern Meccanico Compositions of Gyorgy Ligeti. *Perspectives of New Music, 1,* 192.

23

Spectral Composition

In *spectral composition* the acoustic properties of sound constitute source material for music composition. The term *spectral* refers to the timbral content of sound — the precise mixture of partials (frequencies, amplitudes and initial phases) that make up a sound's waveform (see Chapters 9 and 13 for a discussion of sound and harmonics). Spectral composition is also a label that refers to a group of contemporary French composers (Dufourt, Grisey, Murail, Risset) that work extensively with timbral information. An overview of some of their compositional techniques can be found in An Introduction to the Pitch Organization of French Spectral Music (Rose) by Francois Rose. Many other contemporary composers also work extensively with spectral information as well, including John Chowning, Barry Truax and James Dashow. Spectralist tendencies are clearly observable in the work of earlier twentieth century composers such as Andre Jolivet, Olivier Messiaen, Iannis Xenakis, Edgard Varese and Ben Johnston.

Because spectral techniques are based on the physical properties of sound, computer analysis and synthesis figure strongly in this type of composition. There are two broad approaches to composing with spectral information. The first method employs an analysis/resynthesis strategy — a specific source waveform is analyzed by computer for its harmonic content and this spectral information is then "resynthesized" back into the composition in ways the composer works out. The second approach to spectral composition utilizes *sound synthesis algorithms* to synthesize spectral information directly. We will introduce both strategies in this chapter.

Spectral Analysis

Spectral analysis means to deconstruct a sound (a source recording or real-time audio signal) into its constituent partials. Analysis methods vary according whether the waveform is periodic or aperiodic in nature. One particular method, called the *Fast Fourier Transform* (FFT) lies at the heart of many computer programs that analyze complex periodic waveforms. The French mathematician Jean Fourier (1768-1830) discovered that any periodic wave can be described as a sum of individual sine waves, where each sine wave is described by its frequency, amplitude and initial phase, or starting point. This suggests that there are two different ways to "look at" a sound: as a pressure wave, or as a collection of individual partials. A *time domain* representation of a waveform displays the aggregated wave's changing amplitude (pressure) over time. A *frequency domain* representation plots the changing amplitudes of the individual partials over frequency (Figure 1).

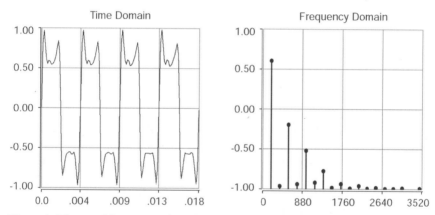

Figure 1. Time and frequency domain representations of a 220 Hz Clarinet tone.

→ nm/23/snd/clarinet.mp3 Clarinet playing A3 (220 Hz).

The FFT algorithm provides an efficient bridge from the time domain to the frequency domain. An FFT analysis proceeds by first "chopping up" the input signal into short time segments called *windows*. By performing the analysis over a series of windows an FFT program can capture the dynamic characteristics of a spectrum as it changes over time. Each window in the analysis defines a "snapshot" of the spectrum to be analyzed. The mechanics of the FFT analysis within a single window are quite complex. Suffice it to say that the FFT acts like a bank of filters — it measures the amount of energy in frequency "bins" that are equally distributed over the entire range of frequencies. This means that the bins of a given FFT analysis should match, or "line up", with the spectral components in the input signal and most analysis programs provide a way to tune the FFT to the specific sound being analyzed. The output from an FFT analysis are *frames* of data that contain the amplitude and initial phase values of each frequency bin. This information can then be displayed, resynthesized, or saved as data in files.

The important thing to grasp here is that — while the time and frequency domains are really just different perspectives on the same thing — the frequency domain representation is particularly useful to the spectral composer because it deconstructs the wave into its discrete components that can then be used to inform compositional decision making. For example, one can see quite clearly from the frequency domain plot in Figure 1 that odd numbered harmonics contain much more spectral energy than do the even harmonics. This acoustic information could be reflected, for example, in the composer's preference for using odd numbers or the ratios 1:3:5:7 to determine critical aspects of the composition.

Some FFT programs allow the results from the sound analysis to·be exported as data files containing the contents from each frame of the analysis. Example 1 shows what data from one frame might look like.

Example 1. Spectral snapshot of Clarinet tone in Figure 1.

```
(define clarinet
  '(1.00  .0842   2.01  .0017   3.00  .0420   4.01  .0029
    5.00  .0251   6.02  .0041   6.99  .0115   7.96  .0006
    8.99  .0032   9.98  .0003  11.00  .0018  11.96  .0003
   12.96  .0006  14.00  .0001  14.97  .0001  15.97  .0005
   17.95  .0002  18.96  .0001  19.07  .0001  22.06  .0001))
```

Example 1 displays the spectral information output by the FFT analysis of the clarinet tone in shown Figure 1. The information contains the first twenty harmonics from the analysis. The data are interpreted pairwise: the first number in each pair is the frequency ratio of a harmonic and the second number is its amplitude. Phase information is not represented here. The example was taken from the file "spectra.clm" from the Common Lisp Music (http://www-ccrma.stanford.edu/software/clm/) source distribution. This file contains a large number of spectral sets that can be used as compositional source material without having to actually perform an FFT analysis yourself.

Spectral Resynthesis

Output from an FFT analysis is simply statistical data. As such it can be mapped, manipulated and processed in various ways to resynthesize the information back into a composition. The nature of this transformation is, of course, up to each composer's imagination (see Chapter 16 for a general discussion of mapping). In Example 2 we define a simple set of tools that allow spectral information to be reshaped into different tonal gestures.

Example 2. Spectral processing tools.

```
(define (spectrum-maxfreq spec)
  ;; return freq of last harmonic in spec
  (list-ref spec (- (length spec) 2)))

(define (spectrum-maxamp spec)
  ;; iterate successive tails of spec and find
  ;; the max amplitude
  (loop for tail = spec then (rest (rest tail))
        until (null? tail)
        maximize (second tail)))

(define (spectrum-freqs spec)
  ;; return only the freq components of spectrum
  (loop for tail = spec then (rest (rest tail))
        until (null? tail)
        collect (car tail)))

(define (spectrum-length spec)
  ;; return number of partials in spec
  (/ (length spec) 2))
```

The spectrum-maxfreq function returns the highest harmonic scaler in *spec*, a list of harmonic and amplitude pairs such as the one shown in Example 1. Since the harmonic pairs in *spec* are ordered lowest to highest the function simply returns the second-to-last element in the list, which is the frequency value of the highest harmonic. The spectrum-maxamp function returns the loudest amplitude in *spec*. Since there is no way to predict which harmonic in a spectrum will be the loudest the function must search the entire spectral list for the maximum amplitude. The *tail* variable holds successively shorter versions of *spec*. On the first iteration *tail* is equal to *spec* but each iteration thereafter sets *tail* to (rest (rest tail)) — the *remainder* of the list beginning at the next pair of elements to the right. As *tail* moves successively rightward though *spec*, the form (second tail) always accesses the amplitude value of the current pair at the front of the list. Iteration continues until *tail* is empty and the predicate null? returns true, at which point the until clause stops the iteration. The spectrum-freqs function iterates *spec* in a manner identical to *spectrum-maxamp* but collects (first tail) — the frequency component of the current pair in *tail*, thus reducing the spectrum to a list of its frequency values.

Given this basic set of tools we can write a general mapping function to transform spectral information into different shapes (Example 3).

Example 3. Rescaling spectral data.

```
(define (rescale-spectrum spec a1 a2 k1 k2)
  ;; rescale spectrum to lie between keynums k1 and k2
  ;; and amplitudes a1 to a2
  (let* ((fund (if k1 (* (hertz k1) (first spec)) 1.0))
         (key1 (keynum fund :hz))
         (key2 (keynum (* fund (spectrum-maxfreq spec))
                       :hz))
         (soft 0)
         (loud (spectrum-maxamp spec)))
    (loop for tail = spec then (rest (rest tail))
          until (null? tail)
          collect
          (list
            (rescale (keynum (* fund (first tail))
                       :hz)
                     key1 key2 (or k1 key1) (or k2 key2))
            (rescale (second tail) soft loud a1 a2)))))
```

The `rescale-spectrum` function rescales a spectrum such that it lies proportionally between the specified key numbers *k1* and *k2* and the amplitude values *a1* and *a2*. If *k1* or *k2* is false their values default to the lowest and highest frequency values in *spec*. If *k2* is less than *k1* then the spectrum will be inverted. The spectrum returned by `rescale-spectrum` is formatted as a list of lists rather than as list of paired values. Reformatting the spectral data allows each partial in the spectrum to be represented explicitly as a sublist containing a frequency and an amplitude value. This reduces the total length of the spectrum by half, and allows each partial to be processed as a single unit of structure. Given this simple spectral toolkit we can now define a musical process that creates tonal gestures from spectral information. The main process `spectral-zither` creates zither-like material from the clarinet spectrum using two "helper" processes. The first helper plays an upward or downward strum of a rescaled spectrum and the second produces random plucks of the same material:

Example 4. Spectral gestures.

```
(define (strum-it play rate dur amp up?)
  ;; play ascending or descending spectrum
  (process for s in (if up? play (reverse play))
           output
           (new midi :time (now)
                :keynum (first s)
                :amplitude amp
                :duration (vary dur .1))
           wait rate))
```

```
(define (pluck-it play rate dur amp len)
  ;; play spectrum in random order
  (let ((pat (new heap :of play)))
    (process while (< (now) len)
             for s = (next pat)
             output
             (new midi :time (now)
                  :keynum (first s)
                  :amplitude (interp (now) 0 amp len (/
amp 2))
                  :duration (odds .2 (* dur 4)
                                     (vary dur .1)))
             wait rate)))
```

The main process `spectral-zither` takes a *spectrum* list (such as the clarinet defined earlier in this chapter) and generates a self-similar series of spectra in which each rescaled version is transposed to a specific harmonic level in the original spectrum. The amplitudes of each partial in the original determines the proportional length of each gesture — the louder the partial in the original spectrum the longer the transposed gesture lasts. Each gesture consists of two parts, a loud initial strum followed by random plucking of the same material. The amplitudes of the random plucks diminish over the length of each gesture.

Example 5. The spectral zither process.

```
(define (spectral-zither spectrum tim1 tim2 key1 key2)
  ;; transpose tonal gestures to successively higher
  ;; positions in spectrum. duration of each gesture is
  ;; proportional to amplitude to the partial it is
  ;; based on
  (let ((spec (rescale-spectrum spectrum
                                tim1 tim2 key1 key2)))
    (process for x in spec
             for k = (first x)
             for a = (second x)
             for topk = (between 100 113)
             for play = (rescale-spectrum
                           spectrum .4 .9 k topk)
             for up? = true then (odds .5)
             sprout (strum-it play .075 2.3 .9 up?)
             sprout (pluck-it play (vary .075 .2)
                              .6 .9 a)
             wait a)))
```

We now generate both upward and downward versions of the spectral zither. The second version uses channel tuning to approximate the spectral microtones.

Interaction 1. Playing the zither.

```
cm> (events (spectral-zither clarinet 10 80 2 6)
           "zither.mid")
"zither-1.mid"
cm> (events (spectral-zither clarinet 100 20 4 3)
           "zither.mid" :channel-tuning 9)
"zither-2.mid"
cm>
```

→ nm/23/snd/zither-1.mid
→ nm/23/snd/zither-2.mid 8 channels, microtones.
→ nm/23/snd/clearbends.mid Clear pitch bends.

1706°F

To conclude this section on analysis and resynthesis methods we examine a spectral composition that was composed with information derived from the FFT analysis of a tam-tam tone. The piece is *1706°F*, for chamber ensemble and electronic sounds, written by the composer Michael Klingbeil. The analysis data for the composition was first organized in Common Music and then manipulated by the composer to create the instrumental parts and synthetic sounds events (samples) which are triggered at appropriate times during the performance of the piece.

The original tam-tam sound was approximately 11 seconds long which resulted in over 300 FFT windows, each corresponding to about 35 milliseconds of actual sound. Rather than try to recreate the tam-tam sound with the instrumental sounds, the composer chose to conceive of each analysis window as a kind of "chord".

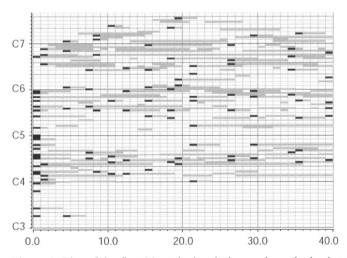

Figure 2. Plot of the first 30 analysis windows where the horizontal axis corresponds to window number.

Common Music was used to manipulate the individual chords, first by finding common tones between each successive chord and then by selecting chords based on the number of non-common tones with its predecessor. These selected chords are highlighted in the preceding graphic. The remaining pitches, shown in light gray, became a structural background layer which was used in part as a basis for the electronic sounds. The melodic and contrapuntal contours of the instrumental parts were then created by choosing from the reservoir of pitches available in each chord. The compositional method was not always strictly algorithmic: at times pitches were selected from a larger corpus (such as all of the pitches found in a particular time window or all the pitches sounding within a particular time region spanning across several windows).

Figure 3. Musical notation of 8 chords selected from the first 9 analysis windows. (Note that the pitches may differ slightly from the graph shown above since some chords were selected using a different method of quantizing frequencies to tempered pitches.)

Selected chords were translated into common practice notation (with quarter tones) to facilitate the free composition of the instrumental parts. In some cases a chord may correspond to only a few seconds of composed music, or in other instances as many as 30 or 40 seconds.

Simple processes are used to generate the electronic sounds. The following is a MIDI simulation of electronic events numbered 40 and 41 in the score. Event 40 simply sounds the pitches of time window 5 in an ascending arpeggio. The pitches are doubled at the octave, the octave plus a fifth, and at two octaves (this is to better simulate the electronic sounds which are actually used in the piece). Event 41 is a chord which sounds all pitches of analysis window 6 simultaneously.

In this example a portion of the data used in the piece is bound to the variable *tam-tam-data*. Each element of the list corresponds to the spectrum of a single analysis window (the first five windows are empty for this example).

Example 6. The tam-tam FFT data.

```
(define tam-tam-data
  '(() () () () ()
    (156.77036815728735 90.637619 259.9496481697027
                     82.718292
     286.574546692396 100.874054 306.25563026238274
                     93.336433
     324.7524389568296 100.055481 337.44764076690535
                     102.149223
     364.6634271878465 230.778137 415.7531705386655
                     119.252495
     606.0946243520343 86.700752 693.632505316461
                     99.007416
     793.6624934018535 122.259544 884.1881093270954
                     157.20726
     933.8675278134929 145.184113 1088.9671367780802
                     89.725365
     1488.6904580535806 101.671417 1511.527861059107
                     104.7155
     1618.8507000903057 84.252243 1713.9968634651475
                     112.454514
     1765.292105410349 89.296089 1890.2215478184416
                     99.125633
     1908.0848686296388 92.404488 1999.0901910667542
                     99.439217
     2041.0190392835411 105.710556 2179.3234227680086
                     88.835609)
    (156.9226656365204 84.869324 260.82045952862836
                     90.014053
     285.1896751834164 111.457977 307.17019597206075
                     99.64637
     336.09609235859693 120.298607 362.75665648480026
                     225.252136
     415.73593078208086 115.339218 655.5235086291844
                     87.095612
     692.9686610934529 82.759056 793.4209536257428
                     108.587471
     850.8079688652781 95.086945 883.5759843738408
                     150.945786
     932.8432789368185 150.02179 1088.3966109501614
                     85.69706
     1490.71509379789 112.47464 1512.3888337014348
                     92.084824
     1619.7171692738077 82.596962 1712.6721745280083
                     102.734337
     1890.1368493016446 97.024925 1908.251766584189
                     94.600105
```

```
          1998.8849421756013  106.950005  2009.4111265591894
                                 83.189438
          2041.6380351691066  102.523079  2402.793452296438
                                 84.39566)))
```

Each window in the tam-tam data is organized as frequency and amplitude pairs. The frequency for each harmonic is recorded in Hertz rather than in scaler form. We can now define two sample chords from the piece:

Example 7. Two sample chord events.

```
(define (event40)
  (let ((data (rescale-spectrum
                (list-ref tam-tam-data 5) .5 1 #f #f)))
    (process for delta in (append (explsegs 3 0.5 4)
                                  (explsegs 4 0.6 1/2)
                                  (explsegs
                                    (- (length data) 7)
                                    2 1/8))
             for s in data
             for count from 0
             each kt in '(0 12 19 24)
             output (new midi :time (now)
                         :keynum (+ (first s) kt)
                         :amplitude (second s)
                         :duration 1.5)
             wait delta)))
(define (event41)
  (let ((data (rescale-spectrum
                (list-ref tam-tam-data 6) .7 1 #f #f)))
    (process for s in data
             output (new midi :time (now)
                         :keynum (first s)
                         :amplitude (second s)
                         :duration (between 8.0 10.0))
             wait 0)))
```

We now generate both chords together slightly offset in time.

Interaction 2. Generating sample chords from 1706F.

```
cm> (events (list (event40) (event41))
            "1706Example.mid" '(0 3.75))
"1706Example.mid"
cm>
```

➼nm/23/snd/1706Example.mid

In the actual piece each pitch of the arpeggio is composed of a simple synthetic tone and a snippet of a tam-tam sound which is comb filtered to sound at the desired pitch. The file 1706Event40.mp3 contains the synthesized sound for Event 40. The chord of event 41 consists of noise filtered with very sharp filters at each frequency of the chord can be heard in the file 1706Event41.mp3. The upper pitches are doubled with a sampled crotale sound and a snippet of a cymbal sound is mixed in. Figure 4 shows the electronic part as it looks in the score.

Figure 4. This excerpt shows the combination of electronic events with the instrumental parts.

→nm/23/snd/1706Example.mp3 Passage in performance.

Spectral Synthesis

An alternate way to work with spectral information is to directly compute it using *synthesis algorithms*. A synthesis algorithm is a software program that calculates a waveform. As a very simple example of this process we will synthesize a spectrum consisting of the *combination tones* of two sine waves. When two sine waves *f1* and *f2* sound together, nonlinearity in the frequency response of our ears causes us to perceive frequency components above and below the sine tones. *Sum tones* are tones that lie at *f1+f2* Hz and *difference tones* lie at *f1-f2* Hz. Since sum tones are above the generating sine waves they tend to be masked but the difference tones can be clearly heard. The file diff.mp3. contains four difference tones, each difference tone is first "previewed" and then generated by pairs of sinewaves.

Example 8. Computing sum and difference notes.

```
(define (combo-notes n1 n2)
  (if (scale= n1 n2)
    '()
    (let ((f1 (hertz n1 ))
          (f2 (hertz n2)))
      (list (note (abs (- f1 f2)) :hz)
            (note (+ f1 f2) :hz)))))
```

The `combo-notes` function synthesizes combination notes by adding and subtracting two notes. If both notes are equivalent in the standard scale then the empty list is returned, otherwise the difference and sum tones in Hertz is calculated and the nearest tempered notes are returned in a list. Since Hertz values are added and subtracted neither input *n1* or *n2* will appear in the output spectrum and the synthesized components will usually be inharmonically related to the original tones.

Interaction 3. Calculating sum and difference sets.

```
cm> (combo-notes 'd5 'e5)
(d2 ef6)
cm> (combo-notes 'a4 'ds5)
(fs3 c6)
cm>
```

In the audio domain this technique is referred to as *ring modulation* and the sum and difference tones are called spectral *side bands*. Ring modulation can be performed on individual pairs of frequencies (sine waves) or on complex waves. In the latter case, each frequency in the first wave combines with each frequency in the second to form an output spectrum that represents the "cross product" of the two inputs. We can implement compositional ring modulation using `loop` to append results returned by `combo-notes`:

Example 9. Synthesizing note sets by ring modulation.

```
(define (ringmod set1 set2)
  (scale-order (loop for n1 in set1
                     append
                     (loop for n2 in set2
                           append
                           (combo-notes n1 n2)))))

(define (play-rings notes rate)
  (process repeat 25
           for k = 70 then (drunk k 3)
           for r = (ringmod (list k) notes)
           for l = (length r)
           output
           (new midi :time (now)
                :duration (* rate l)
                :keynum k :amplitude .6)
           each s in r as i from 1
           output (new midi
                       :time (+ (now) (* rate i))
                       :keynum s
                       :amplitude .3)
           wait (* rate l)))
```

The `ringmod` function returns the spectral cross product of two input note sets. The Common Music function `scale-order` ensures that the notes in the synthesized spectrum are ordered low to high. See Chapter 9 for a discussion of `scale-order`.

Interaction 4. Ring modulated melodic line.

```
cm> (events (play-rings '(c4 e4 g4) .1)
            "rings.mid")
"rings-1.mid"
cm>
```

→ nm/23/snd/rings-1.mid

Frequency Modulation

In the remainder of this chapter we will examine *Frequency Modulation* (FM) as a way to synthesize tonal material for composition. FM audio synthesis was discovered by my teacher John Chowning at CCRMA, Stanford University and Chowning's FM paper The Synthesis of Complex Audio Spectra by Means of Frequency Modulation (Chowning) is a seminal paper in Computer Music. Other good non-technical discussions of FM audio synthesis are available in Computer

Music (Dodge) and in The Computer Music Tutorial (Roads). William Schottstaedt's An Introduction to FM (Schottstaedt) included in the CLM source distribution discusses the theory behind FM and also shows the reader how to design FM instruments in Common Lisp Music. Schottstaedt's FM instrument fm-violin is briefly discussed in Chapter 24 of this book. A number of composers, including John Chowning, have used FM as a compositional technique as well as an audio synthesis technique. FM is a particularly powerful synthesis algorithm because it can describe many different types of spectra using only a few simple control parameters.

Fm synthesis

Anyone who has listened to a good violinist can understand the basic idea behind frequency modulation. One of the ways a trained violinist adds warmth and expression to sound is by rocking the string finger back and forth in a constant manner to add a small amount of *vibrato* to the tone. When the tip of the finger angles toward the violinist the string is shorted by a very small amount and the frequency of the tone rises slightly; when the finger rocks back in the other direction the string is lengthened and a slight drop in pitch is produced. The constantly changing string length has the effect of *modulating*, or altering, the frequency of the main tone by a small percentage on either side of its center frequency. Vibrato is a periodic oscillation with two components: a rate (frequency) and an amplitude. The rate of oscillation is how fast the violinist moves the finger back and forth. This can be measured in Hertz, or cycles per second. The amplitude of the vibrato determines how much the main tone deviates around its center frequency. In this case the term "amplitude" is really describing an amount of change of frequency, or *deviation*. Typical values for vibrato frequency lie around six Hertz with a deviation of about 20 cents, approximately 1 percent around the center tone. The effects of changing the rate and deviation of a periodic vibrato can be heard in vib-1.mp3. The example demonstrates vibrato rates of 2, 4 and 8 Hz with deviations of 1/2. 1 and 2 percent around a 440 Hz tone.

What we have described so far is a system in which one frequency, called the *carrier*, is slightly modulated by another, called the *modulator* Now imagine replacing our violinist with a robot capable of producing vibrato at extreme (audio) rates and with very wide deviations. As the rate of vibrato increases and its deviation becomes wider about the center frequency, the carrier becomes distorted to such an extent and so quickly that modulation is no longer perceived as a changing central pitch but as a changing *timbre*. "Robot" vibrato rates of 20, 40 and 80 Hz with deviations of 10, 25, and 50 percent around a 440 Hz tone can be head in vib-2.mp3 This is FM synthesis. FM synthesis generates a complex waveform by *modulating*, or changing, one wave called the carrier by another wave, called the modulator, at audio rates. This modulation causes spectral sidebands to appear at multiples of the modulator above and below the carrier:

$$\text{carrier} \pm (k * \text{modulator})$$

where k is the order of the sideband, For example, a carrier of 400 Hz and a modulator of 100 Hz produces sidebands at the frequencies shown in Table 1.

Table 1. Sidebands arrangements for a carrier of 400 Hz and modulator of 100 Hz.

c-3m	c-2m	c-1m	c	c+1m	c+2m	c+3m
100	200	300	400	500	600	700

Note that at some value of k the lower sideband will become a negative frequency component. A negative frequency can be understood as a positive frequency with its phase inverted. This means that negative components can be "wrapped around", or reflected, into the positive domain by inverting their amplitudes and summing with any existing sideband located at the same positive spectral position (Figure 5).

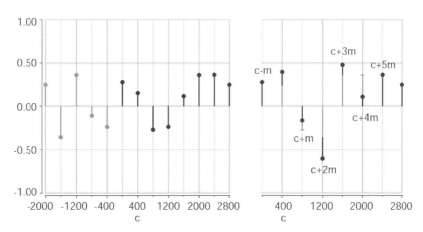

Figure 5. Sideband arrangements for a carrier of 400 Hz and a modulator of 400 Hz. The first graph contains the negative frequency components, the second shows them inverted in the positive frequency domain.

→ nm/23/snd/fm1.mp3 Carrier=400Hz, C:M=1:1, Index=4.

For a given carrier c and modulator m the *c:m ratio* determines the precise arrangement of the sidebands. The *c:m* ratio 1:1 in Figure 5 produces sidebands at integer multiples of the carrier frequency — in this instance FM mimics the harmonic series with a "fundamental" at the carrier frequency. 1:1 is the only ratio that produces all harmonics at the fundamental. All other ratios either produce a fundamental different from the carrier, or do not generate all harmonics, or generate inharmonic spectra (Table 2).

Table 2. C:M sideband arrangements for a carrier of 400 Hz.

c:m	sidebands	result
1:2	400 1200 2000 2800 3600	Odd harmonics.
4:1	100 200 300 400 500 600	fundamental not carrier.
1:pi	400 857 1657 2113 2913 3370	inharmonic spectrum

We can infer a few facts from Table 2:
- For the carrier frequency to be considered the fundamental, the *c:m* ratio must be 1:1 or *m* must be equal or greater than two times *c*.
- For ratios like 1:*m* where *m* is an integer greater than 1 the *mth* harmonic is missing from the spectrum.
- If *c* or *m* are not integers then inharmonic spectra result.

Figure 6 shows the sideband arrangements for a *c:m* ration of 1:*Phi* (the Golden Mean, or approximately 1.618): Notice that when negative inharmonic components wrap around to the positive domain they produce a "denser" spectrum because sidebands do not line up (Figure 3).

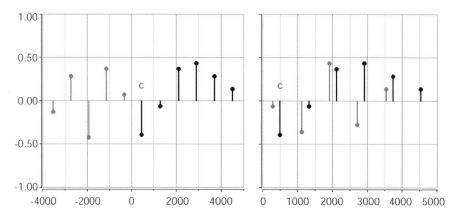

Figure 6. Inharmonic spectra for a carrier of 500 Hz, c:m ratio of 1:phi and an FM index of 4.

→ nm/23/snd/fm2.mp3 Carrier=400Hz, C:M=1:phi, Index=4.

For more information on C:M ratios and their effect on FM spectra see Barry Truax's Organizational Techniques for C:M Ratios in Frequency Modulation. (Truax)

The precise relationship of sidebands to the carrier frequency depend not only on the rate of modulation but also the amount of deviation. Recall that deviation is the amplitude of the modulation — the maximum depth (in Hertz) that the modulation reaches on either side of the carrier. Deviation determines the number and amplitudes of the spectral components. Deviation is typically expressed indirectly, using an *FM index* that relates deviation to the modulation frequency:

> deviation=index*modulator

If the FM index is zero then there is no deviation and only the carrier wave is heard. But as the index increases from zero an increasing amount of energy is "stolen" from the carrier and distributed over an expanding number of sidebands. (Figure 7) The precise amplitude relationships between the sidebands, carrier and FM index is determined by *Bessel functions* that describe what the amplitudes are in each sideband order for a given index. Bessel functions look a bit like dampened sinusoids, and can produce negative amplitude values. Sidebands with negative amplitudes are interpreted as having a positive amplitude but inverted phase.

In general, the number of sidebands k produced on either side of the carrier will equal the closest integer to the *FM Index* plus 1. Since there are two spectral components per side band, and the spectrum also contains the carrier, the total "density" of the spectrum will be approximately $2k+1$. For example, an index of 2.5 will produce nine components: four side bands (eight spectral components) plus the carrier. However, since negative frequencies wrap around they may combine or cancel existing positive frequency components so the resulting spectrum many actually have fewer components.

Composing with frequency modulation

Given a basic understanding of Frequency Modulation we can begin to work with FM synthesis as a compositional tool for computing both harmonic and inharmonic sets given three simple control values:

- a *carrier frequency*, the central tone for the note set.
- a *modulation ratio* that determines harmonicity of the resulting spectrum.
- an *fm index* that controls the number of sidebands, or the density of the spectrum.
-

(fm-spectrum *carrier mratio index* [*spectrum*] [:unique *b*]   [Function]
[:invert *b*])

The fm-spectrum function returns the FM sidebands (frequencies and optionally amplitude values) calculated for a specified *carrier*, *mratio* and *index*. The types of values returned in the spectrum are determined by the value of the *spectrum* argument. If *spectrum* is :raw, then the both frequency and amplitude values are returned for each sideband and the spectrum may include negative frequencies. If *spectrum* is :hertz (the default) then negative sidebands are reflected into the positive frequency domain with their phases inverted. If :spectrum is :keynum or :note then sidebands are returned as key numbers or rounded to their nearest note names. The value of :spectrum can also be a list like (c4 c6) or (48 80) in which case the two values specify *boundaries* within which the spectral components will be fit regardless of which octaves the sidebands were actually located in. If note names are specified as boundaries then the spectrum is returned as notes otherwise key numbers are returned. In either case, the value of the :unique argument is used to determine if separate sidebands that produce identical note values are reduced to a single entry or not. The default value is true. If the :invert keyword is true then the spectrum is inverted before it is returned. If :unique is true then no duplicate key numbers or notes are returned for partials that map to the same spectral positions.

Interaction 5. Generating note sets.

```
cm> (fm-spectrum 220 1 1)
(220.0 440.0 660.0)
cm> (fm-spectrum 220 1 5 :note)
(a3 a4 e5 a5 cs6 e6 g6)
cm> (fm-spectrum (hertz 'c3) 2 5 :note)
(c3 g4 e5 bf5 d6 fs6 fs6 af6)
cm> (fm-spectrum 220 1 2 :keynum :invert t)
(33.0 37.980453 45.0 57.0)
cm> (fm-spectrum 220 1 9 '(a3 a5))
(a3 cs4 ef4 e4 g4 a4 b4)
cm> (fm-spectrum (hertz 'c3) 1.618 6 '(c4 g5) )
(c4 d4 e4 f4 g4 bf4 b4 cs5 d5 e5 f5 g5)
cm>
```

The following example uses fm-spectrum to generate a piano "improvisation".

Example 10. Playing FM spectra.

```
- - - - - - - - - - - - - - - - - - - - - - - - - - - - - - - - - - - - - - - - - - - - - - - - - - - - - -
(define (fm-harmony note )
  (let ((mrat (between 1.0 2.0))
        (indx 1))
    (fm-spectrum (hertz note) mrat indx
                 (list (transpose note -12)
                       (transpose note 12)))))

(define (fm-piano )
  (let* ((rhy (new random
                :of `((q weight 2)
                      (tq :min 3)
                      (, (new cycle :of '(e q e)))))))
    (process for n = 60 then (drunk n 3 :low 40
                                          :high 80
                                          :mode :jump)
             repeat 40
             for s = (fm-harmony (note n))
             for r = (rhythm (next rhy) 70)
             output (new midi :time (now)
                        :keynum n
                        :amplitude .75
                        :duration (* r .9))
             output
             (new midi :time (+ (now) (rhythm 'e 70))
                  :keynum
                  (list-ref s (pick 0 (1- (length s))))
                  :amplitude .7
                  :duration (* r .9))
- - - - - - - - - - - - - - - - - - - - - - - - - - - - - - - - - - - - - - - - - - - - - - - - - - - - - -
```

```
if (odds .6)
each k in s
output
(new midi :time (now)
      :keynum k
      :duration (* r .9)
      :amplitude (between .4 .55))
wait r )))
```

The fm-harmony function returns an FM note set for a specified center note. The modulation ratio *mrat* is randomly selected between 1.0 (harmonic series) less than 2.0, so inharmonic spectra generally result. The *index* 1 produces 2 side bands on either side of the carrier for a total of 5 notes in each spectrum. But since the *spectrum* argument is specified as octave boundaries on either side of the carrier, fewer notes will be returned if transposed sidebands produce the same value inside the boundaries.

The fm-piano process plays 50 spectra generated by fm-harmony. On each iteration the process plays the center tone and either the lowest or highest note in the spectrum. Sixty percent of the time the process also adds the entire spectrum as a chord.

Interaction 6. Listening to fm-piano.

```
cm> (events (fm-piano ) "fm-piano.mid")
"fm-piano-1.mid"
cm>
```

➙ nm/23/snd/fm-piano-1.mid

The Aeolian Harp

We conclude this chapter with two examples of FM tonal synthesis used in *The Aeolian Harp*, a composition for piano and computer generated tape written by the author. *The Aeolian Harp* won the Eric Siday Musical Creativity Award as the top composition submitted to the 2003 International Computer Music Conference. Links to the full score, program notes and a recording are included at the end of this section. All the sounds in this 22 minute composition have their basis in either FM synthesis or in the justly tuned Aeolian scale. The tape music for Aeolian Harp consists of real sounds (primarily wind and plucked piano strings) that have been transformed or colored in some manner appropriate to the composition. These techniques include resonating comb filters, time stretching, and cross synthesis. Cross synthesis was used to create the "singing wind" that occurs toward the end of the composition as wind sounds take on the spectral properties of the Buddhist chant Zen Sho Kada sung by the Rev. Haruyoshi Kusada of Berkeley, California. A short passage from the seventh *Visions Fugitive* by Serge Prokofieff (title Arpa) appears briefly with Zen Sho Kada. The tape part was created using Common Lisp Music, a sound synthesis language developed by William Schottstaedt at CCRMA, Stanford University. All of the melodic and harmonic structures in the piano part were derived through Frequency Modulation. Many of the piano sections follow a similar technique: basic carrier, mratio, and FM index values are first determined using envelopes or patterns and then varied by some slight random amount to produce fresh spectra on each output set. The first example (Example 11) comes from the "bell section" near the beginning of the composition. The piano plays a constant A440 pulse with a harmonic accompaniment generated by FM using a carrier is A440, a mratio and an index:

Figure 7. Center frequency of A4 or A3, mratio between 1.1 and 1.6, and FM index of 2.4.

→nm/23/snd/ah1.mp3 Piano and tape, measures 17–22 (page 2 of score).

Here is a simplified version of the process that generated the bell-like FM chords.

Example 11. FM Bell harmony.

```
(define (fm-bell-notes tone )
  (let ((cen (hertz tone))
        (rat (between 1.1 1.6))
        (ind 2.4))
    (fm-spectrum cen rat ind
                 (list (transpose tone -12)
                       (transpose tone 12)))))

(defun fm-bell (reps rate)
  (let ((tones (new random
                    :of '((a4 :weight 3)
```

```
                              (a3 :max 1)))))
      (process repeat reps
               for tone = (next tones)
               for bell = (fm-bell-notes tone)
               output (new midi :time (now)
                           :keynum tone
                           :duration 3
                           :amplitude .6)
               when (odds .65)

               each k in  bell
               output (new midi :time (now)
                           :keynum k
                           :duration 3
                           :amplitude .4)
               wait rate )))
```

In Interaction 7 we listen to twenty fm-bells.

Interaction 7. Listening to fm bells.

```
cm> (events (fm-bell 20 1.25) "fm-bell.mid")
"fm-bell-1.mid"
cm>
```

→ nm/23/snd/fm-bell-1.mid

The second example from Aeolian Harp demonstrates melodic material generated through FM synthesis. The excerpt comes from the beginning of the long piano solo in the middle of the piece. The entire solo is generated by FM. Each measure in Figure 8 constitutes one FM spectrum. The measures are played at a constant rate no matter how may notes are in the spectral set — the larger the set the faster it must be played. The carrier is always heard as the first note of each measure. The FM index in this section was controlled as a function of time. Over the course of the section the index and note boundaries increase so that the sets become more jagged and chromatic. Figure 9 shows what the spectra look like near the end of this section.

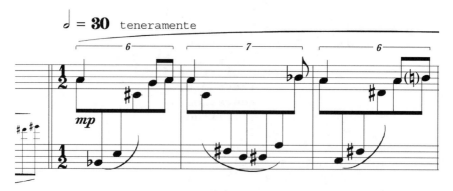

Figure 8. Carrier A4, A3 or A5, mratio between 1.1 and pi, index between 2 and 2.5.

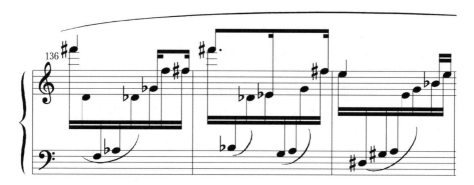

Figure 9. Same process with increased FM index and enlarged note boundaries.

→nm/23/snd/ah2.mp3 Piano solo, measures 118-150 of score.

The following process example is a slightly simplified version of the melodic generator.

Example 12. FM melodic generator.

```
(define (gen-mel cen rat ind low high)
  (fm-spectrum (hertz cen)
               rat ind
               (list (transpose cen low)
                     (transpose cen high))
               :scale-order nil
               :invert true :unique nil))

(define (fm-melody measure ratlow rathigh
                   indlow indhigh blow bhigh)
  (let ((starts '(a4 a4 a4 a3 a4 a4 a5 a4)))
```

```
(process for cen in starts
         for rat = (between ratlow rathigh)
         for ind = (between indlow indhigh)
         for mel = (gen-mel cen rat ind blow bhigh)
         for rhy = (/ measure (+ 1 (length mel)))
         output (new midi :time (now)
                         :keynum cen
                         :amplitude .6
                         :duration .4)
         each n in mel as r from rhy by rhy
         output (new midi :time (+ (now) r)
                         :keynum n
                         :amplitude .4
                         :duration 2)
         wait measure)))
```

The gen-mel function generates an inverted fm spectrum (the "undertones" of the carrier) fit between two boundary notes *low* and *high*. Since :unique is false, the spectrum is not reduced to a set after the spectral components have been fit between the boundaries. The fm-melody process plays a series of FM spectra generated by fm-mel as a single melodic line. Each spectrum represents one measure of music with a constant duration; the more notes in a spectrum the faster they are be played. This example approximates the piano in Figure 8:

Interaction 8. Listening to fm-melody

```
cm> (events (fm-melody 1.8 1.1 pi 2.0 2.5 -24 12)
            "fm-melody.mid")
"fm-melody-1.mid"
cm>
```

→ nm/23/snd/fm-melody-1.mid

The score, recording and program notes of the entire composition are located in this chapter's directory:

→ nm/23/img/ah.pdf . Score (PDF format)
→ nm/23/snd/ah.mp3. Recorded on April 3, 2002 at the University of Illinois; Mei-Fang Lin, pianist.)
→ nm/23/img/ah-pn.pdf . Program Notes (PDF format)

Chapter Source Code

The source code to all of the examples and interactions in this chapter can be found in the file spectral.cm located in the same directory as the HTML file for this chapter. The source file can be edited in a text editor or evaluated inside the Common Music application.

References

Rose, J. (1996). An Introduction to the Pitch Organization of French Spectral Music. *Perspectives of New Music, 34,* 6-39.

Chowning, J. (1973). The Synthesis of Complex Audio Spectra by Means of Frequency Modulation. *Computer Music Journal, 1(2),* 46.

Dodge, C. & Jerse, T. (1985). *Computer Music.* New York: Schirmer Books.

Roads, C. (1996). *The Computer Music Tutorial.* Cambridge: MIT Press.

Schottstaedt, W. (2003). *Introduction to FM* [On-line]. Available http://www-ccrma.stanford.edu/Software/clm/.

Truax, B. (1978). Organizational Techniques for C:M Ratios in Frequency Modulation. *Computer Music Journal, 1(4),* 39-45.

24

Beyond MIDI

All of the algorithms, examples and Etudes in this book have described musical sound in terms of MIDI events and MIDI score files. The simplicity of MIDI has been a convenience for us — a way to generate musically satisfying results while maintaining our focus on larger compositional issues and algorithmic design. Indeed, the MIDI protocol *is* very convenient: it is simple, universally available on all makes of computers and an industry standard that has been adopted by most commercial music software applications. But the benefits of the MIDI protocol — its simplicity and ease of use — come only at the price of limiting compositional expressiveness and control over the production of an acoustic signal. We have already encountered some of MIDI's limitations during the course of this book. For example, we have seen that MIDI has an extremely weak representation of frequency, which it defines in terms of only 128 "key numbers". The protocol has many other limitations as well, including a very slow data rate, poor 7-bit quantization, and an extremely limited channel, or instrument, address space.

But perhaps the most severe restriction that MIDI imposes on a composer has more to do with its nature than its features: MIDI is a *control protocol* and not a *language* for sound synthesis. From the perspective of a composer using MIDI, a synthesizer is a "black box" whose hardwired operations are hidden behind the messages that MIDI transmits. MIDI makes it very easy to use the synthesizer but at the price of control over synthesis algorithms. One solution to this problem is to purchase a number of synthesizers, each with different and distinct capabilities. It is quite common for composers who work seriously with MIDI to have a whole rack full of expensive synthesizers, samplers and effects processors. But many composers eschew MIDI completely in favor of *sound synthesis languages* that permit the specification of audio signals on a sample-by-sample basis. These languages generate sound from score information using audio algorithms, or "digital instruments" that the composer creates.

In this chapter we introduce sound synthesis as an alternative to MIDI sound generation. We will learn how to work with two different sound synthesis languages: Csound and Common Lisp Music. Both of these languages provide the composer with a rich set of audio operators and an ability to design audio instruments from scratch. Since Csound and Common Lisp Music exhibit a certain similarity in their design, which of these languages a composer chooses to work with is largely a matter of preference. Among the factors to consider when selecting a synthesis language are: availability on your computer and operating systems, speed of execution, interactive control, expressive power, extensibility of system, and how well the software is supported. Of course it is not possible in this chapter to explain much about these synthesis languages in particular — these topics can only be properly addressed in books. Computer Music (Dodge) is an excellent introductory textbook that discusses most of the synthesis techniques in use today. Its presentation can be applied to any synthesis language you choose to work with.

Sound Synthesis Languages

A sound synthesis language is a software system that defines audio processing operators called *unit generators* and a syntax for combining these operators to form *instruments*. Each type of unit generator implements a distinct, generic operation on an audio signal. Common unit generators include oscillators, envelope generators, wave tables, delay lines and various types of digital filters. By routing the output of one unit generator into the input of another, a relatively small number of different generator types can be "chained together" in different configurations to implement different synthesis algorithms. Each collection, or network, of operators is called a synthesis *instrument*. Synthesis instruments are often depicted as a graphs or "patches" in which the different unit generators are connected by lines representing the signal's path as it flows from generator to generator.

Synthesis runtime environments
Synthesis languages make a distinction between the activity of designing an instrument and using the instrument to actually create an output audio signal. This latter activity is the responsibility of the synthesis *runtime environment*. The job of the runtime environment is to route external synthesis data to specific synthesis instruments executing inside the environment. This routing may be implemented in or out of real time. Some languages provide a *score file* interface to the synthesis runtime environment. A score file is a text file that contains a time ordered series of *instrument calls*, where each call is roughly analogous to a note in a traditional

music score. An instrument call in a score file associates the name, or identifier, of a synthesis instrument with the parameter data that defines a sound. The parameter data provide the initial input conditions for the instrument's audio algorithm to generate sound output. The synthesis data enters the instrument through its *parameters*, or input variables. Thus the notion of an "instrument call" in a score file is very similar to a function call in Lisp, and as we will see shortly, a synthesis instrument can be implemented as a specialized type of Lisp function.

Instruments and parameters

One of the challenges of working with digital instruments is to learn which parameters produce interesting results. Since each parameter adds an additional dimension of complexity to a digital instrument, composers may spend hours experimenting with parameter values in order to learn about an instrument's acoustic capabilities. The first task in this exploratory process is to understand what each parameter means to the instrument, and what the valid range of values are for each parameter. Since each synthesis instrument implements its own synthesis algorithm, the number and types of parameters vary widely from instrument to instrument. It is not uncommon for synthesis instruments to have twenty or more parameters! An instrument might require a large number of parameters because it uses large amounts of input data (as in the case with additive synthesis instruments, for example), or because the instrument supports many optional features, for example vibrato, glissando, reverberation, and so on. In order to reduce the amount of parameter data in instrument calls, a language like CLM allows *default values* to be associated with optional parameters. This means that a parameter value must only be specified in an instrument call if it is actually different from the value the instrument would otherwise use. Although the order and meaning of instrument parameters cannot be known without consulting documentation, many instruments commonly adhere to a conventional interpretation of the first few parameters:

> *name start duration frequency amplitude*

where *name* is the name or identifier of the instrument, *start* is its start time in the score in seconds, *duration* is its duration, *frequency* is in Hertz and *amplitude* is its amplitude value. The following table shows what two instrument calls might look like for Csound and Common Lisp Music.

Table 1. Example instrument calls in Csound and CLM.

Csound	i1 0 3 440 .5
CLM	(beep 33.2 10.0 8231.43 .75)

In the remainder of this chapter we will learn how to define new musical objects and use them in conjunction with Csound and Common Lisp Music. Although musical sound will be rendered quite differently than by using MIDI, it is important to understand that — when viewed from the perspective of the metalevel — very little will actually change. The only practical differences will be:

- Compositional algorithms will use sound event classes that permit more explicit control over the syntheses of sound than using the MIDI event class.
- Each new sound event class has its own set of sound parameters, depending on the instrument it uses to render sound.
- Frequency will be specified in Hertz rather than key numbers or note names.
- MIDI files will be replaced by Csound or CLM score files and audio files.

Csound

Csound is a synthesis language that runs on most computers and operating systems in use today. As its name would suggest, Csound is written in the C programming language but the actual syntax of the synthesis language is not C. Csound's runtime environment can be controlled by MIDI in "real time" or by input from score files. To generate sound, Csound combines what it calls an "orchestra" of synthesis instruments with synthesis data. Both the orchestra and score are simply text files with information encoded in Csound's specialized instrument and score syntax. (The orchestra file has an .orc file extension and a score file has a .sco extension). The details of Csound's instrument syntax is beyond the scope of this book but it is not difficult to understand its general characteristics. We will start with the orchestra file first. Each synthesis instrument in an orchestra file is identified by a unique *instr*, or instrument number. Example 1 show the contents of of an orchestra file called "blur.orc" that contains a single instrument definition.

Example 1. Contents of the Csound orchestra file "blur.orc".

```
-----------------------------------------------------------------------
sr = 44100
kr = 4410
ksmps = 10
nchnls = 1


;;;
;;; simple oscillator with envelope
;;;
;;; f1: 0  <size>  10  1 0 1 0 1 0 1 0 1 0 1

instr 1
idur = p3
iamp = p4*32767          ; scale logical amplitude
ifreq = p5
iattackt = p6
irelt   = p7

k1       linen   iamp, iattackt, idur, irelt
a1       oscili  k1, ifreq, 1
out      a1
endin
-----------------------------------------------------------------------
```

The instrument defined in Example 1 consists of a single oscillator controlled by an amplitude envelope. The first few lines of the file set the global sampling rate *sr*, control rate *kr* and number of audio output channels *nchnls* for sound synthesis. Our instrument's *instr* number is 1, which means that instrument calls that reference this instrument in the score file will use the name i1. The i1 instrument requires 7 parameters; some of these parameters be seen in the Example 1 listed by their *pfield* names: (p2, p3, p4 and so on). Table 2 lists the parameters and pfields of the i1 instrument with example values for each parameter.

Table 2. i1 instrument parameters identified by their pfields.

	name	time	dur	amp	freq	amp-attack	amp-release
pfield	p1	p2	p3	p4	p5	p6	p7
values	i1	0.0	1.0	.5	440	.1	.1

The next five lines in the instrument's definition initialize local variables used by the instrument. The instrument's duration *idur* is set to the value of the *p3* parameter. The instruments amplitude *iamp* is calculated by rescaling the logical amplitude in *p4* by 32767, which converts it into Csound's internal amplitude scale. The next three lines proceed in a similar way: the frequency *ifreq* in Hertz is set to the value of *p5*, the attack time of the instrument's amplitude envelope *iattackt* is set to *p6* and the envelope's decay time *irelt* is set to *p7*. The actual instrument patch appears in the next two lines; this is the runtime code that is executed repeatedly to generate the audio output signal. In the first line the envelope unit generator linen (line envelope) calculates the current sample's amplitude value *k1*, which becomes the amplitude input to an interpolating oscillator ocili. The oscillator produces a sine wave at the frequency *ifreq* and sets the variable *a1* to the current audio sample. The out statement then writes the current sample to the open audio output file.

Defining a Csound event

Given the fact that we can define different instruments in Csound, each with its own set of parameters and sound characteristics, we must have some means for defining musical events that can output these sound descriptions to Csound scores. More specifically, in order to work with the i1 instrument defined in the "blur.orc" file we must define a new musical event that will output i1 instrument calls to a Csound .sco file.

The easiest way to create a new type of Csound event is to define it in terms of a system defined event class called i. Common Music provides the i event class so that different Csound instrument events can be created simply by *subclassing* this one event class. Recall from Chapter 11 that a subclass inherits all the slots and values declared by its *superclasses*. In the case of the Csound i class, its subclasses will automatically receive the following slot initializations:

:ins *integer*

   The instrument number of the CSound instrument.

:time *number*
        The start time of the sound event.
:dur *number*
        The duration of the sound event.

We will use the defobject macro to define our new sound event class.

(defobject *name* (*supers* ....) (*slots* ...) [(:parameters [Macro] ...)])

The defobject macro defines a new class of object. *Name* is the name of the new class. Following *name* comes a list of zero or more superclasses from which the new class inherit slots and values. Following the superclass list comes a list of *slot specifications*. Each *slot* in the list is either the name of a slot or a list of the form:
        (*slot* [:initform *x*])
If an :initform expression is specified its value *x* becomes the value of *slot* if no initialization is provided when the object is created using the new macro. Following the slot specification list comes an optional parameter list:
        (:parameters *slot* ...)
This list declares the names of the slots that will produce parameter values for the instrument. The order of the slots in this list determines the order the values appear in the instrument call written to the score file. Example 2 shows the definition of a new class of object called i1 that will output sound events for our i1 instrument:

Example 2. Defining a new class of object.

```
(defobject i1 (i)
   (amp
    freq
    (attack :initform .05)
    (release :initform .25))
   (:parameters time dur amp freq attack release))
```

This defobject form defines a new sound event called i1 that inherits slots and values from the i superclass. The defobject expression declares both slots and parameters for our new object. The amp and freq slots for i1 are declared without specifying initial values, which means that these value will always have to be specified when an i1 object is used. The attack and release slots, in contrast, are defined with initial values. If an initialization is not provided, the values for the attack and release slots will be .50 and .25, respectively.

    Following the slot list comes the :parameters declaration list. The time and dur slots that appear in this list were inherited from the i superclass.

Working with the i1 object

Once the `defobject` expression in Example 2 is evaluated we can create `i1` objects, as shown in Interaction 1:

Interaction 1. Creating i1 events.

```
cm> (new i1)
#i(i1 ins 1 attack .05 release 0.25)
cm> (new i1 :time 0 :freq (random 1000) :amp .5)
#i(i1 time 0 ins 1 amp 0.5 freq 693 attack 0.05 release
0.25)
cm>
```

Generating a Csound score file

Now that the `i1` object has been defined we can write a simple example process that outputs `i1` events:

Example 3. Generate i1 events.

```
(define (blur )
   (process repeat 100
             output (new i1 :time (now)
                            :freq (between 20 2000)  ; Hertz
                            :dur .4 :amp .1)
             wait .015))
```

At this point we can generate a Csound score. But before doing so we will first establish an output hook to automatically call the CSound program with our orchestra file and score file whenever the `events` function outputs a CSound score. You can define your own Csound hook function or use the `play-sco-file` hook defined by Common Music:

(play-sco-file *file* [:orchestra *s*] [:options *s*] [Function]
[:output *s*] [:play *b*])

The play-sco-file functions plays the score *file* using the specified `:orchestra` file. `:options` is an optional string of commands that will be passed to the CSound program when it starts. `:output` is the output sound file or "dac" if Csound will generate the audio signal directly to the speakers. By default, the `play-sco-file` function assumes that the CSound program can be started using the shell command: "/usr/local/bin/csound". If this is not the location of the Csound program on your computer, reset the global variable `*csound*` to the appropriate command string that will work on your machine. If you do not have Csound installed on your computer you can generate the score file but you will not be able to run CSound. In this case you should not set an output hook.

Before generating our score we will also define a CSound *header* string to include in the top of the output score file. This string is not examined by Common Music and so can contain any text that is legal in a Csound score file. In our case the header string will contain a CSound *f statement* that defines an amplitude envelope for the `linen` unit generator used by `i1`. At this point we are ready to output events to a Csound score file.

Interaction 2. Listening to blur.

```
cm> (set-sco-output-hook! #'play-sco-file)

cm> (define sco-header  ; define a score header string
        "f1 0 8192 10 0.0   0.41 0.06 0.04 0.00 0.11 0.02
0.00 0.00")

cm> (events (blur) "blur.sco" 0
        :header sco-header
        :options "-d -m0 -A"
        :orchestra "blur.orc"
        :output "blur.aiff")
"blur.sco"
cm>
```

→ nm/24/./blur.sco
→ nm/24/snd/blur.mp3

Example 4 contains the first few lines of the "blur.sco" score file created in Interaction 2:

Example 4. Contents of blur.sco
```
----------------------------------------------------------------
; Common Music 2.4.0 output on 24 Mar 2003, 09:49:38
f1 0 8192 10 0.0   0.41 0.06 0.04 0.00 0.11 0.02 0.00
0.00
i1 0 0.4 0.1 300 0.05 0.25
i1 0.015 0.4 0.1 406 0.05 0.25
i1 0.03 0.4 0.1 975 0.05 0.25
. . .
----------------------------------------------------------------
```

Notice that the f statement from our header string appears before the first instrument call in the score file. After the score file was written our hook function automatically started the Csound program in "/usr/local/bin/csound" and passed it the command options "-d -m0 -A", our score file "blur.sco" and the orchestra file "blur.orc". Csound then generated audio output from the score to the file "blur.aiff".

Common Lisp Music

Common Lisp Music (CLM) is a sound synthesis language written by William Schottstaedt at CCRMA, Stanford University. CLM is fast, efficient, has real-time capabilities and runs on many different types of computers. Despite CLM's name, the software is actually written in Lisp and C. CLM uses C to implement the low-level unit generators that perform the sample-by-sample calculations to generate the audio signal. Lisp provides CLM with an interactive development environment for designing and working with instruments. Since CLM and Common Music share the same Lisp environment, from the novice Lisp composers' perspective they may not appear to be separate software systems at all!

Defining CLM instruments

Like Csound, CLM defines audio signals in terms of synthesis instruments acting on synthesis data. But in the case of CLM, both the audio instruments and the data they use are represented in Lisp. CLM instruments are just specialized Lisp functions that generate audio signals. These instrument functions are defined using CLM's definstrument macro. Definstrument expressions are normally placed in a Lisp source files with a .ins extension and then compiled and loaded into Lisp. An .ins file can contain any number of CLM instruments and is in every way analogous to a Csound orchestra file.

For purposes of comparison, Example 5 shows the contents of an instrument file called beep.ins (nm/24/beep.ins) that contains a single CLM instrument definition. The instrument is called beep and it is equivalent to the i1 Csound instrument defined earlier in this chapter.

Example 5. The contents of the CLM instrument file "beep.ins".

```
(definstrument beep (start dur freq amp amp-env)
  (let* ((beg (seconds->samples start))
         (end (seconds->samples (+ start dur)))
         (osc (make-oscil :frequency freq))
         (env (make-env :envelope amp-env :scaler amp
                        :duration dur)))
    (run
     (loop for i from beg to end
           do
           (outa i (* (env env) (oscil osc)))))))
```

Like i1, the CLM beep instrument uses of an oscillator and an amplitude envelope. The let* establishes local variables used in the calculation of the audio output signal. The variable *beg* is the first sample number to start generating in the audio output file and *end* is the ending sample. The *osc* variable holds an oscillator object and *env* is set to an envelope generator. The run expression establishes the scope of the instrument's *run time* statements: expressions inside the run block execute to generate a stream of audio samples. The run time expression of beep consists of a loop that iterates over each sample number i and sets the variable s to the next sample output from the oscillator *osc* scaled by the output of the envelope generator *env*. The sample s is then written to the open output audio file.

Compiling and loading instruments

Definstrument code must be complied and loaded into Lisp (Interaction 3). Compilation is a process that transforms program code (Lisp expressions) into equivalent low-level machine instructions. Compiled machine code executes many times faster than interpreted program code. Compilation is really a necessity for audio instruments due to the large amounts of data that they compute. For example, a stereo, CD-quality audio signal requires the calculation of 88,200 audio samples for each second of sound!

Rather than listen to the simple beep sound again we will take this opportunity to compile and load two instruments from the CLM software distribution. The main instrument is called fm-violin and it was developed by William Schottstaedt when he was a graduate student at CCRMA. The source code for the instrument is contained in the file v.ins (nm/24/v.ins) located in the same directory as this HTML chapter file. The instrument is an example of *cascade frequency modulation*, in which a carrier frequency is modulated by a complex wave output from a cascade of three modulating oscillators. Despite its inherent complexity, the fm-violin instrument is actually very easy to work with. See Chapter 23 for a general discussion of frequency modulation as a synthesis technique.

Interaction 3. Compiling and loading "v.ins".

```
cm> (cd "/Users/hkt/NM/24/")
"/Users/hkt/NM/24/"
cm> (compile-file "v.ins")
"/Users/hkt/NM/24/v.pfasl"
cm> (load "v")
"/Users/hkt/NM/24/v.pfasl"
cm> (compile-file "nrev.ins")
"/Users/hkt/NM/24/nrev.pfasl"
cm> (load "v")
"/Users/hkt/NM/24/nrev.pfasl"
cm>
```

Lisp Note:
> The file extension for the compiled file will vary with each Lisp implementation.

In Interaction 3 the function compile-file is used to compile the Lisp program file containing the fm-violin instrument definition. The load function is then used to load the complied code into Lisp. It is possible to load interpreted program files as well as compiled files using the load function. In either case, the effect of loading is to evaluate the contents of the loaded file. We also compiled and loaded a reverberation instrument called `nrev` that we will use to add a "hall effect" to the audio output.

When the "v.ins" file is compiled and loaded both the fm-violin instrument as well as a sound event object for the instrument is automatically defined. This means that when you work with CLM instruments you do not have to use `defobject` to define a new object class. This process happens automatically by `definstrument`. The `fm-violin` instrument has almost forty parameters, but only the first four parameters must be specified in order to produce a sound. We can use Common Music's `object-parameters` function to inspect the list of parameters that the `fm-violin` contains.

(object-parameters *object*)   [Function]

Returns a list of sound parameters associated with the specified *object*.

Interaction 4. Listing an object's parameters.

```
cm> (object-parameters (new midi))
(time duration keynum amplitude channel)
cm> (object-parameters (new fm-violin))
(startime dur frequency amplitude fm-index amp-env
 periodic-vibrato-rate random-vibrato-rate
 periodic-vibrato-amplitude random-vibrato-amplitude
 noise-amount noise-freq ind-noise-freq
 ind-noise-amount amp-noise-freq amp-noise-amount
 gliss-env glissando-amount fm1-env fm2-env fm3-env
 fm1-rat fm2-rat fm3-rat fm1-index fm2-index fm3-index
 base frobber reverb-amount index-type degree distance
 degrees no-waveshaping denoise denoise-dur
 denoise-amp)
cm>
```

The fm-morph process

One of the interesting properties of the fm-violin instrument is that it is capable of generating many different types of sound, not just violin timbres. The key to its flexibility lies, in part, with its many optional parameters. We will now generate a sound file that demonstrates the effect of the *fm index* on the fm-violin's timbre. We start by defining a few envelopes that our instrument and process will use.

Example 6. Envelopes for the fm-violin example.

```
(define amp-env '(0 0 2 .5 3 .9 5 .6 75 .2 100 0))

(define morph-weight
  '(0 1 .2 10 .3 20 .35 50 .45 100 .5 100
    .55 100 .65 25 .97 20 .98 10 1 1))
```

```
(define spike-env
  '(0 .01 .2 .02 .3 .05 .35 .09
    .4 .1 .425 .15 .45 .2 .5 2.5
    .55 .2 .575 .15 .6 .1 .65 .09
    .7 .05 .8 .02 1. .01))

(define trough-env
  '(0 9 .2 8 .3 5 .35 4 .45 0 .5 0
    .65 4 .96 8 1 9))
```

The *amp-env* variable holds the amplitude envelope that the fm-violin will use. The other three envelopes are used to calculate parameter values for fm-violin events. M*orph-weight* is the random weight of each note. *Spike-env* controls the duration of each event, durations in the middle portion of the score will last significantly longer than at its start or end. *Trough-env* controls the *fm-index* of the process; its value is 9 (quite large) at the start and end of the process and zero in the middle.

Example 7. The fm-morph process.

```
(define (fm-morph len rhy amp)
  (let* ((w1 1)
         (pat (new random
                  :of `((c1 :weight .3)
                        (c4 :weight, (pval w1))
                        cs4 d4 ds4 e4 f4 fs4
                        (g4 :weight , (pval w1))
                        gs4 a4 as4 b4
                        (c5 :weight , (pval w1)))
                  :for 1)))
    (process for i below len
             for pct = (/ i len)
             for frq = (next pat)
             for lo? = (scale= frq 'c1)
             do (set! w1 (interpl pct morph-weight))
             output
             (new fm-violin :startime (now)
                  :dur (if lo? 8
                           (interpl pct spike-env))
                  :amplitude amp
                  :frequency (hertz frq)
                  :amp-env amp-env
                  :reverb-amount .1
                  :fm-index (if lo? 2.5
                                (interpl
                                 pct trough-env)))
             wait rhy)))
```

Generating an audio file

At this point we are ready to generate a CLM score. There are two possible score files that we can generate: a CLM score file or an audio file. A CLM score file is a text file with a .clm extension that contains a time ordered series of instrument calls. A CLM audio file contains the audio signal itself. We will take this opportunity to generate a stereo CD-quality audio file. Audio files can be generated from CLM in .aiff, .snd or .wav formats simply by specifying one of these as the file extension in the `events` function. A CLM score has many possible initializations, only a few of the most basic are shown here:

`:srate` *number*
>The sampling rate of the audio file. The default is 22050.

`:channels` *number*
>The number of channels in the output audio file. The default is 1.

`:trace` *boolean*
>If true then each event will print its instrument and start time as it is output to the audio file.

`:play` *boolean*
>If true then CLM will play the audio file after it is written. The default value is true.

Consult the CLM documentation on `with-sound` for the complete list of audio file initializations. At this point we are ready to output our audio file:

Interaction 5. Generating audio output from fm-morph.

```
cm> (events (fm-morph 400 .1 .2) "morph.aiff" 0
            :srate 44100 :channels 2 :reverb 'nrev)
; File: "morph.aiff"
; Channels: 2
; Srate: 44100
; Reverb: NREV
"morph.aiff"
cm>
```

➡ nm/24/snd/morph.mp3

Common Music Notation

We conclude this chapter with a brief discussion of Common Music Notation (CMN), also written by William Schottstaedt at CCRMA, Stanford University. Common Music Notation is a program that transforms Lisp expressions into a musical manuscript that is saved in an Encapsulated Postscript file (EPS). CMN has no editor and is not designed as a substitute for notation programs. However, it does an excellent job of music manuscripting and it is particularly useful for producing visual output from algorithms. The algorithms can use `midi` objects to represent the basic note data that CMN will display. While CMN's time-line and layout algorithms are very sophisticated, best results can be achieved by following two simple guidelines. First, the `midi` event's keynum property should contain note names rather than key numbers. Second, to minimize problems with rhythmic quantization, time values should be specified using exact ratios of a quarter note. This will be discussed in more detail in the next section.

The CMN score

A CMN score is generated by specifying a file with an .eps or a .cmn file extension to the `events` function. In either case a EPS file containing the manuscript is generated. If a .cmn file is specified then a CMN input file will be saved along with the EPS output. A CMN input file is a text file that contains the Lisp expressions that generated the EPS manuscript. These expression can then be edited in any text editor to produce a more refined or detailed score. A CMN score supports many initializations, consult the CMN documentation for a complete listing. The most basic initialization are defined here:

:exact-rhythms *boolean*

> If true then the CMN score parses time values as exact rhythms. Exact CMN rhythms are ratios of the *quarter note*, not the whole note. For example, 1 means quarter note, 1/2 means eighth, 1/4 means 16th and so on. Using exact rhythms will avoid quantization errors that might otherwise occur if CMN parses note events containing time values specified in seconds.

:title *string*

> The title string to display in the output manuscript.

:size *number*

> The overall size of the score. The default value is 40; 24 produces a moderately small staff.

:staffing *list*

> A list of staff descriptions, see the next section for more information.

CMN staff descriptions

A list of *staff descriptions* provides a way to determine the exact staff that each event will appear in when it is output by an algorithmic processes. The list of staff descriptions is specified to the :staffing initialization of a CMN score when it is created by the `events` function. Each staff description is a list in the format:

(*id* [:name *s*] [:clef *sym*] [:meter *list*])

The first element *id* in the staff description is an integer identifier for the staff. Events output by a process are matched against all the staff ids in the score to determine which staff the object will appear in. In the case of MIDI events, the *channel* number of the MIDI event is used to specify this staffing value. The :name attribute is an optional string name for the staff. If a :name is not provided the name of the staff will be set to "staff-*n*" where *n* is the *id* of the staff. The value of the :clef attribute is an optional symbol clef name or a list of clef names. If this value is not specified then CMN will use whatever clef it thinks best. If the clef value is :both then the grand staff is used. If the value is a list of clefs it limits CMN's clef choices to the clefs mentioned in the list. The :meter attribute is an optional meter list for the staff, where the first element in the list is the number of beats per measure and the second is the measure beat. Example 8 shows the definition of a staffing list for a score with three staves of music:

Example 8. Example staff definitions.

```
(define trio-staves
  '((0 :name "Cello" :clef :bass :meter (4 4))
    (1 :name "Oboe" :clef :treble :meter (4 4))
    (2 :name "Flute" :clef :treble :meter (4 4))))
```

The staffing list in Example 8 species that any MIDI event with a channel value of 0 will appear in the staff named "Cello", channel 1 events will be written to the "Oboe" staff and channel 2 events will appear in the "Flute" staff.

Creating a CMN manuscript

We first define a little example process that outputs MIDI events to our CMN score:

Example 9. defining a process to output CMN files.

```
(define duet-staves
  '((0 :name "Viola" :clef :alto :meter (4 4))
    (2 :name "Flute" :clef :treble :meter (4 4))))

(define (duet-cmn stf len nts)
  (let ((nts (new heap :notes nts))
        ;; choose quarter or two eighths
        (rhy (new random
                  :of `(1 ,(new cycle :of '(1/2 1/2))))))
    (process while (< (now) len)
             for n = (next nts)
             for r = (next rhy)
             output (new midi :time (now)
                             :duration r
                             :keynum n
                             :channel stf) ; link to staff
             wait r)))
```

Because our CMN example involves exact rhythms, the time values in the *rhy* pattern are expressed using CMN rhythm ratios. (Since these values are proportional we could scale them by an arbitrary tempo factor if this process were to be used for both MIDI file and CMN file output.)

Interaction 6. Outputting a CMN file.

```
cm> (events (list (duet-cmn 0 12 '(c3 d ef f g))
                  (duet-cmn 1 12 '(c5 d ef f g)))
            "duet.eps"
            :staffing duet-staves
            :size 24
            :title "Hiho!")
Manuscripting duet.eps...
"duet.eps"
cm> (events (list (duet-cmn 0 12 '(c3 d ef f g))
                  (duet-cmn 1 12 '(c5 d ef f g)))
            "duet.cmn"
            :staffing duet-staves
            :size 24
            :title "Hiho!")
"duet.cmn"
cm>
```

The file duet.pdf (nm/24/duet.pdf) is a PDF version of duet.eps and the file duet.cmn (nm/24/duet.cmn) contains the CMN input expressions that created it.

Chapter Source Code

The source code to all of the examples and interactions in this chapter can be found in the file beyond.cm located in the same directory as the HTML file for this chapter. The source file can be edited in a text editor or evaluated inside the Common Music application.

References

Dodge, C. & Jerse, T. (1985). *Computer Music*. New York: Schirmer Books.

Subject index

STUDIES ON NEW MUSIC RESEARCH
ISSN 1384 1203

1. *Signal Processing, Speed and Music.*
   Stan Tempelaars
     1996 ISBN 90 265 1481 6 (Hardback)

2. *Musical Signal Processing.*
   Edited by C. Roads, S.T. Pope, A. Piccialli and G. de Poli
     1997 ISBN 90 265 1482 4 (Hardback)
        ISBN 90 265 1483 2 (Paperback)

3. *Rhytm Perception and Production.*
   Edited by Peter Desain and Luke Windsor
     2000 ISBN 90 265 1636 3 (Hardback)

4. *Representing Musical Time - A Temporal-Logic Approach.*
   Alan Marsden
     2000 ISBN 90 265 1635 5 (Hardback)

5. *Musical Imagery.*
   Edited by Rolf Inge Godoy and Harald Jorgensen
     2001 ISBN 90 265 1831 5 (Hardback)

6. *Notes from the Metalevel. An Introduction to Computer Composition.*
   Heinrich K. Taube
     2004 ISBN 90 265 1957 5 (Hardback)
        ISBN 90 265 1975 3 (Paperback)
        ISBN 90 265 1958 3 (CD-ROM)